KNOWN
AND
NEAR

The Relationship With Jesus You Were Born to Have

KATIE ROCKETT

Draw Near

BOOKS

Cover art by Gracie Beyer, Katie Rockett, & Meredith Eastman

Scripture quotations are taken from the following translations:

Bold emphasis added to Scripture quotations is the author's.

To Jesus, Brian, and Daddy:

Jesus, my whole heart and my every day is *Yours*. You are *everything* to me. Use these words to help people everywhere find the same love, purpose, freedom, and *joy* in a relationship with you that I have found.

Brian—only second to Jesus—no person on earth has known and loved me the way *you* have. You have cherished and cared for me in a way that has healed me and brought me the greatest joy. Thank you for believing in me and encouraging me to *write*. I love you deeply.

Daddy, you have taught, trained, encouraged, rescued, and loved me my whole life. I wouldn't have the life I have without *you*, too. You have been and *are* one of the most tremendous and *treasured* gifts of my life.

TABLE OF CONTENTS

Chapter 9: *Our Hunger*

Part 6: *The Fruit*

Chapter 10: *He Changes Us Personally*

Chapter 11: *He Uses Us Publicly*

Part 7: *The Promises*

Chapter 12: *Truths to Hold On To*

Chapter 13: *Stay Close*

You Were Made for This

Every person is born to personally *know* Jesus—not just to know *about* Him. When Paul wandered through Athens in Acts 17, he witnessed a city weighed down by the worship of countless gods. Among the many monuments, one shrine caught his eye, and it bore this inscription: *"To an Unknown God."* With gentle yet brave boldness, he proclaimed, *"I have come to introduce you to this God whom you worship without even knowing"* (Acts 17:23 TPT). He then went on to explain that He was the One who made the world and all nations, and His purpose was that *"every person would long for God, feel their way to Him, and find Him—for He's the God who is easy to discover!"* (Acts 17:27 TPT). Like the Athenians, many of us have a silent shrine in our hearts—small, sacred, sometimes half-forgotten—reflecting faith in God, perhaps even in Jesus, but stopping short of intimacy. Too often we worship Him—believing in Him and honoring His Name, perhaps attending church and even serving on Sundays—without *knowing* Him. Yet, He whispers, waits, and welcomes us into so much more than that. He is the God who is wonderfully wide open and easy to discover, inviting every seeking soul into not just a surface belief but a real relationship with Him that runs deep.

In fact, a real relationship with Jesus—*true* intimacy with Him—is what the deepest parts of us truly long for because it is what we were made for. Without being fully filled with Him, we feel empty, drifting, and uncertain of our value and purpose, like a song missing its melody. We were born deeply needing Him *near*, unknowingly aching to *know* Him, and nothing else can satisfy that sacred longing. However, when we step into a real relationship with Jesus—and He floods every corner of our being with His presence, power, and purpose—we come alive. Life bursts as joy rises, and we are fully fulfilled—rooted in the reason we were created. We were made for this divine connection, and until that relationship is *right*—and He rests *right* at the center of our whole lives—we never feel truly *right* ourselves.

Through every page of this book, we will trace the tapestry of the radical, radiant relationship Jesus longs to have with each of us. We'll begin in Eden, where the first created people walked with God in wonder; then, we'll follow the Fall that fractured fellowship and fragmented hearts. We'll witness the miraculous mystery of Jesus' birth, His sacrificial suffering on the Cross, and the silent shadow of His three-day burial—only to erupt in the glorious dawn of His resurrection and His Spirit poured out, offering a brand-new, healed, whole, and powerful life to anyone who chooses to trust Him and walk closely with Him. Along the way, common questions will be courageously and clearly answered, guiding our understanding and stirring our hearts. Later chapters will show how to nurture the relationship we were born to have, offering practical paths to deepen intimacy with Him. We will confront the challenges and schemes of Satan, discover how to overcome obstacles, and witness the astonishing fruit Jesus produces both in and through those who are truly His. Finally, we will celebrate the steadfast promises He makes to those who pursue Him, cling to Him, and remain faithful through every trial. Through every topic and turn of this book, one magnificent message will remain markedly clear: Jesus made us to be **known** and **near** to Him—and it is *still* possible to experience the full, flourishing relationship with Him we were born to have.

PART 1

The Garden

CHAPTER ONE

The Beginning

"Yahweh-God scooped up a lump of soil, sculpted a man, and blew into his nostrils the breath of life. The man came alive—a living soul!"—Genesis 2:7 (TPT)

The First Breath

Adam's freshly formed eyes fluttered open for the very first time. Inhaling anointed air streaming straight from the lips of his Creator, Adam looked into the flawless, full-hearted face of the One who had dreamed him up, designed him, and destined him for a life filled with Him eternally. Before either spoke a single syllable, Adam knew one truth immediately: he was *loved*. He was *wanted* by a Wonder. He was safe, secure, and *smiled* upon. His identity—who he was and Whose he was—was inherently known and unmistakably clear. He *belonged* to the One who was undeniably near. His presence surrounded Adam externally, and His Spirit—the very breath and blaze of Heaven's power—saturated him internally. Before Adam ever touched a task—before he tended a garden, named a creature, or even uttered a word—his God was not just his Creator but a Father *and* Friend who was **known** and **near.**

This is how the first beautiful breath of human life began. No sin existed, and no shame twisted Adam's understanding of God's unbroken approval and affection for him. There was no striving for status and no stage set for self-proving. Instead, he received immediate intimacy and automatic affection. Pure, perfect love pulsed between them, forging full *joy*. Delight steadily spilled, drenching both hearts. Within minutes of breathing Eden's air, Adam's deepest desire became *being loved* and *loving back* the One who drew him from dust. Between them lay deep, decisive trust. He was irrefutably a righteous and holy God who cherished the man He made, and, in return, the man treasured the God from which he came. The most beautiful relationship that had ever existed and would *ever* be—that between humanity and Divinity— commenced at the crux of creation.

Placed With Purpose

The Lord had *"planted a garden in the East, in Eden, and there He put the man He had formed"* (Genesis 2:8 NIV). Yes, next, *"The Lord took the man and put him in the Garden of Eden to work it and take care of it"* (Genesis 2:15 NIV). This glorious garden was not generated and germinated for just functional factors but for *relational* reasons. This was the place the Lord had prepared for the one He created to cherish— where all their walking, talking, and enjoying of one another would unfold. After opening his eyes and observing the most breathtaking scenes any human has ever seen, Adam wasn't left to simply *wonder* or to senselessly *wander*. The Lord intentionally placed the newly made man in a garden that was meant for both relationship *and* rulership alongside Him—a sacred partnership to steward His creation.

The Lord then brought all the animals He had assembled to Adam and allowed him to know and name each one—adding collaboration to their relationship. He thereafter toiled and tended to the earth alongside His Creator in all aspects and assignments. This shared stewardship was a sweet song, not a straining shackle—another form of worship and connection. They didn't just enjoy each other's company; they also took pleasure in their *partnership*. They joyfully walked side by side and worked task by task—bringing order to the earth and blessing it with balance, blooms, and beauty all around. From the very beginning, their relationship deepened not only through conversation but also through their joint stewardship and rulership of creation. *This* is what the Lord desires with each of us who breathe this beautiful earth's air—*still*.

Freedom With Boundaries

He also granted Adam generous freedom to enjoy the earth—establishing only one beneficial boundary to barricade him from harm. The Lord instructed, *"You are free to eat from any tree in the garden, but you must not eat from the tree of the knowledge of good and evil"* (Genesis 2:16-17 NIV). At this point, evil existed only beyond the earth's realm; the Lord alone knew *all* and was the ultimate judge of right and wrong. This command was not a reasonless restriction but a loving act of *protection.*

Furthermore, it was an *invitation* to trust God and walk in dependence on His wise counsel, character, and care. The tree wasn't a trap; it was a test of trust. By giving him a choice, the Lord granted Adam freedom—the chance to love Him *willingly.* Love that isn't *chosen* isn't real love. Obedience that isn't *optional* is control. God didn't craft a controlled, rigid robot; He created a choice-driven man with a free will. Adam had the ability to choose Him or to walk away, the capacity to trust Him or go his own way. Without the commandment and the tree, he wouldn't be *free.* Without freedom, Adam couldn't fully, *truly* love. In both His precious love and perfect justice, God offered Adam the most fulfilling, life-giving relationship with Him—yet it was never forced. The Lord chose Adam decisively and irrevocably, but He granted Adam the chance to choose Him in return *voluntarily.* We *still* get this incredible choice today.

The First Human Relationship

Adam lived with everything that was *good,* but he lacked something greatly needed: human companionship. The Lord said, *"It is not good for man to be alone; I will make a helper suitable for him"* (Genesis 2:18 NIV). Although Adam had the richest relationship with the Lord, He knew that human connection was also an essential, indispensable need for this being He'd made in His own image. Man's desire for relationship reflects God's greatest attribute: He, too, is *relational* to His core. Adam's longing for relationship was not a flaw; it was a detail of his divine design. He created Adam to experience love—both with Himself *and* human companions. This reflects the relational heart of God, who treasures togetherness, trust, and tenderhearted ties that connect Him to people *and* people to each other.

In fact, the Bible says, *"God **is** love"* (I John 4:8 NIV). Love is not content to sit still and stay silent. It must be passionately poured out and passed around. Love longs for something—or *someone*—to receive it, relish it, and revel in it. God created people to be the objects of His affection—upon which He would pour *Himself* for them to experience and enjoy (Deuteronomy 10:15). Not only does He desire that we receive His love straight from Him, but by making people, He gave us a way to experience His affection, passion, and partnership in physical form, too. Human connection becomes one of the clearest ways we live out the love we lavishly receive from the Lord. So, Adam's need for Eve wasn't about weakness; it was always about revealing and reflecting the *full* richness of God's love.

Therefore, the Lord caused Adam to fall into a deep sleep and then formed Eve from his side. He took a rib—not a bone from his head as if to rule over her or from his feet as if to trample her. He took a bone from his side, which was near his heart and under his arm. This symbolizes their closeness and equality—the absence of superiority or inferiority. They were to be deeply connected and equally respected. When Adam awoke and beheld her, his heart readily rejoiced, and he excitedly expressed these words: *"This is now bone of my bones and flesh of my flesh!"* (Genesis 2:21-23 NIV). The first human relationship was built and began literally in God's presence and according to His plan. Adam did not have to go in search of her; she was brought right to him by the One who knew and loved him best. A relationship with God came first—and then flowed divinely directed relationships with others.

This is a gift He *still* gives to His people today. For those in relationship with Him, He divinely directs delegated people into their lives—some for a season and others for the full stretch of life—to receive and share His love in the most life-building, love-giving ways. He *still* knows it's *"not good for man to be alone."* In His wisdom and goodness, He places particular people onto our paths to both point us to more of Him *and* to pour out more of His love into our lives.

The Greatest Relationship

That's exactly what all three—Adam, Eve, and God—enjoyed

together most: *relationship*. The first two humans didn't just exist in paradise; they were enveloped in *Presence*. They spent their days not just tending to creation but marveling at it—naming animals, touching petals, tasting fruit, all while walking and talking with their Creator. They lived on earth, but their hearts were anchored in Heaven. His company was not intimidating or unusual; it was constant and familiar. Adam and Eve's normal lives included walking with God, hearing His voice, and knowing His nearness—without fear, without distance, without shame.

He was a God who drew *near*. Genesis 3:8 (ESV) says, *"They heard the sound of the Lord God walking in the garden in the cool of the day."* Interaction with Him wasn't rare; it was their rhythm. They lived life *together*. They lingered in conversation. They listened. They learned. They laughed. His voice wasn't distant thunder; it was the familiar sound of *love*. Their relationship was conversational, pure, and unbroken; it was built on closeness, trust, and delight. This wasn't a side-note of creation; it was the primary point. This was the Creator's deepest desire fulfilled: not just to be worshipped from afar but to be *known*—to dwell with His people, to walk with them in the cool of the day, to be *near* to them in the most *real* and radical way.

What We Were Made For

This is *still* His primary passion for all people today. Like Adam and Eve, we, too, were birthed for belonging, born to be loved. We were made for our Maker and Friend to be **known and near**. We—*each* of us—began as a deep desire and dream in the Lord's heart. He foreknew each of our faces and voices—our beauty, personality, and ability—and determined that He wanted *one* just like each of us. Compelled by love too vast to keep to Himself—out of passionate longing for *relationship*—He envisioned us before we were born and then purposefully and personally knit us together in our mother's womb (Psalm 139:13). He would say this to *each* of us as He said to Jeremiah: *"Before I shaped you in the womb, **I knew you intimately**. I had divine plans for you before I gave you life"* (Jeremiah 1:5 TPT). We each existed in His heart before we ever entered this earth—and, detail by detail, He molded and made each of us exactly as visualized in *His* holy imagination.

He does not create *casually* either. We were *"fearfully and wonderfully made"* (Psalm 139:14 AMP). The word "fearfully" comes from the Hebrew word *"yare,"* which means to be in awe, to revere, to respect deeply. Our Father *carefully* created each of us—with a sense of sacred seriousness. He made each of us with the most sanctified purpose and special care. With each life, God labored like an artist in awe—with hands trembling with wonder as He crafted a creation unmatched, unique, and utterly beloved. This is what it means to be "fearfully made." Additionally, the word "wonderfully" comes from *"pala,"* which means to be set apart, distinguished, and marked by uniqueness. None of us are copied from a common, reusable mold; all of us are unique in our looks and in our wiring. Even our weaknesses and quirks were honed by His hand (2 Corinthians 12:7-9). We are each a one-of-a-kind, divine *masterpiece* woven together with remarkable reverence and intricate intentionality. We are also each the physical product of a peerless passion in His heart—uniquely personal yet equally powerful for all.

This is true of *every* person. No matter the situations surrounding our births, the Father planned for us to be brought into being. For those born into cruel, crushing circumstances—poverty, abandonment, abuse, trauma, or even unplanned pregnancies—this truth becomes deeply powerful and redemptive. Even if we were born unwanted by people, we are *wholly* wanted by God. He *"knit"* each of us together (Psalm 139:13 AMP). This wasn't indifferent; it was *intentional.* A person's worth is not determined by how he or she was delivered into the world but by the One who designed him or her. Even if born to parents who weren't ready or who were absent—even if conceived through a traumatic event—*no* person is a mistake. The Lord's value of each individual is not dependent upon or often reflected in peoples' view of him or her. Even to the people overlooked and unloved, the Lord passionately proclaims, "I see you. I know you. I formed you. I love what I made! I meant for you to be born and to become Mine!" Each life began by God's hand, not by human failures. To any person who has struggled with feeling unwanted, who has been told his or her birth was an "accident," or who is wrestling with identity and shame, know this: each life is a miracle made by the Master, not a mistake made by a man. The One who purposefully dreamed up each person is the same One who passionately desires to pull *each* close and pour out His power, peace, and purpose into each life—no matter *how* it began.

He breathed His breath into *every* born being and brought *each* to this earth—to know Him well, to walk and talk with Him, and to partner with Him in governing this earth. It is not His will that we wonder who we are and wander near and far—looking for identity and love. It's all found in *Him*—in *relationship* with Him. Though this earth is far from Eden, what Adam enjoyed before sin, we can regain again: the *same* intimacy with the *same* Lord—experiencing real closeness with Him, enjoying His constant presence, and engaging with Him in His work on this earth. All the joy, the peace, and the purpose that flows from knowing Him—we can *still* experience on this flaw-filled earth as if it's flawless Eden.

This is possible because of the One who came and carved a way for us to have unbroken fellowship with Him on this broken earth. He boldly and beautifully spilled His love in the form of blood. He came **near** and made His love **known**. He came to radically restore the relationship with our Creator we were born to have. His Name is **Jesus.**

CHAPTER TWO

The Fall

"When Adam sinned, the entire world was affected. Sin entered human experience, and death was the result. And so death followed sin, casting its shadow over all humanity, because all have sinned."—Romans 5:12 (TPT)

Relationship Severed by Sin

Although joy welled through Eden, there was *one* who witnessed it all joylessly. An angered enemy watched in horror as the God who had cast him out of His presence created beings that carried His image. He writhed in wrath at the sublimity of creation because he had surrendered his own splendor—some of the greatest beauty Heaven had ever seen. He had also forfeited his own closeness with his Creator. He had lost everything—all hope and all of Heaven—with only Hell to face. He had been known as *Lucifer*, the "Morning Star"—a name now shadowed by eternal darkness and despair (Isaiah 14:12 NIV).

Ezekiel 28 provides one of the most striking glimpses of Lucifer's original beauty, position, pride, and fall. Although this passage is directed towards the King of Tyre, it shifts into a dual reference to Satan himself. He's described as *"the seal of perfection, full of wisdom and perfect in beauty"* (Ezekiel 28:12 AMP). He was not devised to be evil; he was designed by God as a majestic being, a masterpiece of wisdom and beauty. The Lord even adorned and decorated Lucifer with every precious gemstone—all inlaid with gold (Ezekiel 28:13 AMP). He was also *"anointed as a guardian cherub"*—personally *"ordained"* by God (v. 14). Appointed to the class of angels who were near the throne of God, he was set apart for a holy purpose—involving worship. He dwelled *"on the holy mount of God"* and *"walked among fiery stones"*—meaning that he had personal access to the presence of the Almighty (v. 14). Then, the passage addresses him directly: *"You were blameless in your ways from the day you were created until wickedness was found in you"* (v. 15). This evil didn't come from God; it arose within Lucifer through *pride*. The speech then speeds on like this: *"Your heart became proud on account of your beauty, and you corrupted your wisdom because of your splendor"* (v. 17). His *pride* was his perilous downfall. This connects with Isaiah 14:12-15 (NIV) where Satan secretly schemed inside, *"I will ascend to Heaven…I will make myself like the Most High."* Lucifer wanted God's *throne*, not God's *heart*. He began to worship his own beauty and brilliance instead of the One who bestowed it. He turned inward, adored himself, and desired to *be* worshipped rather than *to* worship.

Scripture indicates that this being—along with other heavenly beings—possessed moral agency and the capacity to obey or rebel as well. Like humanity, angels were not forced into loyalty but were capable of choosing disobedience. No being in all existence was created to be controlled or coerced to love and worship the Lord. This beautiful being—the one called Lucifer—turned inward and rebelled of his own volition. He then faced calamitous consequences.

Satan was cast out not because the Lord is impetuous or petty but because evil cannot exist in His holy presence. Scripture declares this about our flawless Father: *"Your eyes are too pure to look on evil; you cannot tolerate wrongdoing"* (Habakkuk 1:13 NIV). Heaven's glory is a refuge for the righteous, and in its light, sin cannot linger. Satan's pride and rebellion made him incompatible with Heaven's holiness. Therefore, he—along with the other angels who fatally followed him— was expelled from Heaven and hurled into eternal exile. Revelation 12:7–9 (ESV) describes the dramatic heavenly battle when Satan and his angels were defeated and driven out, declaring that *"there was no longer any place for them in Heaven."* As he fell towards Hell, he said farewell to his splendor, beauty, joy, peace, fruitfulness, and the presence of God forever. The Bible also foreshadows his final end: he will be *"thrown into a lake of fire"* where he will be *"tormented day and night forever and ever"* (Revelation 20:10 NIV). Lucifer's rebellion didn't rattle our Lord. God rendered righteous judgement and removed him from glory, and Satan's final defeat is already written at the end of his story.

So, picture Satan's indignation as he watched the Creator form the earth and fill it with vibrant vegetation and vitality of every shape and shade. Next, ponder his heightened horror as He derived a living being from the dust and decorated him with divine strength; then, He drew life from the man's rib, creating a woman and crowning her with splendor similar to what Satan surrendered. The devil's rage and jealousy at this scene cemented vengeance in his heart. However, this foiled foe could not afflict the Almighty, so he advanced towards the object of His affection, His most prized possession: the *people* He made in His image.

Even Satan knew people were designed to be **known** and **near** to the Almighty. Since he couldn't destroy God the way He'd devastated him, he determined to decimate the greatest desire of God's heart: His *relationship* with the people He created to cherish. Even Satan understands this about our existence: if we live, it's because we were dreamed up and desired by God. Revenge on God is his aim, but *we* are his target—and destroying our *relationship* is his greatest goal. Satan seeks to subvert and sever us from the God-nearness we were born to embrace and enjoy. He longs for each soul to dwell and die in the same godless place—the same emptiness and darkness—that ensnares him.

So, imagine him sneaking, spying, and seething over the daily rituals and rhythms of life on the uncorrupted earth—all the perfection that covered the ground and the loving, life-giving relationship cherished between Adam and Eve and their God. The laughter, the love, the fullness of joy—it fervently fueled his *fury*. In his agony and anger, he plotted his pernicious payback. He would bring death to this earth that exuded only life, and he would blight this relationship that extended only love. He would reduce it *all* to ruin. He would drown the earth in defilement and divide the people from their God by their guilt. He knew the one principle that protected it all—the peace, the joy, the security, and the relationship—was their *obedience*. So, he would tempt them to first *distrust* and then to *disobey*.

The scheming, slithering enemy in disguise—glaring through a snake's hate-filled eyes—sought out the woman. The fact that Satan—shrouded in serpent form—approached her and spoke seems strange to us post-Eden people. They lived in a pre-fallen existence—absent of deceit, darkness, dread, and perhaps even the division between animals and humans we know today. Though a speaking snake sounds scary to us, it wasn't to Eve. Nevertheless, he spoke to her, his words like poison pouring into her perfect trust in God. He cunningly questioned, *"Can it really be that God has said, 'You shall not eat from any tree of the garden?'"* and she readily responded, *"We may eat fruit from the trees of the garden, except the fruit from the tree which is in the middle of the garden. God said, 'You shall not eat from it or touch it; otherwise, you will die'"* (Genesis 3:1-3 AMP). The serpent challenged the claim: *"You certainly will not die! For God knows that on the day you eat from it, your eyes will be opened [that is, you will have greater awareness], and you will be like God, knowing [the difference between good and evil]"* (v. 4-5 AMP). There was the thought that torpedoed her trust. He had lied about her Lord. He appealed to the free will she had been given. He irritated the itch of her natural want and inched her to the disobedient decision that destroyed it all. He didn't tempt her to kill, steal, or destroy—just to take *one* bite of *one* piece of fruit from the *one* tree she wasn't to touch. It seemed harmless. It seemed small. It even seemed *sensible.*

She listened to His farce and looked at the fruit and *"saw that the tree was good for food and that it was delightful to look at, and a tree to be desired to make one wise and insightful,"* so she took a piece, ate it, and then shared it with her husband (Genesis 3:6 AMP). Immediately, their eyes were awakened to evil, their awareness amplified—just as Satan had said, but it wasn't "good" like he had sworn. Instantly, they felt deeply wrong and darkly ashamed—so dramatically *different.* Corruption and condemnation consumed them to their core, and they scrambled to cover the now-humiliating nakedness they bore.

This absolute annihilation was the enemy's aim. He knew the cost and consequence of even the most diminutive disobedient decision. So, he did to Eve what he does to *us* still: he talked her out of obedience to God with convincing, justifying arguments—but all the while aiming to assail her *relationship* with Him. The bite must have been bursting with flavor because she boldly brought it to Adam. The enemy didn't even have to address the man; Eve approached him herself. She spread the sin, and the enemy grinned. He had *won*. His determined damage had been done. Shame purloined their peace, and their sin parted them from Love that never ceased. Death devoured all life. Sin savagely spewed shame and strife. Yes, the enemy destroyed the earth's perfection, wielding *disobedience* like a knife.

Hiding in Shame

The suddenly shame-filled, strife-stricken couple hid from their Creator. They had torn their trust in Him and twisted the earth He had given them. They had boldly betrayed Him—and they were badly broken. Their shame shoved them into the shadows to hide—driving them *away* from their Holy Father and Friend for the first time. They now *feared* facing Him. They retreated to bushes and buried their faces in bottomless sadness. They knew they deserved punishment—banishment from His presence—so they endeavored to execute it themselves.

Yet, they didn't understand that their Father's love ran *long*—longer than their disobedience, deeper than their downfall, reaching for them even as they lay drowning in their defiance. Let's not miss his response to the two who were tempted and tricked and then tossed their relationship with Him aside: He did not leave them in hiding. He did not turn His back in hurt and heave them into the ramifications of their rebellion. In His deep, undying, never-quitting, never-changing-His-mind love for them, He *still* pursued them. Just as before, He walked in the garden and called their names (Genesis 3:8-9)—the same tone, the same love, the same heart and intent, the *same* pursuit *still*.

They stepped into His presence, this time hanging their heads in heavy shame instead of lifting their eyes in loving delight and worship. He immediately inquired, *"Who told you that you were naked? Have you eaten [fruit] from the tree of which I commanded you not to eat?"* (Genesis 3:11 AMP). Adam blamed Eve, and Eve berated Satan. The Lord quickly called out and cursed the Satanic snake. He then communicated the consequences of their choices: toil and trial would tax their days. Conflicts and challenges would crowd their paths. Sweat and tears would perpetually pour—and they would ultimately experience a physical death, returning to dust once more.

Yet, *mercy* endured. He shed the blood of an animal to clothe His people, covering them with garments of grace (Genesis 3:21). Though He expelled them from Eden's embrace, it was to protect them—to prevent them from eating the fruit of "the tree of life" which would keep them alive in their earthly anguish eternally (Genesis 3:22-24). Their days on this broken earth would now be brief and bound by consequence—but beneath and behind it all was the boundless, unbroken love *still* beating in the Father's heart for His beloved humans.

The Consequences & His Care

How could the charging of consequences have been *real* love? Wouldn't *true* love completely erase their errors and the consequential terrors? We must understand that God is both deeply loving *and* perfectly just. Instead of wiping everything clean and just re-setting the perfection of Eden, He chose something far more costly: a plan of *redemption*—one that reveals who He really is and how radically He loves more richly than a simple reset ever could.

If the Lord had just effaced the effects of the Fall, it would have made human free will mean nothing at all. It would have been unjust and controlling for Him to just flush the fruit of Adam and Eve's free choices and start again. This wouldn't reflect real love or the character of a relational God. It also wouldn't have portrayed His perfect justice, which *requires* penalty. If He simply removed their sin, He would no longer be righteous. Justice punishes rebellion; it doesn't just pass over it. However, His mercy always moves *with* His judgement. Instead of making mankind pay for their sin forever, He chose to provide the payment *Himself*—through the staggering sacrifice of His Son (John 3:16). In this way, the consequences remain real—but our unbelievably loving Father and Friend absorbs the ultimate penalty *for* us.

Additionally, if the Lord had simply wiped the world afresh after the Fall, we would never have glimpsed the glorious depths of His love or the wonder woven into His character. We would not know what forgiveness truly feels like, how fiercely and fully the Lord loves even the most fallen, what grace genuinely means, or what a Redeemer really is. Our God did not intend to be called merely Creator. He longed to be known as Redeemer, Comforter, Shepherd, Healer, Savior, Father, and Friend. Many, many hollows of His heart and facets of His face towards us are revealed through the long, painful story of redemption. He has always known what He is doing, what He will do next, and where He will draw it all to its destined close, and each of His marvelous movements magnifies His love—more than we could ever fully fathom. As Ecclesiastes 3:11 (NIV) explains, *"He has made everything beautiful in its time…yet no one can fathom what God has done from beginning to end."* Through *all* time, His every movement in every moment—minute or mighty—will *always* arise from His amazing mercy.

So, even with His first two people—saddened and shamed Adam and Eve—He didn't crush them; He *covered* them (Genesis 3:21). Even in His judgment, He journeyed in mercy. This spilling of sacrificial animal blood and the shrouding of shame gave us the first glimpse of His glorious plan. He would bear the full burden of sin *Himself.* He would soon send His Son to the Cross. He would spill His *own* blood and pay the cost. Jesus would die to deliver us, to draw us back into the *life* that was lost.

This offering was not an on-the-spot, passionate reaction to their perverse actions. This sacrifice—this story—was premeditated. It was planned and penned *before* He created. If people sinned, His Son would be sent. **Jesus** was the plan all along. He is *"the Lamb who was slaughtered* **before** *the world was made"* (Revelation 13:8 NLT). He stood ready for redemption before creation. If the Fall happened, it wouldn't be *final.* He would reveal that He's a Creator who carefully crafts but also a Redeemer who readily restores. Not only that—but He's a Friend who would lovingly lay His life down for even the lost (John 15:13). Our faithful Father would pay the highest price to be **known and near** to *each* of us—no matter what wrongs we've wrought. Our fallen enemy may have fractured the earth, but the Fall would fail when Jesus' Blood prevails. The Father's faithful *love* would have the final word, and through His Son's life on this earth, it would be *fully* and *forever* heard.

CHAPTER THREE

The Human Condition

"The corruption that was in us from birth was expressed through the deeds and desires of our self-life. We lived by whatever natural cravings and thoughts our minds dictated, living as rebellious children subject to God's wrath like everyone else. But God still loved us with such great love..."—Ephesians 2:3-4 (TPT)

The Spread of Adam's Sin

Just as the Lord declared, Adam and Eve's sin certainly did deal out death. Each of us is born and bound to eventually experience a final breath in our bodies. However, it also caused a worse death—the one the Lord warned would befall Adam, Eve, and all born after them if they bit the forbidden fruit, the one the enemy said would never come: *spiritual death.*

Whereas Adam and Eve opened their eyes for the first time with a fully living body and a wholly thriving spirit automatically connected to God, all of us who've come after them arrive in this world wailing *physically* and failing *spiritually*. We are born with spirits disconnected from God, unable to know, love, or obey Him without divine help (Ephesians 2:1). We also inherit a fallen condition—with a nature that is automatically sinful and selfish. We are each *"a sinner from birth"*—sinful even from the moment our mothers conceived us (Psalm 51:5 TPT). This sin builds a barrier between our God and us (Isaiah 59:2). Even worse, we are born as *"slaves to sin"* (Romans 6:17 NIV,

John 8:34). Sin naturally controls our desires and decisions; we're like puppets on a string in the hands of Evil. We may feel like we're making our own movements, but the sin within us delegates our every direction. Therefore, we are *"by nature, children of wrath"*—born under God's judgement because of our fallen nature (Ephesians 2:3 ESV). No matter how fiercely we fight to be flawless, we *all* fail to fully follow or please God (Romans 8:8). We enter life lifeless and lost in the way that matters most. We are born physically but in desperate need of a re-birth spiritually.

How is this fair when it was Adam's sin that brought darkness in, not *ours*? This happened because of how we're all connected. Adam wasn't just the first human; he was the first representative, or "head," of *all* humanity. Whatever he elected to do, he selected on behalf of *all* people who would come after him. Just as the leader of a nation declares a war and it affects all people within its borders, so Adam's choices impacted all of us because we're within the same body (Romans 5:12). Romans 5:19 (NLT) reveals this: *"Because one man disobeyed God, many became sinners."* When God created the human race, He intended for us to be a united family or *body*—connected not just biologically but also spiritually and covenantally. Again, Adam was the first God-appointed *head*. Acts 17:26 (TPT) articulates, *"From one man, Adam, he made every man and woman and every race of humanity."* Our lives are not isolated; they are intentionally interconnected. The Lord did not create us as partitioned pieces; we are branches of *one* body. So, when our first "head" fell, he brought the whole body down with him.

This is why God sent a new Head—*Jesus*. Jesus came as humanity's new representative to choose *for* us again. As in Adam we all fell, in Jesus, we can all rise again. I Corinthians 15:22 (NIV) claims, *"As in Adam all die, so in Christ all will be made alive,"* and Romans 5:14 (AMP) relays this: *"Adam is a type of Him (Christ) who was to come [but in reverse—Adam brought destruction, Christ brought salvation]."* By allowing sin to spread through one, God made it possible to thread salvation through *another* One. So, what may seem unfair on the surface actually reveals the close connection God built into the human race *and* the brilliance of His redemptive plan. He allowed the risk of a fall by one man but always planned to bring radical redemption and righteousness through the One who would come later. *Jesus* would arrive ready to redeem and rebuild the body broken by Adam. This was only possible because of the Lord's system of representation. This system is not rigged or repressive; it is *redemptive*. It paved the path for providential *mercy* to march magnanimously in.

The Cry of Every Heart

So, each is born under the egregious effects of Adam's sin. We arrive alive on the outside but dead on the inside. When an infant's mouth releases its first cry, so does its *heart*. Each newborn knows of hunger, discomfort, and fear—and longs to be **known** and **near** to someone who'll give love and nourishment. Just as a brand-new baby cries for closeness to his or her mother, so our hungry, love-thirsty souls yearn to be near and fully known by our heavenly Father. We arrive aching and empty spiritually, our souls silently crying for the fullness that can come only from the Father. We are born separated from Him and desperate for Him—even before we have heard His Name. As we grow, our hearts helplessly hunger for the pure, perfect Love we were created to crave. Many try to fill the hollow within with people and pleasures, grasping for whatever seems to satisfy, but we will never *really* feel full on a diet of anything but *Him*.

Reaching for Relationship

Since we were created for closeness with the Lord, our first move to soothe the spiritual ache inside is to seek significant, sustaining relationships with others. We are wired for warmth, wonder, and wholehearted intimacy. When we wander without the Lord—or wrestle with weakness in our walk with Him—we work to get others to meet our weightiest relational needs. We turn to treasured friendships, family members, and romantic partners to take in the joy, security, and affirmation we truly crave from *Him*. We do this desperately because we have a deep need to be delighted in and *known*.

We are actually born with God-instilled questions in our being: Am I noticed and known? Am I accepted and loved? Am I a delight? Am I enough? —and so on. The Lord intended to fully answer these questions for us Himself—forging deep confidence, contentment, and completeness. However, many people look to human beings instead to answer these subconscious questions and fulfill these deep-seated needs—but because people are imperfect and can never perceive us as *perfectly* and *personally* as the Lord can, they give us the wrong answers to these questions. Whereas God's answers heal us, others' answers harm us. Every time we experience being misunderstood, abandoned, or rejected, we feel unworthy and unwanted, and it makes us crave connection even more—unfortunately, even with *anyone* anywhere.

Many people move from person to person desperately pursuing the "one" who will love them perfectly and provide a sense of "completeness." However, here's the truth: none of us will ever find the kind of unconditional, never-disappointing, always-at-the-highest-level love we really need in a human being. Even the godliest partner or friend cannot content our deepest desires—even within a healthy, Christian marriage. From our core, we crave the love and presence of God. We perpetually hunger and thirst for *Him*.

This is exactly what Jesus explained to the woman at the well—the lady who had looped from husband to husband looking for *real*, lasting love. About the natural well, He noted this: *"Everyone who drinks this water will be thirsty again"* (John 4:13 AMP). Then, He heralded this about Himself—the *spiritual* well: *"But whoever drinks the water that I give him will never be thirsty again…The water that I give him will become a spring of water [satisfying his thirst for God] welling up [continually flowing, bubbling within him] to eternal life"* (John 4:13-14 AMP). The water we *really* thirst for—His Spirit living within us, releasing constant revelation of His love, grace, and full acceptance of us—can only be found in *Him*. We were *made* to be marvelously filled with Him, and no human "well"—not even the godliest ones—can quench our deepest thirsts.

Seeking Success

Others chase success and strive for achievement to make them feel complete. This is because we not only have a deep desire to be loved; we also have a natural need to be *enough*—to feel seen, special, and significant. However, without receiving revelation of our *real* worth from the Lord, we restlessly reach for recognition, working to prove our value to people—and even to ourselves. Achievements become our evidence, the measurable marks of meaning: grades, gains, goals, gold stars, promotions, paychecks, and popularity. However, the perpetual pursuit of higher achievement incessantly whispers: "If you'll do more, you'll finally be *enough*." Again, without revelation from God about our *real* worth, we will search for significance in our successes—but we will *never* secure it. No matter how much we achieve, acquire, or accomplish, we're still shadowed by the sense that we're somehow not sufficient, never *truly* enough.

From an early age, we are rewarded for what we work at and win, not for simply resting in and being who we are. Our identity in our society is tied to triumphs, but even the most thunderous cheers cannot calm the quiet cry of never feeling quite enough. *Achieving* becomes another way to alleviate the ache for importance inside. Many spend their lives building an impressive image—both online and in person—overworking and acquiring a sense of identity through productivity, chasing titles and degrees, seeking approval through accomplishment after accomplishment, and setting goal after goal. They keep running and reaching rising levels, but they can never out-accomplish that anguish inside. That ache is not for applause; it's for *Him*. It's for the One who sees us and can softly, steadily speak our sacred worth to us even as we just sit at His feet—doing *nothing*.

Piling Up Possessions

Many make money and materialism their main aim. They reach for *things* to fill the God-shaped void inside. This first comes from our human desire to feel safe and secure. To many, money feels like a shield that can protect them from poverty, pain, and powerlessness. It gives the illusion of control in a chaotic world. Proverbs 18:11 (NIV) proclaims, *"The wealth of the rich is their fortified city; they imagine it a wall too high to scale."* Many put their trust in money instead of the One who made them. They also base their identity on their possessions. Society tells us that our worth is tied to what we wear, own, and drive. Materialism becomes a counterfeit identity, but here's a transforming truth: we are *not* what we *have*.

People also love the quick dopamine hit of happiness that comes from a purchase over the deeper joy that comes from surrendering and sitting in God's presence. However, the new fascinating thing always fades. The void returns. The ache *remains*. If people don't know the Lord personally, they instinctively try to fill their soul with things that only feed the body or a fleeting fancy. Even real Christians can fall into this—forgetting that life doesn't come from material things but from the One who made us. Let's take note of this truth: *"Whoever loves money never has enough; whoever loves wealth is never satisfied with their income"* (Ecclesiastes 5:10 NIV). The ache isn't for *stuff;* it's for *Someone*. The void in us is shaped for relationship with God, not the accumulation of things. Only our God gives security that can't be stolen, worth that doesn't depend on success, joy that doesn't fade, and peace that outlasts possessions.

Pursuing Pleasure & Escape

People also pursue pleasure and escapism to distract them from the spiritual emptiness they experience inside. Our longing for joy, peace, rest, and freedom is real—but apart from the Lord, we chase it in shallow, short-lived ways that only leave us *emptier* in the end. We respond to loneliness, shame, regret, anxiety, or even just boredom by reaching for something to distract or numb ourselves. Pleasure becomes a form of self-medication—something that soothes the internal ache but doesn't solve it. We too often seek *relief* from what we feel instead of full *restoration* of what needs to be healed.

We also frequently mistake pleasure for *peace*. Pleasure is easier and more immediate than the true peace that comes from cultivating a relationship with God. All the easily accessible scrolling, binging, drinking, eating, and hooking up—it's *right* there, often rendering just the right distraction. However, the effect fades instantly because indulgence doesn't heal. It doesn't create the kind of *deep* and *lasting* joy we so desperately crave. People seek feel-good highs to mimic the holy happiness they were made for—the kind of joy that *only* comes from Jesus. Binge-watching, streaming, and scrolling to drown out silence only soothes for a second. Pornography or sex to feel cared for and connected only satisfies momentarily. Partying and thrill-chasing to feel alive and find fun only distracts temporarily. Daydreaming and fantasizing take people to a world where they feel safe and in control only briefly. Over-scheduling helps people avoid quiet moments that would expose their emptiness just ephemerally. Escapism may give a rush, but only the Lord can give *rest*. Only *He* provides peace that pacifies our every personal storm, joy that doesn't depend on circumstances, rest that restores, and love that lasts limitlessly. Pleasure can distract us from the deep-down ache, but only presence—*God's* presence—can downright *heal* it.

Creating Identity & Self-Expression

Others hyperfocus on identity and self-expression to successfully fill the space in them meant for God. People naturally search for meaning and belonging and a solid sense of self, but too many people grapple with this without the guidance of the One who gave them existence. When we turn inward to inquire who we are, we invent a version of ourselves that we hope will provide peace, purpose, and praise—but our self-invention always proves inadequate. Here's why: every person longs to be truly *known* and *accepted*. When this isn't experienced in a relationship with God, people endeavor to launch an identity loud enough to be looked at, lauded, and loved. Self-invention and self-expression become a way to scream, "This is who I am! Please accept and love me!" Still, without God, being "seen" doesn't satisfy the human starvation to be known and loved on a *spiritual* level.

Remember that we also war with an enemy who wants none of us to pursue or perceive our *true*, God-given identity and image. So, within our sordid society, he pushes this propaganda: *"You* can decide *who* you are and even *what* you are!" This feels freeing, but it forces the formidable burden of self-creation on fragile shoulders. Instead of resting and *reveling* in being made in God's image—whether born male or female—people exhaust themselves trying to propose, prove, and protect who they think they "really" are or "need" to be. When people don't know they're *already* passionately loved and purposed by God, they pursue identity labels, passions, affiliations, and even communities that promise acceptance and significance. They think that finding a fitting identity will lead to finally feeling whole. However, no self-made label—no career, gender, sexuality, personality, fashion sense, or passion—can carry the weight of giving a person *true* spiritual and eternal *worth*.

Many people keep reinventing, rebranding, and reshaping themselves—even surgically—hoping the *next* version of themselves will finally feel "right" and forge peace. Others opt to form online personas to acquire affirmation. Many will even alter appearances, names, and labels after trauma to regain control of their lives and story. Some decide to dive head-first into ideologies and subcultures in search of lasting belonging and purpose. The examples are endless. Expression becomes performance—aiming for applause. Identity becomes a boundless burden—one that's never fully brought to rest. The ache remains—*still.*

Here's the transcendent truth: we don't have to guess our true identity; we were *given* one before birth. We come into this world created purposefully, loved unconditionally, known fully, and named already. Real identity isn't repeatedly reimagined; it's *received* through relationship with the Father who first fondly formed us in His heart before He fashioned us with His hands.

Living in Religion

Ironically, some focus on measured morality to forge a feeling of "rightness." Many people search for approval, order, and meaning through some sort of religion—even in Christian churches—but they stop short of *relationship.* They settle for rules without intimacy, hoping that doing good will be enough to make them feel whole, accepted, and at peace. However, religion without real closeness with Jesus becomes a way to try to earn love, cover shame, and feel worthy—but *this* leaves the spirit just as contrite as outright rebellion.

Deep down, people know they're broken, and they want to be "fixed." Following rules and religion becomes a way to prove that they have been "saved." However, trying to *earn* worth through goodness keeps the soul enslaved in a pattern of guilt, fear, and performance. Also, grace is humbling. Many people don't want to admit that they can't save or fix themselves. They would rather perform than surrender. They prefer having a sense of control through religion than putting their trust in grace. Too many *"have a certain enthusiasm for God, but not in accordance with [correct and vital] knowledge [about Him and His purposes]. For not knowing about God's righteousness [which is based on faith], and seeking to establish their own [righteousness based on works], they did not submit to God's righteousness"* (Romans 10:2-3 AMP). Religion can polish the outside, but it can't demolish wrong on the inside like receiving *His* righteousness does. We can honor Him with our lips but have hearts that are *far* from Him (Matthew 15:8). Religious structure and schedule can make us seem moral, but it isn't spiritual, and it doesn't save us. Doing good to offset our mistakes can make us feel better, but it doesn't cleanse us. We cannot out-perform or out-shine our shame; only *He* can shear it. We cannot erase our list of sins; only *He* can shred it. We can attend church, repeat prayers, follow rules, do good deeds, make mistakes, repent, and "do better" repeatedly—but many of us are just wearing religion like a robe hiding our unaddressed and unhealed hearts. Our faith is a mask instead of a mirror—and the void *remains.* Our "morality" only manifests more misery. Religion doesn't truly refine or renew us from the inside out. Morality isn't the same as intimacy with God. Religion is *not* relationship.

Born Needing a Savior

Only a *real* and *right* relationship with God can fill the inherent void every human has inside. Ecclesiastes 3:11 (AMP) explains this: *"He has planted eternity [a sense of divine purpose] in the human heart [a mysterious longing which nothing under the sun can satisfy,* **except God***]."* That ache in every human heart—that deep, day-to-day desire within each of us— that's the place meant for our God. Just as He molded Adam, He made us to literally breathe *His* breath, carry *His* image, walk in *His* plans and purposes, and enjoy *His* closeness. However, we've also—like Adam— experienced spiritual death. We are born deeply sensing our separation from our God, and we desperately spend our days reaching for a remedy.

We are also born *broken.* We come into this world bent in wrong directions—with souls full of twisted vines reaching where they shouldn't. Built in us from the start is a selfish, sinful nature—already wanting what's wrong, automatically wandering into what's wayward, aptly committed to promoting and protecting ourselves above others, and ancestrally influenced by passed-down patterns and problems. We each arrive on earth with issues and fractures that only the Lord can fix: natural and deep inclinations towards lying, anger, fear, violence, addiction, greed, sexual perversion, idolatry, mental and emotional strongholds, poverty or materialism, shame and insecurity, and so on. From our first breath, we not only need love but also *healing* and *freedom*. Yet, we begin life separated from the only One who can completely set us right. We are born in need of a *Savior*.

So, our Creator—whose love never lessens no matter our messes—set in motion His pre-creation plan of salvation. If His people fell, His love would not fail. He would *not* be without us. He would *still* long to pull us close and pour out His love. So, He had planned the Way for us to be **known and near,** the Way for us to have the relationship with Him we were born to have—*still.* Our enemy had not emerged victorious. The fullest enforcement of the Father's justice and the greatest demonstration of His love was *yet* to come. He'd send a Savior, and sin would not win. He'd send His Son. He'd give us **Jesus.**

PART 2

The Savior

CHAPTER FOUR

The Sacrifice & Salvation

"Nearly everything under the law was purified with blood, since forgiveness only comes through an outpouring of blood…Under the old system, year after year, the high priest entered the most holy sanctuary with blood that was not his own. But the Messiah did not need to repeatedly offer Himself year after year, for that would mean He must suffer repeatedly ever since the fall of the world. But now He has appeared at the fulfillment of the ages to abolish sin once for all by the sacrifice of Himself!"—Hebrews 9:22, 25-26 (TPT)

Sacrifices for Sin

When sin shattered Eden, God started a system. He would *still* be **known** and **near** to the people He made. He would *still* pave a path—for those who would pursue Him in faith—to have a profound, personal relationship with Him. Yet, sin stood squarely in the way of this—for *"the wages of sin is death"* (Romans 6:23 NIV). In fact, *"without the shedding of blood, there is no forgiveness"* (Hebrews 9:22 NIV). So, following Adam and Eve's fall, the Lord established a pattern to pay for personal sin.

It started like this: *"And the Lord God made garments of skin for Adam and his wife and clothed them"* (Genesis 3:21 NIV). This is widely understood as the first symbolic act of animal sacrifice, and it was done by the divine hand of God. Blood was shed to shroud their shame. The payment for sin is gory because sin itself is gruesome. Sin is sinister, and requiring such a sacred sacrifice for it only reveals God's justice, holiness, and—yet again—*mercy*. In God's design, blood equals life: *"For the life of the body is in the blood…It is the blood, given in exchange for a life, that makes purification possible"* (Leviticus 17:11 NLT). When blood is shed in sacrifice, it's a visible, visceral picture: an innocent life being given in place of the guilty. In His holiness, God cannot ignore sin. In His justice, He must deal with it, not just dismiss it. However, in His mercy, He does not require our blood immediately; He allows a substitute.

This is the system—the shedding of the innocent blood of animals—that the Lord required of His people following the Fall. Many of God's people—Abel, Noah, Abraham, Job, and many others—all built altars and brought animal sacrifices directly to Him. Individual believers presented offerings themselves, professing their sins to God. Then came the day of Moses: the Law was given, and a formal priesthood was established. God directed that only the priests from the line of Aaron, of the tribe of Levi, could perform sacrifices at the Tabernacle (and later the Temple). The people brought their animals and laid their hands on them, transferring their guilt to the creature while the priests performed the actual sacrifice (Leviticus 1:4). Some offerings served a single sinner while others sustained an entire nation. Time and time again, these sin-atoning sacrifices were submitted. Yet, it was *"impossible for the blood of bulls and goats to take away sins"* (Hebrews 10:4 NIV). Even with the *"steady stream of sacrifices offered year after year, there still was nothing that could make our hearts perfect before God"* (Hebrews 10:1 TPT). Just as quickly as they atoned for their sin, they'd fail again; their hearts were never cured. Their consciences remained smeared, and sin was never *fully* seared. There was only one Way it could be completely cleared: a final sacrifice made by the Father Himself—the perfect Lamb that Heaven revered.

Every drop of blood from each dove, pigeon, goat, bull, ram, and lamb led up to the once-and-for-all sacrifice that our God graciously gave *Himself*. He would send the final Lamb—straight from His heart and Heaven. Our God so loved the world—so cherished His people and so longed for *real* relationship with them—that He would send His only Son to completely clear sin (John 3:16). On the earth, John the Baptist heralded Him *"The Lamb of God, who takes away the sin of the world"* (John 1:29 NIV). He is the Redeemer at the heart of God's grand redemption plan and story. He is **Jesus**, whose very name declares salvation: "the Lord saves" (Matthew 1:21). This sacred Savior—our selfless, shining Jesus—spoke to the Father: *"Since your ultimate desire was not another animal sacrifice, you have clothed me with a body that I might offer myself instead! Multiple burnt offerings and sin offerings cannot satisfy your justice. So, I said to you, 'God—I will be the One to go and do your will, to fulfill all that is written of me in your Word!'"* (Hebrews 10:5-7 TPT). Our Lord *willingly* became our Lamb. By His Blood, He *bought* us back—paying the price for our forgiveness and freedom from sin—and *brought* us back to the place where it's possible to truly experience Him as **known** and **near**— and to have the relationship with Him we were born to have.

His Undying Desire for Relationship

It's worth noting that through all the sin and sacrifices of the Old Testament, the Lord still passionately pursued *relationship* with His people. He promised redemption to Adam and Eve—speaking of the "seed" of a woman who would ultimately subdue and smash the serpent's head (Genesis 3:15). He constituted covenants with mighty— but *imperfect*—men like Noah and Abraham. He called Moses to lead and liberate His people and gave them the Law as a lifeline for living in relationship with Him. He then commissioned him to construct the Tabernacle, a sacred space to host His holy presence on earth—with the Ark of the Covenant resting in the Holy of Holies as His symbolic throne. The Lord also appeared to people in burning bushes, in pillars of cloud and fire, on Mount Sinai, and through theophanies—visible manifestations of God, often appearing as the angel of the Lord. God's presence in the Old Testament was often seen and sensed, mighty and moving. It always revealed His holiness, His nearness, and His tender desire to dwell intimately with His people, drawing them to discern and delight in Him even then.

God also persistently proclaimed His heart through His prophets. Through Jeremiah, He cried out that He longed to treat His people as His *children* and bless them with His best, and He yearned for them to call Him *Father* (Jeremiah 3:19). In Isaiah 54:5, God spoke even as a loving *Husband* to Israel, showing His tender desire for relationship. He also promised through a prophet that there would be a new Covenant written *on* hearts, not tablets—that He would implant

His Word and Himself *within* them, showing His desire for intimate, internal relationship (Jeremiah 31:31-34). He even fervently foretold this about the future: *"I'll pour pure water over you and scrub you clean. I'll give you a new heart, put a new spirit in you. I'll remove the stone heart from your body and replace it with a heart that's God-willed, not self-willed. I'll put my Spirit in you and make it possible for you to do what I tell you and live by my commands…You'll be my people! I'll be your God!"* (Ezekiel 36:26-28 MSG). He would come closer than He'd ever been since the Fall—flooding every life and fully transforming each heart. He would restore the radical, external-*and*-internal closeness first felt in Eden.

Clearly, even after the Fall, God repeatedly pursued humanity to restore fellowship—through covenants, deliverance, presence, promises, and prophetic hope—showing that *relationship* was always His heart's desire. It was *still* His sacred, most-prized dream. One day, it would be finally restored and faithfully fulfilled—once more—through **Jesus.**

Jesus On the Earth

At last, that long-awaited day arrived: Jesus, our Savior, stepped into our skin and onto this earth. He could have come down as a striking King—arms loaded with unseen treasures and a mouth uttering truths of untold measures—but He didn't. He came in the same way we do: He began as an embryo in the womb of a woman and was born as a baby. He grew up in a literal human body and faced actual human experiences, emotions, and limitations—except without sin. He *chose* this so that He could identify with us completely (Hebrews 4:15), live the perfect life we couldn't (Romans 5:19), and die in our place as one of us (Philippians 2:6-8). Yes, He arrived *low*—as a baby laid in straw—to fulfill the Father's salvation plan for all. For centuries, a Messiah was prophesied and promised—One who was birthed from the line of David and the offspring of a woman (Genesis 3:15, 2 Samuel 7:12-13). As the "seed" of a woman, He would crush Satan (Genesis 3:15). As the son of David, He would reign forever (Luke 1:31-33). As the Lamb of God, He would be offered as a perfect, sinless human in *our* place.

He was sent *truly* as the Father's Son, too. Mary, His mother, was a virgin when she gave birth to Jesus. She was told by an angel, *"The Holy Spirit will come upon you…Therefore, the child to be born will be called holy—the Son of God"* (Luke 1:35 ESV). This shows that Jesus was *truly* God's Son, not just a "good" man. He was free from inherited sin since He wasn't born through a sinful, human father. His birth was also a miraculous sign that salvation is God's work, *not* ours.

We'd expect the Father to have His Son begin in a princely palace, but He had Him birthed in a barn. It was prophesied that the Messiah would arrive in Bethlehem (Micah 5:2)—a tiny, trivialized town—and then grow up in Nazareth, a place people put down (John 1:46). Jesus was born to an uncelebrated young woman in a stable and became an unwealthy carpenter's son. He was even described later as a man with no beauty or majesty to attract us to Him (Isaiah 53:2). This was divinely *deliberate*. Through His arrival and even His appearance, our extraordinary God revealed that *no* one is too ordinary—too *low*— for Him to notice, understand, and love. Jesus came humbly *for* the humble—not for the high-class and highly honored. He would be followed for the *right* reasons—not for prestige but for *hunger*. He didn't come to impress the crowds but to save the crushed. He came as one who is approachable and relatable. He *intentionally* walked among the poor, the sick, and the broken. He even called a group of imperfect misfits to be His closest companions and disciples. Yes, the Father sent His Son *low*—the Holy One of Heaven swaddled in sinew and skin—to raise us *up* again.

From His humble beginnings, Jesus grew up as a child into a teen and then into a young adult on the earth He came to redeem. From the time of His birth in a barn to His crucifixion on the Cross, He lived for thirty-three years. However, He didn't launch His public ministry until the age of thirty. What did He do for three decades before He began preaching, teaching, and reaching out and healing lame limbs? He lived as a *human*. Jesus was both fully God *and* fully man (John 1:1-14, Philippians 2:5-11, Colossians 2:9). On the human side, He arrived like we do, and He got tired (John 4:6), became hungry (Matthew 4:2), and grew thirsty (John 19:28). He didn't just experience joy; He endured grief, compassion, anger, and *deep* sorrow (Hebrews 4:15). He also confronted every temptation we will ever contend with but never sinned. Jesus *fully* experienced humanity. Before He died for us, He wanted to *live as* us. He would return to Heaven as our High Priest—one with firsthand understanding of and compassion for our condition (Hebrews 4:14-16). He would experience hurt, loss, betrayal, ridicule, pain, fatigue—everything but sin and sickness. Then, He would experience death—the one meant for *us*.

Jesus was also *fully* God on the earth. Many have called Him a "good teacher" or a "prophet"—but He was completely God in flesh. Though He stood on the earth, He had stood before time; He was eternal (John 1:1-3, Colossians 1:16-17). Jesus said that He and the Father were "one" (John 10:30), so He, too, was all-powerful, all-knowing, wholly holy, and ever-unchanging. He, the Son, is *"the image of the invisible God, the firstborn over all creation,"* and the Father was *"pleased to have all His fullness dwell in Him"* (Colossians 1:15, 19 NIV). Jesus wasn't just sent by God; He *was* (and *is)* God—made knowable and visible in human form. Jesus portrayed the Father's passionate heart, perfect nature, and profound glory. He had the power to forgive sins, accept worship, perform miracles by His *own* authority, and conquer sin and death—something only *God* could do. Also, coming to this earth as both fully human *and* fully divine was something only *God* could do, too. To truly save us, Jesus had to reach up to God and down to humanity and bring us back together forever. He did this by dying as a sinless man—to represent all of humanity, bearing all of its sin—*and* as God—to offer a perfect, infinite sacrifice strong enough to conquer sin and death once and for all.

His death revealed His love and healed His people to the fullest extent—but so did His life on earth. The steps of our Savior on our soil made known the most marvelous parts of His heart. Yes, He demonstrated His divine power. He preached and performed wonders nearly everywhere He stepped and spoke. He repaired blind eyes and restored lame legs. He even radically raised the dead—but He also took a seat at tables and broke bread. He sat, ate, and laughed with people— *imperfect* people. Many reprimanded Him for sitting with sinners, but He told them this: *"It is not the healthy who need a doctor but the sick. I have not come to call the righteous, but sinners"* (Luke 15:1-2, Mark 2:15-17 NIV). Jesus welcomed the wrong and shared life with the lost; *they* were His mission.

He also proved that He didn't just care about crowds; He would show up for just *one*. The Gospels brim with parables about seeking out just *one* who is lost (Luke 15) and stories of Jesus detouring through a town, by a cave, or near a well to have *one* life-changing encounter with *one* hated human. On the earth, Jesus showed us that He's a God who sees and seeks out *each* of us—no matter our messes. He's the Lord who tenderly touches lepers and fully forgives adulterers. He dynamically delivers the demon-possessed and lovingly lifts loads off the stressed. He weeps with those who weep and leads us as His cherished sheep. He would pour out and prove His powerful care in every purposeful step He took on this earth—even as He fell to His knees in Gethsemane and warred to yield His will. Both the misery of His impending mission and the mercy of His unending magnanimity seeped through His skin as sweat and blood (Luke 22:44). Still, our Savior successfully submitted and stood to His feet—then set out to *our* Cross to fulfill *His* Father's will and make our salvation complete.

Jesus On the Cross

After being betrayed and bought-out by a follower and friend, Jesus acquiesced to arrest. Leaders put Him to the test—challenging Him with His own quotes and their own questions. Yet, our Lamb remained reticent (Isaiah 53:7). He could have demonstrated His divinity in one dynamic breath, but He stood strong in the prophesied cross-examinations that came before the Cross. *Love* made Him last through every challenge, thorn, and lash that pierced His back, brow, and breast. *Passion* pushed Him through a pernicious, near-fatal flogging. By the time He came to the Cross, His skin hung in shreds, but His surrender held like steel. With huge, horrific nails hammered into His holy hands and feet, our Lord was lifted up on the Cross. As He hung there, men mocked Him mercilessly, and soldiers cast lots for His clothing. Over this offensive scene, Jesus released this radically redemptive prayer: *"Father, forgive them, for they don't know what they're doing!"* (Luke 23:34 TPT). He forgave them even as He hung dying for their freedom.

There's another He forgave from the Cross, too: a tormented thief who hung heavy-heartedly on his own cross next to Jesus. To His left and His right stood two other crosses carrying two more condemned men. One of the men who hung there mocked Jesus, but the other one repented and requested mercy. Jesus replied, *"I promise you—this very day, you will enter paradise with me!"* (Luke 23:43 TPT). This man's last-minute salvation became a preview of our own—an atonement that comes through prayer and faith, *not* by works. He would spend eternity in relationship with Jesus but never spent *one* day in religion.

Relationship—*still* His foremost focus and fire—burned in His heart even as His body began to burn out. He addressed His mother Mary—concerned for her security even in His misery—pointed to John, and appointed them as each other's new mother and son from that day on (John 19:26-27). Many believe this new family formed at the foot of the Cross also foreshadows the new family of faith forged by His Blood. We would *all* become brothers, sisters, mothers, and fathers—one family united in *Him*. *This* family would be the fruit of *that* fateful, fatal day.

Yet, that day dimmed into darkness after Jesus made those arrangements for His mother. As He reached the climax of the Cross—His own separation from His Father—the sun disappeared over the Son, and despair swallowed the sky. For three full hours, the sunless sky stood as a somber sign of God's searing wrath, poured upon Jesus as He shouldered the sins of the world (Matthew 27:45). Jesus cried out, *"My God, My God, why have you abandoned me?"* (Matthew 27:46 MSG). For the first and only time, Jesus experienced the agonizing absence of His Father—the rightful result of human sin—so that *we* would be rescued from this place so grim. The fracture in His fellowship with the Father plunged Him into the pinnacle of pain on the Cross. The flawless, faultless Son fully absorbed the forsakenness that should have been forever *ours*.

This revelation rushed Him to His final breath. He requested a sip of wine to moisten His mouth so that His last words could be heard, and as He swallowed, He surrendered, shouting, *"It is finished!"* (John 19:30 NIV). He bowed His head, giving His Spirit up to the Father and His life up for the world. Jesus had achieved His aim and completed every claim. The final penalty for sin was paid in full. The Old Testament prophecies and sacrificial system were finally fulfilled. Nothing else was needed for our full forgiveness; His holy work was wholly wrought. The Way back to God was opened. His last words were not a cry of defeat but a victorious declaration. *Relationship* with the Lord—the way it was always meant to be—had been restored.

His Presence Poured Out

Symbolically and powerfully, just as Jesus gave up His Spirit, it's as if the hand of the Father forcefully ripped the veil in His Temple from top to bottom (Matthew 27:51). This curtain—traditionally believed to measure sixty feet high, thirty feet wide, and four inches thick—was the enormous, elaborate barrier that separated the Holy Place from the Most Holy Place (Holy of Holies) in the temple. This vast veil symbolized the separation between God and humanity. Only the High Priest could enter the Most Holy Place—and only once a year on the Day of Atonement (Leviticus 16, Exodus 30:10, Hebrews 9:6-12). The torn-in-two curtain meant direct access to God was now made possible through Jesus. God Himself broke down the brocade blockade, emphasizing that Christ's sacrifice fully satisfies the requirement for atonement (Hebrews 10:19–20).

The instant the veil tore timed faithfully with Jesus' final breath, showing that *His* sacrifice had fulfilled what the temple sacrifices could only foretell. It also signaled the sunset on the old temple-bound offerings; a *new* covenant would now rise like the sun with the Son over the earth. Hebrews 10:19–20 (TPT) explains that Jesus opened *"a new, life-giving way"* into God's presence. Jesus' shedding His Blood and the Father's shredding His veil shows the gospel is for *everyone*, not just the priestly elite. Now *all* people would have full and free access to their Creator, Father, and Friend—just as Adam did. Through Jesus, the Father restored His presence to humanity as intimately as experienced in Eden—but this time, not just in a garden but within *every* willing heart.

Also, as Jesus released His last breath and the Father ripped apart the holy veil, the earth violently quivered and quaked (Matthew 27:51). The weight of the Son's death surged through everything in existence and caused a physical shaking, breaking rocks into shards. God's full wrath and judgement had *heavily* hit the earth, causing upheaval of the old order. The Cross had resoundingly released the preeminent power of God. Yet, the pulse of His power didn't just shatter stones; it split sealed tombs. Long-dead, long-forgotten saints sprang to life, startling the streets of Jerusalem (Matthew 27:52-53)—a staggering sign of the resurrection yet to come. Jesus' death demolished Death itself, driving it to deliver the faithful. Tombs trembled, saints stood alive, and resurrection ruled, roaring through the realm of the redeemed, proclaiming that through Him, eternal life now reigns for *all* who would believe (1 Corinthians 15:20–23).

One *unbelieving* man—a centurion—stood by and stared at it *all*, and as he witnessed the wonder of Jesus' last words, the world shaking, and dead people waking, he wailed in absolute awe, *"There is no doubt, this was the Son of God!"* (Matthew 27:54 TPT). Even *this* man's conclusion and conversion was the result of the Cross and the Presence breaking out of the Temple. Though the Cross looked like loss, it lifted spiritual eyes and enlightened souls. The centurion's confession is a glimpse of the transforming power of Christ's sacrifice, able to soften hearts and reveal truth even in unlikely people. A Roman officer—part of the oppressive system that crucified Christ—became the first to declare His divine identity after His death. This foreshadows the future: rulers, rebels, and *every* nation will come to see Jesus as Lord. This Cross, this Jesus, and this relationship with Him was never meant for just one particular group; it's for *every* tribe and tongue. On the day Jesus died, the Lord made Himself available to every heart—even the *hardest* ones—on the entire earth.

Jesus Comes Back to Life

Jesus was dead. It looked like defeat. Yet, divine design didn't derail; it drove *on*. Down to every detail, His destiny unfolded. Joseph of Arimathea and Nicodemus took Him down from the Cross, wrapped Him in linen and spices as the Law prescribed, and laid Him to rest. Even with His lifeless body lying limp, He continued to complete what the prophets foretold. Isaiah 53:9 declares that the Messiah would be with a rich man in His death. Every act, every arrangement, affirmed God's absolute authority. Jesus' burial proved His death was real—and purposeful. Even when defeat seemed definite, divine plans were quietly, powerfully advancing.

Jesus' body—lifeless and linen-wrapped—was placed in a tomb that had been newly cut from rock (John 19:41, Matthew 27:60). A stout, sturdy stone sealed the entrance to ensure no one would tamper with His tomb. Pilate—reminded of Jesus' promise to rise again in three days—ordered soldiers to stand guard day and night, ensuring Jesus' followers would not break in and burgle His body. With a stone sealing Him in and soldiers stationed out, Jesus would not be touched (Matthew 27:62-66). This was man's attempt to stop God's plan, but these appointed watchmen would only become witnesses to the Miracle they meant to muzzle.

While His body lay in the guarded tomb, Jesus descended down to the place of the Dead—to the lower parts of the earth, a place often understood as Sheol or Hades. He voiced His victory to the vanquished spirits in this prison (I Peter 3:18-20, Ephesians 4:8-10). Yes, before He rose up, He rushed down—to the darkest dimension, to the place of *Death* itself—and announced His triumph over *all* sin, *all* death, and *all* Hell. Before He resurged to His tomb, He snatched up the keys to this revolting realm—taking up *full* authority. In Revelation 1:17-18 (MSG), John records this message released from the lips of the Resurrected Jesus: *"Don't fear: I am First, I am Last, I'm Alive. I died, but I came to life, and my life is now forever. See these keys in My hand? They open and lock Death's doors; they open and lock Hell's gates."* Now, there is no place too low, too dark, or too hopeless where His victory cannot reach. Jesus conquered *all*. His grip is greater—His authority higher—than the hold of addiction, sickness, sin, grief, depression, generational iniquity—*any* dark, deadly thing that would dare to destroy one of His devoted ones. Because *He* defeated darkness, *we* can, too.

One who personally knew this to be true was one of the women who came to visit Jesus' tomb: Mary Magdalene—out of whom He had cast seven demons (Luke 8:2). She and another woman named Mary arrived early on Sunday morning with spices to anoint Jesus' slain body (Matthew 28:1). They honored Him—even in their grief and mourning—and they would soon discover that He honors those who draw near *even* in doubt and difficulty. As they approached the tomb, the earth began to shiver and shake yet again. Their eyes jolted up and witnessed an angel of the Lord descending from Heaven—with an appearance like lightning and clothes like sparkling snow. He rolled the stone away from the tomb and rested upon it (Matthew 28:2-3). The soldiers froze in fear, but the women waited in wonder for words from the angel. This powerful pronouncement poured from his lips: *"There's no reason to be afraid. I know you're looking for Jesus, who was crucified. He isn't here—He has risen victoriously, just as He said! Come inside the tomb and see the place where our Lord was lying!"* (Matthew 28:5-6 TPT). He tasked them with telling this truth to the other disciples, and as they rushed home with this resurrection news, they ran into the Resurrected Lord *Himself.* He appeared to them on their way, and as they fell at His made-new feet, He, again, told them to toss their tears and fears aside and go share the Truth (Matthew 28:9-10).

Jesus later appeared to many others: two question-asking disciples on the road to Emmaus and to His depressed disciples locked behind doors (Luke 24:13-35); to discouraged Peter and doubting Thomas (Luke 24:34, John 20:24-29); to seven struggling disciples attempting to fish and then to His mission-ready disciples on the Mountain of Galilee (John 21:1-14, Matthew 28:16-20)—plus *many* more. He proved His resurrection to *real* people—and He presented it *personally.* He revealed it *relationally.* Even in His first resurrected appearances, He shows His heart again: He was alive, and He would meet people face to face—even those in confusion, grief, and fear. He was (and *is*) truly the Lord who would be **known** and **near** to *all.*

Jesus Ascends

For forty glorious days, the Resurrected Jesus appeared to people—as living, luminous proof that death had been defeated. He walked, He talked, and He revealed His resurrected reality—proclaiming His purpose and proving His power on the earth once more. In these in-person speeches, He reaffirmed His majestic identity and mission (Luke 24:44-48)—showing how every scripture in the Law, the Prophets, and the Psalms pointed to Him and was perfectly fulfilled in His sacrificial death and victorious resurrection, securing forgiveness and freedom for all who would believe. He also commissioned His people: *"Go and make disciples of all nations…teaching them to obey everything I have commanded you"* (Matthew 28:18-20 NIV). This was The Great Commission—a clear call to spread the message of salvation world-wide. He also promised His Spirit: *"You will receive power when the Holy*

Spirit comes upon you, and you will be My witnesses!" (Acts 1:8 NIV). Jesus told them not to leave Jerusalem yet but to wait for this promised Helper, who would empower them to live boldly and fully carry out His call for their lives (Acts 1:4-5). So, Jesus' resurrection was not the conclusion but the *commission*—an unstoppable surge of salvation, sending His followers into the world to shine His light and share His life by the power of His Spirit.

Then, on His final day on earth, He led His disciples out near Bethany (Luke 24:50). He held high His holy hands and blessed His friends. As He spoke, He was taken up into the skies before their very eyes, and a cloud of holy glory hid Him on the horizon (Acts 1:9). As they stood staring at the sky, two angels appeared and announced: *"This same Jesus, who has been taken from you into Heaven, will come back in the same way you have seen Him go into Heaven!"* (Acts 1:11 NIV). Alive and victorious, Jesus headed to Heaven, but He would be back *again*.

Upon His return to the heavenly realm, Jesus took a *seat*. Mark 16:19 (ESV) states, *"Jesus, after He had spoken to them, was taken up into Heaven and sat down at the right hand of God."* Hebrews 1:3 (ESV) seconds this: *"After making purification for sins, He sat down at the right hand of the Majesty on high."* His sitting down designated His work was *done*. His sacrificial mission was made complete. He was then crowned King over *all*—with absolute authority in Heaven and on earth. He was exalted *"to the highest place"* and given *"the Name that is above every name"* (Philippians 2:9-11 NIV). From this seat of authority, Jesus became our High Priest and Intercessor. Day and night, Jesus *"is at the right hand of God interceding [with the Father] for us"* (Romans 8:34 AMP). He *"lives to pray continually for [us]"* (Hebrews 7:25 TPT). This means that our Jesus endlessly stands in the gap for us, pleading on our behalf. He is the Mediator between us and the Father. He *continues* to represent us before the Father, reminding Heaven that our sin has been paid for, that we are righteous in Him, and that we are rightfully *His*.

This does not mean that Jesus is trying to persuade the Father to love and accept us; He is *representing* us with perfect righteousness. His intercession and presence next to the Father is a constant reminder that our debt is paid in full; He is living proof of our redemption. He covers our sin and secures us in the favor and love of the Father continually. This should give us confidence in approaching Him, not fearing rejection, *because of* Jesus (Hebrews 10:19-22). This should give us courage, too: He speaks our literal *names* and *needs* in Heaven every day. When we feel unworthy, Jesus is warring for us by name. When we find ourselves unsure of how to pray, Jesus is already praying *for* us specifically. When we are attacked, Jesus is avidly advocating for us already. When we sin *and* repent, Jesus speaks up— not to plead for our pardon but to declare, "I paid for *that!*" We are constantly being remembered, represented, and defended in the heavenly courts. His work on our behalf didn't end at the Cross; it continues *personally*—and *eternally*.

Ten days after His ascension, Jesus sent His Holy Spirit—just as He had promised (Acts 2). In a stunning scene, the Spirit flooded and filled all who belonged to Him—igniting the birth of the Church. This was a community commissioned to boldly broadcast the Gospel, beautifully love one another, and bravely live as one Spirit-shaped family. The Spirit didn't just birth a new people; He brought a new, deeply *personal* nearness to the Lord. His power and presence poured into every believer individually, reviving what the Fall had ruined. In that sacred outpouring, the fatal effects of the Fall flatlined, and the dead spirits of these first believers surged with life. By His Spirit, the Lord becomes deeply **known** and **near**—restoring His people, collectively *and* personally, to the intimate relationship with Him they were born to have.

What This Means for Us

As Jesus hung on the Cross, all of our *sin* hung on *Him*. Yes, *"it was because of our rebellious deeds that He was pierced and because of our sins that He was crushed"* (Isaiah 53:5 TPT). Truly, *"Yahweh laid the guilt of our every sin upon him"* (Isaiah 53:6 TPT). As Jesus was fastened to the Cross, *every* one of our sins—past, present, and future—were firmly fused *to* Him as if *He* had committed them. He took the *full* wrath of God— which doesn't mean reckless rage but rather God's righteous judgement against evil—for *every* one of our sins. Jesus drank the *full* cup of the Father's fury—the one He dreaded drinking in Gethsemane (Matthew 26:39, Jeremiah 25:15). He sipped it to the bottom, absorbing the entire penalty for *all* sin so that we wouldn't have to taste a single drop.

It's like this: imagine us all—saturated in our sin—standing in the middle of an open field watching a vast, violent thunderstorm roll in—with a sky deadly dark, thunder detonating deafeningly, and a dreadful bolt of lightning directed our way. God's wrath—the penalty for our sin—is the lightning coming *right* and *rightly* to us because of our guilt. However, Jesus—directed *by* the Father out of love for us—*willingly* steps in front of us with arms stretched out wide—yes, in the shape of a cross. He takes the full force of the lightning strike for us, in *our* place. We weather the wind and witness the flash, but we are untouched by the torrential blast because *He* consumed it *all*. He didn't just divert *most* of it. He stood in our place and took it *all*.

Because Jesus absorbed God's righteous judgement for our sins in *full*—down to the last drop and jolt—there is no wrath remaining for those who trust in Him and walk in *real* relationship with Him. Jesus has rescued us from the coming wrath (I Thessalonians 1:10 TPT)—and there is now *"no condemnation [no guilty verdict, no punishment] for those who are in Christ Jesus [who believe in Him as their personal Lord and Savior]"* (Romans 8:1 AMP). Because of Jesus' death and resurrection, God no longer condemns us for our sin. Our guilt is gone. The punishment was paid. Since this is true, we can come with confidence to His throne—even when we've sinned. Here's a verse to never forget: *"Since we have a High Priest who has entered Heaven…let us hold firmly to what we believe. This High Priest of ours* **understands our weaknesses***, for he faced all of the same testings we do, yet he did not sin. So, let us* **come boldly** *to the throne of our gracious God. There will receive His mercy, and we will find grace to help us when we need it most"* (Hebrews 4:14-16 NLT). When we've sinned, we do not have to hide. We can go straight to the throne of God with boldness and confess our sin. Since it has been *already* paid for, we will only meet *mercy*—no judgement, no anger, no cold shoulder, no verbal thrashing. *All* wrath and punishment were poured out on Jesus. Therefore, even as we stumble into sin in the moment, it is sin already swallowed by the Cross; its punishment was fulfilled before we even fell.

Even though each wrong choice has been covered, we still need to *confess* it when we commit it. For those already in relationship with Jesus, confession is about *relationship*, not salvation. Consider these words: *"If we confess our sins to Him, He is faithful and just to forgive us our sins and to cleanse us from all wickedness"* (I John 1:9 NLT). This says *"faithful and just"*—not "merciful and kind"—because Jesus already paid for it. It would be unjust for Him to punish the same sin twice. Even though we're forgiven, we still sin daily, and sin affects our *relationship* with God, not our legal standing with Him. Think of a parent and child: when a child disobeys, he is not disowned, but it has disrupted closeness and trust with the parent. Confession restores *closeness*. It also changes us. Saying our sin helps us see it as God does, which leads to cleansing, transformation, and a deeper walk in doing what's right. It keeps our hearts soft, honest, and dependent on Him and growing in His grace.

Not only did Jesus purchase our forgiveness, He also bought our peace, freedom, and healing. Peer into these phrases from Isaiah 53:4-5 (AMP): *"He has borne our griefs, and He has carried our sorrows and pains...The punishment [required] for our well-being fell on Him, and by His stripes (wounds), we are healed."* It wasn't just our sin that hung on Jesus; our addictions, pains, and sorrows clung to Him, too. Jesus took every one of our strongholds—our *stuck* places—and our broken hearts—our *bruised* places—to His grave so that we don't have to take them to our graves. His work on the Cross didn't just cover our guilt; it reached into *every* kind of brokenness caused by sin. He came to restore *all* that sin ruined.

This means that in addiction, we can reach for *complete* freedom—through *Jesus*. In anxiety, depression, shame, and fear, we can receive *complete* healing—through *Jesus*. In relational conflict and division, we can call out for *complete* clarity and concord—through *Jesus*. In physical pain, we can embrace *complete* recovery—through *Jesus*. In heartache, in loss, in despair, in grief, we can rest in supernatural comfort and *complete* peace—through *Jesus*. When we face inner pains and outer problems, we can turn to the Cross, too. At the Cross, Jesus not only carried our sins but also our *sorrows*—purchasing the healing of every inner wound and the power to overcome every outer storm, securing supernatural breakthrough for every burden we will ever bear.

Because He rose, we can rise, too—in *every* way, inside and out, even in the most crushing circumstances. When the grave could hold Him no longer, every dead part of us—and every dead-end story—rose *with* Him. We don't have to *stay* addicted, hurt, broken, or bruised on this earth—because His death and resurrection carry a *miracle* for *every* mess we will ever face. His rising does more than redeem; it transforms our shattered places into sacred spaces, our failures into fountains of grace. Every struggle and shadowed corner of our lives is now made hopeful and holy—a canvas for His *glory*. Our trials become the stage on which we meet His strength, our pain the doorway to His presence—and in all of it, He *delights*.

Isaiah 53:10 (TPT) says this: *"Even though it pleased Yahweh to crush Him with grief, He will be restored to favor. After His soul becomes a guilt-offering, He will gaze upon His many offspring and prolong His days. And through Him, Yahweh's deepest desires will be fully accomplished."* What are His "deepest desires"? *We* are. It's always been His *people*. He has always wanted us to be both *whole* and *wholly* His. Because of the Cross, He can become truly **known** and **near**—and through real *relationship* with Him, every waking moment can be spent walking with Him, experiencing *forgiveness* in every sin and *freedom* in every situation.

How to Receive Salvation

How do we receive this gift? How do we accept *Jesus*? How do we begin this *relationship* with Him that He longs to have with us? It's so simple yet so powerful. Romans 10:9-10 (NIV) gives us the clear how-to: *"If you declare with your mouth, 'Jesus is Lord,' and believe in your heart that God raised Him from the dead, you will be saved. For it is with your heart that you believe and are justified, and it is with your mouth that you profess your faith and are saved."* Faith and belief in Jesus—*who* He is and *what* He's done—in the heart makes us *right* with God. Verbally confessing this confirms the reality of our saving faith. *Real* belief makes it out of the mouth; it doesn't just stay hidden in the heart.

This moment can happen alone or with another person guiding us into this salvation-receiving confession. Many have prayed this in public gatherings while others have prayed with a particular friend; still, others have prayed this privately—all alone. Whenever and with whomever this prayer is prayed, the result is the same: *salvation*—the beginning of the relationship with the Lord we were *born* to have.

Here is an example prayer of salvation:

"Jesus, I choose You. I believe you are Lord, the Son of God, and that you died for me and rose again. I turn from my sin and trust You to completely forgive me. I receive you as my Savior and Lord. Come into my life, and make me new. I want to follow you from this day forward. I want you to be **known and near.** *Right now, I begin the relationship with You I was born to have. In Jesus' Name, Amen."*

That's it. When we pray this and *mean* it, we step from death to life—washed, welcomed, and awakened into a brand-new beginning with *Jesus.* We immediately step into our *own* relationship with Him—and a whole *new* life.

PART 3

The Relationship

CHAPTER FIVE

All Things New

"Our faith in Jesus transfers God's righteousness to us, and he now declares us flawless in his eyes. This means we can now enjoy true and lasting peace with God, all because of what our Lord Jesus, the Anointed One, has done for us. Our faith guarantees us permanent access into this marvelous kindness that has given us a perfect relationship with God"—Romans 5:1-2 (TPT)

A New Life Begins

Immediately—when receiving salvation from Jesus—we are miraculously made *new*. Our dead spirits—that have been breathless since birth because of sin—come to *life*. It's as if we are newly formed Adam receiving the anointed breath of God into our beings and then flinging our spiritual eyes open for the very first time. Our innermost being awakens in awareness to the Lord and His life *within* us, *around* us, and *for* us. He is now **near** and can be **known**.

The Bible calls this salvation experience being "born again." Jesus taught, *"I assure you and most solemnly say to you, unless a person is born again [reborn from above—spiritually transformed, renewed, sanctified], he cannot [ever] see and experience the Kingdom of God"* (John 3:3 AMP). He tagged on this truth, too: *"That which is born of flesh is flesh [the physical is merely physical], and that which is born of the Spirit is spirit"* (v. 6 AMP). When we are born physically, we inherit human life but not spiritual life. We must *choose* to experience a supernatural, inner birth by confessing faith in Jesus and becoming *His*. When we yield our lives to Jesus, His Spirit awakens our sleeping spirits, sparking our hearts with fire for *Him*.

It's as if we are born as a beautiful candle with a wick but no flame. We are built to carry and shine His light, but sin smothers the wick, leaving us in desolate darkness. This is the human spirit apart from God—present but not alive in the way it was created to be. However, the moment we surrender our lives to Jesus, He removes the sin; then, His Spirit strikes a match and ignites our spirits with divine life. We are now aglow with *Him*—burning, flickering, and giving off His light. We have been lit to *life* spiritually by His Spirit. We can now see and sense Him personally, and we can also be taken up into His hand to light up the dark, dying world around us.

With this new birth and new light comes a whole new *person*. When one surrenders to Jesus, *"he is a new creature [reborn and renewed by the Holy Spirit]; the old things [the previous moral and spiritual condition] have passed away,"* and, *"new things have come [because spiritual awakening brings new life]"* (2 Corinthians 5:17 AMP). At salvation, we become a new creation with a new *nature* (Ezekiel 36:26-27). The former life fades. Our identity before coming to Jesus, our bondage to sin, our guilt and shame, our hopelessness and separation from Him— it all dies and disappears. In the place of all of that, we receive a new identity, a new heart and mind, a new power to walk in freedom, and a new purpose. We don't experience all of this immediately externally, but it does happen instantly *internally*. It will *all* unfold—our new nature steadily surfacing like gold—as we grow in *relationship* with Jesus for the rest of our lives.

The first step of salvation—the initial confession of faith and surrender to Jesus—is monumental. It's *pivotal*. That simple but serious first prayer changes *everything*. It's the initial step into so much *new*.

Newly Forgiven, Freed, & Filled

As soon as we say "amen" when praying for salvation, we receive *full* forgiveness for *all* of our sins. All past sin is eradicated and erased—removed *"as far from us as the east is from the west"* (Psalm 103:12 NLT). We stand completely clean as if we've *never* sinned. Even our future failures—we *already* have forgiveness for those, too. As soon as we surrender, Jesus credits our "heavenly account" in full—applying His covering for any sin we will ever commit. When we make a mistake and then confess it to Him, full forgiveness is already ours. The sin has *already* been paid for with Blood. When we are truly *His,* forgiveness is always truly *ours.* While on this earth, we may never be fully sinless, but His mercy for us is endless. This means we don't have to carry the grievous weight of guilt—*or* fear our Father's rejection. Every step we take is gloriously gloved by His grace, and every mistake is met with His measureless forgiveness. This isn't a get-off-free ticket tucked into the hands of a wrong-hearted person who would waywardly say, "I'll just sin now because I know He'll forgive me later!" This is an assurance anchored in the spirit of a right-hearted person who sincerely says, "I don't want to sin at all!" but still makes mistakes. Those whose hearts are wholly His will never fall too far away—*or* too many times. His forgiveness—finalized and freely given—will *never* run dry for them.

This mind-blowing miracle happens at salvation, too: we are *freed* from the command and control of sin within. Romans 6:6-7 (NLT) declares, *"We know that our old sinful selves were crucified with Christ so that sin might lose its power in our lives. We are no longer slaves to sin. For when we died to Christ, we were set free from the power of sin."* As mentioned before, we are born as puppets on sinful strings that are pulled by a hidden, horrific puppeteer: Satan himself. He is *"the commander of the powers in the unseen world"* and is *"the spirit at work in the hearts of those who refuse to obey God"* (Ephesians 2:2 NLT). However, as soon as we surrender to Jesus, it's as if He takes a sword and immediately severs Satan's strings attached to us. Not *one* is left intact. He *completely* frees us from evil's fetters. This does *not* mean we won't still experience temptation—and even still falter and fail in frail moments—but it *does* mean that we now have no obligation to obey the ongoing urges of our sinful nature (Romans 8:12). Without Jesus, we had no ability to shut out sin, but with Him, we have the authority—the *freedom*—to shout a triumphant, "No!" and shut down every temptation and win.

We may be freed from sin at salvation, but we will still fight with it during our formation. For the rest of our lives, we will undergo spiritual transformation, continually increasing in hatred towards sin and improving in holy desires. After being freed from the prison of sin and stepping into the light, we must learn to walk again—to tread *rightly*—after years of captivity. At times we will stumble—and old habits may continue to pull and prey on us—but as we keep getting back up and barreling forward, we will find that we are only taking one victorious step after another. Over time, those triumphs transform us and take us to the *totally-free* places that Jesus bought us with His Blood.

An equally extraordinary event we experience at salvation is that we are not only forgiven and freed, but we are also *filled*. When we confess faith in Jesus, we are immediately given the gift of the Holy Spirit. Ephesians 1:13 (NLT) makes this clear: *"When you believed in Christ, he identified you as His own by giving you the Holy Spirit, whom He promised long ago."* When we are filled with the Holy Spirit, we are flooded with God Himself. He is an equal part of the Trinity—the Father, Son, and Spirit (Matthew 3:16-17, Matthew 28:19). Our Father plans and sends, the Son comes and redeems, and the Spirit indwells and empowers. Both our Father and Jesus longed and looked forward to our receiving His Spirit. Even before He left the earth, Jesus declared this truth to His disciples: *"It is to your advantage that I go away; for if I do not go away, the Helper (Comforter, Advocate, Intercessor—Counselor, Strengthener, Standby) will not come to you; but if I go, I will send Him (the Holy Spirit) to you [to be in close fellowship with you]"* (John 16:7 AMP). When Jesus was on the earth, He could only be in one place at a time externally. His Spirit, however, can fill us internally and surround us personally, giving *each* of us the closest kind of fellowship and friendship with the Lord.

The Holy Spirit becomes our never-failing, always-there Friend. It is His *delight* to help, encourage, teach, lead, strengthen, counsel, and pray for us (John 16:7, 12-15; Romans 8:26-27). He even *speaks* the very thoughts of God to us. Scripture says, *"No one can know a person's thoughts except that person's own spirit, and no one can know God's thoughts except God's own Spirit. And we have received God's Spirit…so that we can know the wonderful things God has freely given us"* (I Corinthians 2:11-12 NLT). When the Holy Spirit moves into us, we are not only mindful of our own musings, but we can literally lean in and listen to the thoughts of God—and He's so near that we can hear even His gentlest whispers (I Kings 19:11-12). By choosing to put His own Spirit inside of us, He comes as close as He possibly can—to *each* of us personally. It's the

Holy Spirit who comes this **near** and makes God intimately **known**. *He is the One who fosters the friendship with the Father we were always meant to find.*

A New Family

When we surrender to Jesus, we also step into a new *family*. We are personally, permanently *adopted* by the Father. We each become His *child*. His Word says that those who believe in Jesus become *"adopted as sons [as God's children with all rights as fully grown members of a family],"* and The Father sends *"the Spirit of His Son into our hearts, crying out, 'Abba! Father!'"* (Galatians 4:5-6 AMP). We are *"no longer a slave (bond-servant), but a son"* and *"also an heir through [the gracious act of] God [through Christ]"* (v. 7 AMP). The wonders in these words reveal His wide, wholehearted love for those who willingly want and worship Him.

By adopting us, the Father *chooses* us. The Father declares, "I see you. I want you. I *choose* you to become My *child* forever." This kind of love is deliberate and deeply affirming. Through adoption, the Father makes a covenant with us; it is a binding promise—*not* based on our performance. Adoption is also a redeeming love. It moves us from one condition to another—from the kingdom of darkness into *His* Kingdom, from vulnerability into security, from outsider into *family* (Colossians 1:13). We are born spiritual orphans—cut off from the Father because of Adam's sin—and through our surrender to Jesus, the Father adopts us and makes us *His*. This is transformational, too. Adoption doesn't just provide a name or a home; it pivots our identity, inheritance, and future. We belong to a new *place* and have a new *position* that comes with ceaseless *provision* and countless *promises*.

The Lord could have chosen to call us His servants, soldiers, subjects, or slaves, but none of these reflect His true heart towards us. No word could work but His "child"—His *son* or *daughter*—and the tender relationship it implies. The Father's heart is pure and perfect towards us. He cares for us with *"deepest affection"* and *"watches over [us] very carefully"* (I Peter 5:7 AMP). He longs for us to *"have the power to understand, as all God's people should, how wide, how long, how high, and how deep his love is"* (Ephesians 3:18 NLT). He eagerly desires that we *experience* this love personally, and through this understanding alone, we will *"be made complete with all the fullness of life and power that comes from God"* (Ephesians 3:19 NLT). He never just wished for us to be on "His side"; He has *always* wanted us *by* His side experiencing His very powerful, personal love at all times.

It's also one of the highest honors of the Holy Spirit to release this revelation into our hearts. He desires to build and broaden our view of God as a Father—to the point that we don't just call Him "God," but we can't help but cry out *"Abba"* to Him—a term of closeness and endearment that translates in our language as "Dad," "Daddy," or "Papa" (Romans 8:15, Ephesians 4:6). He longs to move us into *that* and out of *this:* a *"spirit of slavery"* that always fears God's disapproval and judgement, has no intimacy with Him, and hurries to hide when mistakes are made (Romans 8:15 AMP). As His adopted child, we step into full acceptance and affection with Him—complete, constant approval that we do not have to earn. He wants us to have an endless awareness of His nearness and the tenderness of His heart, never fearing His judgement or a change of mind towards us. He *remains* our tender Father even when we falter.

Our Father longs for us to truly see, savor, and rightly relate to who He *really* is. When we envision Him, we should see the face of a Father—smiling and loving—one who *delights* in us. Sitting with us, listening to us, and pouring His wisdom into us excites Him. Raising us up—patiently guiding and shaping us into His image—lights Him up with joy. Providing for us—according to *His* riches—ignites His heart with pure pleasure. Even when we mess up, mistakes don't move down our standing with Him. His love doesn't lessen; He just pulls us close and tenderly teaches us the lesson in it. Just as a human parent rushes to the side of his or her fallen child, so does our Father. When we stumble and fumble, He just moves in *closer.* He does not step into the role of Judge, so we don't have to slip back into the sheer fear of a slave. Jesus bore our *full* judgement and left us with only love and mercy to meet when we've fallen off our feet. Yes, His conviction and discipline will come (Hebrews 12:5-13), and natural consequence from our sin ensues—but His love *endures.*

So, let's be careful not to put the wrong face on our Father. He does not wear the mask of earthly flawed fathers or other austere authority figures we've encountered. Don't envision a dad's disappointed demeanor—and don't picture a distant, detached face devoid of feeling either. See an expression of affection and admiration—one that stays the same through our triumphs *and* tumbles no matter how long we've been His. We can envision this same face— this *same* loving look—at *every* stage of development in Him. He smiles just as broadly over the brand-new child stumbling through first steps as He does over the one who's now marching in decades-worth of revelation and relationship. To *all* of His children—new *and* experienced—He is loving and kind, not irritable or rude, keeping no record of wrongs, never giving up or losing faith, remaining hopeful and enduring through *every* circumstance (I Corinthians 13:4-7). To *all* of us, He is the Father watching and waiting for us *even* when we wander off— then wonderfully showering us with gracious gifts and lavish love when we come back home (Luke 15:11-32). He is loving and kind beyond belief—yet He wants it *believed* in every heart and mind.

The more we believe in the Father's perfect love for us, the more *fear* leaves us. All dark clouds of impending doom—all feelings of insecurity and anxiety—fade away. When we *know* His *"perfect love,"* it *"expels all fear,"* and *"if we are afraid, it is for fear of punishment, and this shows that we have not fully experienced His perfect love"* (I John 4:18 NLT). We must ask the Holy Spirit to continually deepen our understanding and experience of the Father's love. He will bring us to such a place of revelation that His *pleasure* towards us pervades and permeates the inner atmosphere of our lives. We will continually feel security instead of anxiety. His perfect peace will make all fear cease. Let's know this: His *constant* feelings for us are love, desire, joy, and pleasure—even when we are just sitting, doing nothing. Like a physical parent, His heart surely swells when we do something that reflects Him—but His heart is *always* at a place of want, commitment, and delight in us—even in non-spiritual moments. While we are eating dinner, brushing our teeth, doing homework, picking up our kids from school, working in our yards—in *any* ordinary moment—He is literally rejoicing over us with gladness or exulting over us with singing (Zephaniah 3:17). So, His favorite move we make is to include *Him* in all our moments—*not* just the "spiritual" ones. We make His heart happiest when we turn and talk to Him when we drive to work or school, wash dishes, load laundry, go for a walk, practice basketball, or mow the grass. That's when He excitedly exclaims, *"This* one *gets* it! *This* is what I've wanted since Eden!"

In this great pleasure towards us, He's also positioned us as His *heirs* and procured a glorious future for us. In fact, as His children, we are co-heirs with Christ and will inherit all that *He* does as we walk the same path of obedience and self-denial He did (Romans 8:17 NLT). Right along with Jesus, we receive a place in His Kingdom (Luke 12:32, James 2:5), His Spirit (Ephesians 1:13-14), *every* spiritual blessing (Ephesians 1:3), His glory (Romans 8:30), and eternal life (Titus 3:7). We have been adopted and written into the Father's will—right alongside our Jesus. This has always been His plan and pleasure—even when we existed only as desires written into the walls of His heart.

New Authority

When we fused into the Father's family, our feet were also fixed firmly onto our enemy's neck. As His children, we have our Father's *authority* over all the power of Satan. When we receive salvation, the authority we lost through Adam's fall is restored back to us; we are recommissioned into our original purpose. Remember that we were created for both relationship *and* rulership with the Lord.

Adam and Eve were given dominion—authority to govern—over the earth (Genesis 1:26-28). The Hebrew word for "dominion" is "*radah*," which means to rule, to reign over, to manage, to govern, to have authority or oversight—but with *care*, not crushing domination. This is royal, governing language. The Lord established Adam and Eve as His vice-regents—His appointed governors to manage and steward the earth under His leadership. They were commissioned to be fruitful and multiply, to fill the earth, and to fearlessly subdue it. Yes, this means the literal caring of land and stewarding of resources and life on earth; however, they weren't just to *tend* to Eden. They were to *expand* it. They were to bear His image as wise and loving care-takers but also as His representatives on this earth—spreading His presence and order throughout the whole world. Working alongside the Father, they were to create culture, form families, and broaden the beauty and harmony of His Kingdom on earth. They were ambassadors of Heaven, ruling creation under His authority—kings and priests in Eden.

This was the position Satan pined after. He couldn't reign in Heaven, but he *could* rule over humanity. He could construct his own kingdom and craft his own corrupt culture on this created earth. He just had to get them to obey *him,* not the Lord. Then, when Satan succeeded, Adam and Eve egregiously gave their God-given authority to Satan, who then became *"the god of this world"* (2 Corinthians 4:4 ESV). He acquired access to human hearts—to influence and control them and the world's systems. He attained the power to tempt, deceive, and oppose God's purposes, lying and leading people away from the Truth and *real* righteousness. Satan now ruled where God's image-bearers should have reigned. The earth became his stage and human hearts his instruments of destruction and corruption.

However, Jesus came to unseat this usurper. Jesus appeared as the Second Adam (1 Corinthians 15:45, Romans 5:17), and he reclaimed *all* that Adam relinquished—including spiritual authority—and restored it to humanity. Jesus didn't just rescue us from sin; He reinstated our original calling: authority over the enemy; power to heal, bind, loose, and proclaim; stewardship of creation; and spiritual dominion. Jesus declares this to His people: *"I have imparted to you my authority to trample over his kingdom. You will trample upon every demon before you and overcome every power Satan possesses. Absolutely nothing will harm you as you walk in this authority"* (Luke 10:19 TPT). In giving us His authority, Jesus restored Eden's commission. We become ambassadors again (2 Corinthians 5:20), we walk anew in our role as kings and priests on the earth (Revelation 1:6, 5:10), and we exercise spiritual dominion to advance God's Kingdom (Matthew 16:19, Matthew 28:18-20). He restored to us both our relationship *and* our rulership.

It's paramount that we perceive what this authority permits. First of all, we have been given *Jesus'* authority (Luke 10:19), and we have even been *"seated with Him in the heavenly realms"* (Ephesians 2:6 NIV). We share in Jesus' victory and rule, and we exercise spiritual authority from a place of unity *with* Him. We are *seated* with Jesus, but we must learn to *stand* against the enemy like Jesus. With the authority Jesus has given us, we no longer have to be shaken and shoved around by Satan. We are to trample *him;* he can no longer tread on *us*—unless we let him (Luke 10:19). In fact, we are promised this: *"Submit to [the authority of] God. Resist the devil [stand firm against him], and he will flee from you"* (James 4:7 AMP). When we align our lives with Jesus' truth and authority, we can stand firmly against the enemy's lies, temptations, and accusations. When we speak up and shut him up, he has no legal ground to stay, so he flees. This also applies to confusion, insecurity, shame, fear, and even infirmity. Anything the enemy throws our way, we can catch—in the authority of Jesus—and toss it right back on him. We have been set *apart* from and *above* Satan. He literally lies and tries to bully us from under our feet. We now stand in power over him, and he meets defeat when we speak.

We've also been given this authority: *"I assure you, whatever you forbid on earth will be considered to be forbidden in Heaven, and whatever you release on earth will be considered to be released in Heaven"* (Matthew 18:18 TPT). To "forbid" or "bind" means to prohibit or restrict. To "release" or "loose" signifies allowing or permitting something. This implies that we have been imparted the authority and the responsibility to bind demonic activity or anything that contradicts God's will and to bring and bestow healing, peace, deliverance, and God's promises. *We* get to decide what is forbidden and fostered in all our atmospheres—in our hearts, in our homes, in our workplaces, and even our world. We do this by standing up and speaking out in prayer. Even as we pray things as simple as, "Fear, *go*! Peace, *come*! In Jesus' Name!"—Heaven is released, and Hell is repressed. We can even send forth healing into bodies (Mark 16:17-18, James 5:14-15), deliverance into souls (Mark 16:17), and peace into situations (John 14:27, Philippians 4:7). As the Father's sons and daughters and Jesus' co-heir, we are not to pray passive, survival prayers; we *get* to pray massive, revival prayers.

We've also been granted authority to advance God's kingdom on the earth. Consider Christ's concluding challenge to His chosen disciples before His ascension: *"All authority (all power of absolute rule) in Heaven and on earth has been given to Me. Go, therefore, and make disciples of all the nations [help the people to learn of Me, believe in Me, and obey My words], baptizing them in the name of the Father and of the Son and of the Holy Spirit, teaching them to observe everything that I have commanded you"* (Matthew 28:18-20 AMP). Jesus has given us abundant, authoritative anointing to share Him with the world—to preach and teach the Word, to disciple and build the Church, and to lead the lost to their Savior. We have been made *"ambassadors for Christ, as though God were making His appeal through us"* (2 Corinthians 5:20 AMP). As we speak, share, and show the world Jesus, we don't move in our own power but in the authority that Jesus made *ours*. We speak and act with Heaven's full backing, releasing sovereign spiritual influence everywhere we go. No matter the resistance that rises against us, the One who is living within us is *far* greater than the one lurking in this world (I John 4:4). We sit, stand, speak, and share with the same authority that dethroned the devil. We are heirs of Heaven carrying out holy work who never have a reason to tremble before Hell.

We aren't to wait on Jesus alone to carry out His work. Let's not make this common mistake: when a need arises—when a move or miracle is required—we ask Jesus to "do something" while we do *nothing*. Many of us watch and wait for His hand to move, not realizing He has already placed the power—and often even the provision—in *ours*. Often, He is waiting for *us* to step up, speak out, and act in the authority He has already entrusted to us. We say, *"Jesus, give this hungry man bread!"*—and He retorts, *"You give it to him!"* We shout, *"Jesus, stop this attack!"*—and He replies, *"You command it to go in My Name!"* We squall, *"Jesus, move this mountain!"*—and He reminds, "I said if *you* tell it to go, it *will* move!" (Mark 11:23-24). Peter set the example when he gutsily grabbed the hand of the beggar—who had been lame since birth—and proclaimed, *"I have no silver or gold, but what I do have, I give to you. In the name of Jesus Christ of Nazareth, rise up and walk!"* (Acts 3:6 ESV). The man then rose on renewed legs. Faith and the power in the Name of Jesus healed the man, *not* Peter. Peter understood that the power comes from Jesus, but *he* could exert *His* authority.

This partnership is also powerfully presented in Ezekiel 37:1-14 when the Lord led Ezekiel to a vast valley full of long-dead, dry bones. The Lord asked him if the bones could live again; Ezekiel responded by saying that's a miracle only *God* could complete. Instead of crying out, "Watch this!" and commanding the bones to come alive, the Lord *partnered* with Ezekiel in this miraculous moment. He told Ezekiel exactly what to speak to the bones, and as he said it, the Lord did it. This scene carried on in stages: the Lord continued to tell Ezekiel what to say, and as the words were spoken by the *man,* the power was released by the *Lord*—until the brittle bones became a breathing, living army standing on feet. This is the pattern for our partnership. We draw near to Him and hear His whisper. He speaks and steers. We follow and obey—declaring and doing *exactly* as led. His power then showers, surges, and stirs the impossible into existence.

Jesus restored this radical *rulership* along with our right relationship with Him. He desires that we daily deepen in both. They go and *grow* together. The more we mature in *knowing* Him, the more we will move in knowing when we are to speak and act on His behalf. The further we advance in listening to Him and obeying His every whispered word—whether Word-written or Spirit-spoken—the greater we will walk in this authority. Let's know that this, too, was the Father's dream in Eden. It's always been His desire to develop and drive His Kingdom and make miracles happen on this earth *with* us—in partnership with His cherished *children*.

A New Boldness

With this new identity and authority comes a new security—a new *boldness*. We have been completely forgiven, freed, and filled. We have been adopted as sons and daughters. We have been given mighty spiritual authority. Yet, we may look at our hearts and hands and still see them as dirty. We don't feel royal—or even *loyal* at times. We are still tempted, still get tripped up, and still feel tied down. In reality, we can *feel* like a mess, which keeps us from approaching the Lord with boldness. Yet, we *still* can.

In fact, the Bible beckons us to come to Him with confidence: *"Because of Christ and our faith in Him, we can now* **come boldly and confidently** *into God's presence"* (Ephesians 3:12 NLT). Another version reads like this: *"We have boldness and confident access through faith in Him [that is, our faith gives us sufficient courage to* **freely and openly approach God** *through Christ]"* (Ephesians 3:12 AMP). Hebrews 10:19 (TPT) heralds this truth, too: *"He welcomes us to come into the most holy sanctuary in the heavenly realm—* **boldly and without hesitation.** *"* Because of *Jesus*, we can have *boldness* in approaching the Lord. That word "boldness" is the Greek word *"parrēsía,"* which means this: outspokenness, courage to speak freely, and fearless confidence. This boldness is not arrogance;

it's the spiritual freedom and confidence we have because of what *Jesus* has done for us. Whereas in the Old Testament, only the priest could enter into God's presence (the Holy of Holies), *we* now have continual, personal access. Jesus is the door we walk through, and our faith in Him is the key that lets us in. (Notice that the key is *not* our spiritual progress or sinless performance.) We come because of *His* righteousness, not our own rightness. We don't have to wait to feel "worthy" to walk and talk with the Lord. We can approach Him without fear, dread, or hesitation—even when we've been weak or wrong. We have full access—no matter what's transpiring in our lives—because we are not outsiders begging for mercy. We are cherished children coming to our faithful Father. We are *always* wanted and welcome.

Here's how the Father *sees* us: *"You are holy and blameless as you stand before him **without a single fault**"* (Colossians 1:22 NLT). How could He view *us* as faultless? It's certainly not because of anything we've done, but because God, in all His fullness, chose to live in Christ and reconcile everything to Himself through His Blood on the Cross—including those of us who were once separated from Him by sin (Colossians 1:19-21). Because of what Jesus has done, the Father now perceives us as *perfect.* He sees us "in Jesus," not "in our mistakes." When we put our faith in Jesus, we experience an extraordinary exchange: Jesus takes our sin, and we are given *His* righteousness. This means we are no longer judged by *our* performance but on *His* perfection. We do not come before the Lord as ourselves alone but as people completely *clothed* in Jesus. We now exist *"in Christ"* (2 Corinthians 5:17, Ephesians 2:6). We are wrapped in Him, covered by Him—all of our ugly dissolved in His holy. This status is declared, *not* earned. The Father doesn't say, *"You're holy and blameless without a single fault,"* because we've become morally flawless; He declares this over us because Jesus paid for our sin and made us spotless. Even when we fall short, we are not kicked out of His presence or knocked lower in His perspective. He corrects, disciplines, and teaches as a loving Father, but He *never* withdraws His righteousness *or* our right standing with Him.

Our relationship with Jesus is secure—even as our character matures. Think of it this way: *positionally,* we are already holy and blameless before God (because of Jesus); *practically*, we are being made holy and blameless in how we live (by the Holy Spirit's work in us). Look at this verse: *"By one sacrifice he has made perfect forever those who are being made holy"* (Hebrews 10:14 NIV). We have been *justified* (made perfect in our spiritual standing), but we are being *sanctified* (growing out of our sinful nature and *into* His nature in our natural lives). We live in an already-not-yet tension. Here's the "already": Jesus' sacrifice has concretely secured our status before the Lord. Here's the "not yet": we are still being transformed by the ongoing work of the Holy Spirit in our daily, earthly lives. So, in real life, we are still "messy," but when we come before the Lord, instead of seeing our flaws and failures, He sees this: the obedience of Jesus, the beauty of holiness already purchased, a child He has adopted and embraced—*not* someone trying to be enough but someone *already* made enough through Jesus.

This doesn't suggest that we can't come to Him and talk about our weaknesses and struggles. We are to bring these *boldly* to Him. Remember this verse: *"This High Priest of ours understands our weaknesses, for he faced all the same testings we do, but He did not sin. So let us* **come boldly** *to the throne of our gracious God. There we will receive His mercy, and we find grace to help us when we need it most"* (Hebrews 4:15-16 NLT). Our Lord peers at us positionally in Christ—perfect, righteous, blameless—but He also perceives us personally and *compassionately* as His child still in process. He still knows our natural condition, and He deeply cares about the pain, fear, and sinful tendencies with which we contend. Jesus is not just our Savior; He is also our Sympathizer. On our earth, He took on our humanity in its entirety. He *truly* understands our weaknesses. He *totally* gets us. When we come into God's presence, Jesus isn't just the reason the Father accepts us; He's also the One who understands exactly what we mean when we state our struggles. We never have to explain to Jesus what it feels like to be *us*. He *fully* knows. There's not one fear, tear, or care that we can't share with Him. There's not one thing so hopeless or horrible that we have to hide it. We come before Him perfect but messy—and no matter what battle or burden we're bringing, we can bring it *boldly*.

The Next Step: Water Baptism

The next step after receiving salvation—this whole *new* life—

is to celebrate it publicly. We do this through *water baptism* (Acts 2:38, Galatians 3:27, Matthew 28:19-20). Being baptized is our first public act of faith. This is a valiant, visible step through which we declare, "I have *truly* made Jesus the Lord of my life!" We rejoice in this choice and the new life it's brought surrounded by our *new* family—our brothers and sisters in Christ. We stand before them broadcasting to all that our repentance and relationship with Him are *real.* We have left our old life behind and stepped boldly into the new life He has birthed.

Water baptism doesn't save us—Jesus' grace did—but it does do something powerful in us. Romans 6:4 (NLT) reveals this: *"For we died and were buried with Christ by baptism. And just as Christ was raised from the dead by the glorious power of the Father, now we also may live new lives."* Next, 1 Peter 3:21 (AMP) proclaims this: *"Baptism [which is an expression of a believer's new life in Christ] now saves you, not by removing dirt from the body, but by an appeal to God for a good (clear) conscience, [demonstrating what you believe to be yours] through the resurrection of Jesus Christ."* As we step into water and then are submerged beneath by a pastor or leader, the person we *were* and the guilty conscience that came with it are wonderfully washed away. This is a work of grace the Lord grants as we take this next step. As we rise from the water—which is symbolic of Jesus' resurrection—we receive a spiritual joy, a lightness; we literally feel the *newness* of the life we've just begun.

Water baptism is a step that Jesus both demanded *and* demonstrated. Jesus declared these words: *"Whoever believes and is baptized will be saved"* (Mark 16:16 ESV). He also stressed that we must be *"born of water and the Spirit"* (John 3:5 ESV). Knowing how momentous this is, He even modeled this move of obedience for us (Matthew 3:13-17). When He approached John to be baptized in the Jordan River, John tried to stop Him, saying that it was *he* who needed to be baptized by Jesus, *not* the other way around. Yet, Jesus responded that it was proper to do this *"to fulfill all righteousness"* (Matthew 3:15 NIV). Then, as John lifted Jesus up from the water, the heavens swiftly swung open, the Holy Spirit descended from above like a dove, and the Father proclaimed an affirming message over His Son: *"This is My beloved Son, in whom I am well-pleased and delighted!"* (Matthew 3:17 AMP). When we are baptized in water, the curtains across the sky may not open wide for us to witness Heaven's wild roar of rejoicing, but there is *certainly* a celebration (Luke 15:10). The cheers of those standing nearby—our new family of faith on the earth—echo the holy handclaps and hallelujahs heard in Heaven for *each* of us as we rise from the water clean, new, and *His*. If we listen closely in our hearts, we, *too,* will hear the Holy Spirit voicing the Father's affirmation: "*You,* too, are my *beloved* child, and I delight in *you!*" This moment—this *next* step—becomes another miracle that moves us into more of all the *new* that **Jesus** has made true.

CHAPTER SIX

The Holy Spirit

"Jesus instructed them, 'Don't leave Jerusalem, but wait here until you receive the gift I told you about, the gift the Father promised. For John baptized with water, but in a few days from now, you will be baptized in the Holy Spirit…I promise you this—the Holy Spirit will come upon you, and you will be seized with power!'—Acts 1:4-5, 8 (TPT)

Who is the Holy Spirit?

His wisdom designed and devised the entire universe. He was the very breath breathed into the beginning man and woman. He appeared in tents, clouds, and fires in the genesis generations. He later anointed, led, and worked miracles through the Son of God on this very earth. It was *His* robust power that resurrected the slain Savior. He was then poured out powerfully upon the early church, baptizing them in fire and fueling them with might that won't tire. He is the One who is *still* spilled out and poured into the lives of all who will surrender to Jesus. He convicts, convinces, heals, frees, transforms, teaches, reminds, encourages, empowers, and emboldens the children of God. *He* is the Holy Spirit. He is the One—the part of our triune God—who comes to literally live *in* us. *He* is the One who makes our God **known** and **near** and miraculously gives us the relationship with Jesus we were born to have.

No other power surpasses that of the Holy Spirit, and He lives *in* and *with* each of us. The Bible calls Him our Helper, Encourager,

Counselor, Comforter, Advocate, Intercessor, Strengthener, and Standby (John 14:16 AMP, TPT). We did not receive a mini-me Jesus who cutely sits on our shoulder constantly cueing us to choose correctly. We have received in *full* the very Spirit that fills our very Father. Consider this truth: *"No one can know a person's thoughts except that person's own spirit, and no one can know God's thoughts except God's own Spirit. And we have received God's Spirit (not the world's spirit), so we can know the wonderful things God has freely given us"* (I Corinthians 2:11-12 NLT). We literally have the same Spirit residing in us that the Father has abiding in Him—just as Jesus did on the earth. In any moment, we can know *His* thoughts and feelings and operate in *His* understanding and power. This is *the* miracle of miracles, and we should never get over it—*or* stop growing in our grasp of it.

Too many people give their lives to Jesus, receive the *gift* of the Holy Spirit, and then leave the wrapping half torn. They carry around a "still-stuffed gift bag," never realizing what treasures are buried inside. Too few understand how very **known** and **near** He can be— how strongly we can feel Him, how frequently we can hear Him, and how powerfully we can live out of *His* strength and abilities. Let's be people who fully unwrap the gift and step into the *whole* experience of the Holy Spirit.

The Baptism of the Holy Spirit

There's more to experience with the Holy Spirit than our first moment of salvation. It starts like this: the Holy Spirit draws us to Jesus and opens our eyes and hearts to Him (John 6:33), and when we speak out our initial salvation prayer, the Holy Spirit arrives to reside within us. Imagine at this point, we are each a cup filled to the brim with water—the Holy Spirit contained within us. However, there's *more*. The Bible clearly tells us that Jesus plans to not just fill us but *baptize* us in His Holy Spirit. Even John the Baptist proclaimed that Jesus would *"baptize...with the Holy Spirit and with fire"* (Matthew 3:11 NLT). Jesus longs to lead us into the fullness of His Holy Spirit—the same Spirit who first drew us to Jesus. He wants each of us to advance from being a cup filled with water to a cup fully submerged *in* water. Imagine throwing that water-filled cup into an entire swimming pool. The cup is no longer in control, containing the water; it's now fully submerged in and moved *by* the water. *This* is what Jesus invites us into: a life intimately intertwined with and immersed in His Spirit.

This "baptism in the Holy Spirit" shows up in Scripture in Acts 2—the day the Holy Spirit was first poured out on God's people. He came powerfully—even *visibly* and *audibly*—upon the believers gathered together in that Upper Room. The Bible says that tongues of fire appeared above their heads, and each spoke in unknown tongues. There are other similar stories throughout Acts—such as in Acts 19 when Paul asked a crowd of new Christians if they had fully received the Holy Spirit when they believed. When they said they had not heard of this, Paul laid his hands on them; then, *"the Holy Spirit came on them, and they spoke in tongues and prophesied"* (Acts 19:6 NIV). There are *still* stories like this today. He *still* desires to flood and fill us like this. The full baptism of the Holy Spirit is *still* given to anyone who asks. Just as we commit our lives to Jesus, we must submit to the Holy Spirit. We must ask to be fully submerged and soaked through with Him. We must offer our entirety, obediently opening ourselves to His *total* control—including our *tongues*. The Holy Spirit desires to have command of our hardest-to-handle part: our mouths (James 3:1-12). The sign that we have totally surrendered and been thoroughly submerged into a relationship with the Holy Spirit is that He takes over our mouths and moves them with the syllables and statements of a heavenly language. He gives us the ability to "speak in tongues"—in *His* language and on *His* level.

Speaking in Tongues

This is the point where people in the pews pull apart. One mention of "tongues," and the Church scatters in opinions and denominations based on traditions and experiences. Still, the fact firmly stands that the Bible features three baptisms: blood (salvation), water, and Spirit (1 John 5:6-8). We cannot ignore the final baptism promised from the Father *and* the very lips of Jesus. *He* Himself declared that He would baptize with His Spirit. He even dictated this demand to the apostles: *"Don't leave Jerusalem, but wait here until you receive the gift I told you about, the gift the Father has promised! John baptized you with water, but in a few days from now, you will be baptized in the Holy Spirit"* (Acts 1:4-5 TPT). They had been called to win the world, but they were told *not* to travel and try it until they were "baptized in the Holy Spirit." He then revealed that they would *"receive power and ability"* when the Holy Spirit comes upon them and that they would *then* be His *"witnesses"* to tell people about Him (Acts 1:8 AMP). He knew they would not be able to *be* or *do* what He called them to in their own strength and skill; they would falter and fail in completing the Father's will if they were not flooded with the fullness of His Spirit.

Here's what many of us miss—and why so many Christians live beneath the power available to them: at salvation, the "old" man dies while the "new" one comes alive; during water baptism, the "old" man and guilty conscience are washed away; and during Spirit baptism, we receive the power to actually walk in the new life we've been given. Many Christians get stuck in that middle part—trying to walk out the new life in their own strength without the full force of the Holy Spirit. The enemy fights to keep us fixed here because he fears most a man or woman fully baptized in the Spirit of God. They are too free, too close to the Father, too full of His *fire*. It is the *enemy* who has stirred up so much misinformation and controversy around the most powerful gift ever poured out from Heaven onto this earth. It is the *enemy* who has chopped up and divided the Church over the very Spirit of God.

At the mention of "tongues," many minds and hearts shrink—shaped by the belief that it's forbidden, fit only for a bygone age, or meant for a few privileged followers. Others want nothing to do with it because they've witnessed people get weird with it, and others have observed people operate in this gift in a disorderly, unbiblical—even *obnoxious*—manner. There are some points of confusion that can be made clear.

First of all, the Bible talks about two kinds of speaking in tongues. There is a *public* speaking in tongues that always includes interpretation and builds the people who hear it, and there is a *private* speaking in tongues that has to do with personal edification. The Bible provides a list of "the gifts of the Holy Spirit" that *He* chooses to give people at certain times, and all of these gifts are meant to edify the *body* of Christ (I Corinthians 12). In this list is the gift to "speak in an unknown language" *and* the gift "to interpret what is being said." Not everyone gets to operate in these two gifts. When this occurs, a person may speak in tongues aloud over a crowd; then, someone else is given the interpretation from the Holy Spirit to speak out—just seconds after—the message in tongues. This can happen with a heavenly tongue being spoken followed quickly by the interpretation in the predominant language of the people present, *or* it can transpire like this: a person is given the ability to speak in a language from another country, and someone from that nation miraculously hears and interprets a message from God in his or her own language (exactly like what happens in Acts 2). This particular gift to "speak in tongues" is the *public* gift, and it builds up *everybody* in the building.

However, we can each be given the ability to speak in a *personal*, private "prayer language." This is found in I Corinthians 14 where Paul prompts *all* believers to learn to both prophesy to exhort others *and* to speak in tongues to encourage themselves. He teaches that when we speak in tongues, we *"edify"* ourselves personally, and then he even writes, *"I wish that all of you spoke in unknown tongues"* (1 Corinthians 14:4-5 AMP). That word *"edify"* is the word *"oikodomeō,"* which means to construct a house; to promote growth in Christian wisdom, affection, grace, virtue, holiness, and blessedness; and to restore, rebuild, or repair. When we pray in a personal prayer language given to us from the Holy Spirit, it powerfully expands and enriches our spirits while diminishing and debilitating our "flesh"—*every* time we pray this way.

How do we receive this personal prayer language? We simply *ask*. We ask Jesus to "baptize us fully in His Holy Spirit," and we make a determined decision to deeply surrender to the direction and development of the Holy Spirit, dedicating *every* part of ourselves to *His* use. As He pours Himself over us like this—and we turn even our *tongues* totally over to Him—He will cause *His* words to well up in our mouths, and we will speak in a heavenly language. If this does not happen the first time it's requested, we can *keep* asking. We should continue to spend time sitting with Him and seeking Him. He will reveal and remove any barriers as we keep moving towards releasing *all* control to Him. This is a gift He longs to give *each* of us, and He certainly will in one miraculous moment.

This should be cleared up, too: *people* can get "weird," *not* the Holy Spirit. Sadly, there are people who do things for "show" in the church. Desiring to draw attention to themselves, they might manufacture a move of the Holy Spirit or even speak in tongues out of turn—in a way that's unbiblical. The entire chapter of 1 Corinthians 14 gives guidelines for the use of tongues and spiritual gifts, and it starkly states that no one should speak in tongues out loud before a crowd if there is not an interpreter (v. 27-28). A personal prayer language is *real*, but it is not something to flaunt before a group. In fact, I Corinthians 14 gives insightful instruction on exactly *how* and *why* there should be "order and peace" in a church meeting as people move in the gifts of the Holy Spirit. Yet, there are moments when what appears unusual is actually the unmistakable movement of the Holy Spirit. At times, His presence presses so heavily upon a body that it bends beneath the weight of His glory. Hearts may tremble, tears fall, and souls shudder under the quiet power of His conviction. Still, the Spirit does not call His people to perform or draw attention to themselves; His work is never a repeated spectacle but a sacred encounter pointing beyond us to *Him*. Some may even long to relive a genuine experience or imitate what they have seen in another, but when someone repeatedly seeks the spotlight or loudly loses control, that is *not* the Spirit at work. Still, we should not allow His mysterious movements to frighten us. We should still desire encounters with Him we have never known, embracing what's *real* and *holy*—even when we've witnessed others act out of order.

Why should we each pursue this gift? Speaking in tongues privately is powerful. The Apostle Paul professed this: *"I will pray in the Spirit, but I will also pray with my mind engaged"* (I Corinthians 14:15 TPT). Why would he pray both ways, and why should we? Praying in our private, Holy-Spirit-given language *"edifies"* us personally (v. 5). When we pray this way, it *builds* our spirits. It incredibly increases the power of the Holy Spirit within us and supercharges our sensitivity to Him. Recollect those old radios with dials. Recall how the knob had to be turned just right to tune into the station we wanted to hear clearly—and if we were even just slightly too much to the right or left, we could faintly hear it, but it was mixed with static. Praying in tongues with hearts *genuinely* surrendered to the Spirit "dials us in" perfectly to the voice and feelings of the Holy Spirit without interference. The more we pray in tongues, the more we can perceive Him with precision.

Speaking in tongues personally also produces His fruit in us and propels us in moving in the gifts of the Holy Spirit. It grows us in joy, love, peace, patience, kindness—the full list from Galatians 5. It also can *empower* and *embolden* us to lay hands on the sick and see them healed and on the bound and see them freed—right before our very eyes. Through this precious gift, Heaven's very power is poured into us—*and* the world around us. It is also helpful to be able to speak in this heavenly tongue when we don't know *what* or *how* to pray for a situation. Often, we feel a nudge to lift someone or something before God but don't know what to say. In those instances, we can intercede through the Spirit's own language, and He will voice to Heaven exactly what is needed. There are moments, too, when we simply don't know what to do, and as we pray in tongues, it will pull forth the counsel of God, and plain revelation of the next step will suddenly spill into our minds from the Spirit. This is because the language He gives is *His* own, a holy tongue that opens the door for us to hear Him clearly and speak with Him on His level, a conversation that rises all the way to Heaven. We *get* to speak these sacred syllables and sounds as we stand on the soil of this earth. This is a phenomenal *privilege*—a rare and radiant *gift*—to stand on this land yet speak the sacred language of our Lord.

Again, this is a gracious gift He wants *each* of us to grasp and gain. That's why Paul proclaimed that he wished *all* spoke in tongues (I Corinthians 14:5). Being baptized in the Holy Spirit and receiving the ability to pray in a personal prayer language is for *all* of us. Again, we simply *ask* Him for this gift. As we seek to become this surrendered and saturated with the Spirit of God, He will fill our mouths with *His* words. When we first receive our prayer language, it may emerge as a few simple, repeated sounds—like a small child experimenting with the first syllables of a brand-new tongue. As we progress in praying this way, our syllables will evolve and expand over time—just as it did in our primary language as children. We must then do it daily with *boldness* and *faith*. The enemy will sinisterly say to us that we sound "stupid" or are "making it up" because he can't *stand* it. It is a language he cannot understand, but he *does* comprehend its power. When we have received a prayer language, we must press through these troubling thoughts and pray this way frequently. Persisting in this kind of prayer throughout the day plants and perfects a power in us that nothing else produces, like fire moving through every chamber, igniting strength and warmth throughout the whole being. Again, this is a gift for *every* believer—and though it may start small, it will greatly grow, and there's nothing the enemy can do to stop its life-changing, fiery flow.

Here's a concluding challenge: ask to be "baptized in the Holy Spirit" daily—even multiple times a day. Remember that the movement our heart makes in this is to *fully*, seriously surrender to the Holy Spirit. Each time, we are committing to Him complete access and control to *all* parts of us. Recall again the analogy of the cup being flung fully into the swimming pool, and let's consider this: we have a flesh that can creep to the edge of the pool, start climbing back out, and aim to reclaim command. What if we repeatedly asked to be baptized in the Holy Spirit and resubmitted to *His* leadership again and again? What would happen if we *daily* asked at intervals to be baptized in His Spirit—at dawn, at noon, and at dusk—repeatedly plunging into His Spirit, letting the full tide of His presence wash over us once more? Waves of His wonder-working power would roll through us without end.

Relationship With Him

Even after being baptized in the Holy Spirit, we must totally take in this truth: the Holy Spirit waits at the gate of our *will*. The Father has given us two divine gifts: the *Holy Spirit* and our *free will*. He did not craft us as puppets or robots that He controls; He gave us full freedom to *choose* Him and to bend and blend our will with His. He also did not leave us to lean on our own strength or skill in fulfilling His will. He has filled and flooded us with the same omnipotent Spirit who lives and breathes in *Him*. The Holy Spirit's highest aim is always to shape us into His likeness and empower us to respond as He would in every moment. However, He sits on the edge of His seat within us *waiting* on our will to lean to Him. He is present—*so* present—but He mostly *presents* Himself in the instances He's invited. So, let's understand this: we possess the Holy Spirit within us—and He can pour out the power, purpose, and Person of God in *any* moment in us and through us—but, because of our free will, He constantly waits on our submission *and* permission.

The Holy Spirit was given to us to *help* us constantly—in every moment, with every mood and movement (John 14:16-17)—*and* to speak to us steadily (John 16:13, Revelation 2:7). There is a continual closeness—a constant awareness—with the Holy Spirit that we can experience that few have fully stepped into. Here's what's possible: to be so intimately intwined and tuned-in to Him that His gentle whispers and nudges are rarely missed, that His feelings and thoughts are experienced constantly and instantly alongside our own with ease. It's attainable to not go a moment without being aware of Him. It's achievable to not make one movement without Him. The answer is in learning to *abide* in Him.

To abide—*"menō"*—means to remain, to not depart, to continue to be present, to endure, to not become another or different, and to wait for or await one. Put all together, this means that we learn to *stay* aware of the Holy Spirit when we learn to stay anchored in *surrender*. We often only yield to Him in certain moments throughout a day, and the rest of it is mostly spent doing and saying whatever we think and feel. We flop back and forth from attention to Him to submission to *ourselves*. Think about this: we become aware of the Holy Spirit's presence—what He's doing, saying, and wanting—when we very intentionally make Him the focus of a moment like when we pray, read the Word, worship, or ask Him a question and listen. When we aren't *attuned* to Him, we aren't *aware* of Him. That's why many of us have powerful points alone in His presence—but during the up-and-about parts of our days, we are mostly aware of only our *own* thoughts, feelings, frustrations, wants, and tasks. Any time we make a moment or movement *about Him*, we will be aware of Him and then can hear Him, receive power or perceive a word, and operate in His fruit right there on the spot constantly.

How do we make this happen? We *surrender* our daily lives— every piece and part of our day to Him—on a constant and complete level. Look at this verse: *"For all who are **allowing themselves** to be led by the Spirit of God are sons of God"* (Romans 8:14 AMP). We must *let* Him lead us all day long. We take this position and remain here all day, every day: *"The way I love you is like the way a servant wants to please his master, the way a maid waits for orders from her mistress. We look to you, our God, with passionate longing **to please You** and discover more of your mercy and grace"* (Psalm 123:2 TPT). This must be the firm position of our hearts that we reset resolutely each morning and then repeatedly all day long.

Here's how this habit happens in the hustle: we get ready in the morning turning our thoughts, fears, and worries into conversation with Him. We drive to work or school with Him. We literally *walk* with Him. We turn to Him on the inside even while tackling tasks and conducting conversations on the outside. We release repeated requests: "*Holy Spirit*, what do I say or do?" "*Holy Spirit*, keep me calm, and help me respond like You." "*Holy Spirit*, show me what You see in these people, this room, this moment right now." "*Holy Spirit*, what do you want me to do with these few minutes?" "*Holy Spirit*, what do you desire to show me?" Constantly consult Him. Without ceasing, want what *He* wants. Let's not immediately pick up our phones or turn to our own thoughts in spare moments; let's learn to lean into *Him* instead. The more we mindfully make moments *His*—our rising, driving, working, planning, spending, thinking, and even waiting in line or resting at home—the more we will live near Him and hear Him. When solid surrender—which means constantly turning to Him in all things—is where our hearts remain, our lives will grow in constant *abiding*. Plus, when we turn to Him, He'll always tilt our hearts away from sin, waste, worry, offense, and discouragement—every single time. We will also feel Him, hear Him, and know Him more intimately than we imagined possible.

Let's hold this truth close: the Holy Spirit is perpetually present and pines to pour out in us what is in *Him*. Yet, He waits behind our will—waiting for us to simply *ask*. When we do, the gate of our will opens wide, and *He* flows forth. Let's make this our highest habit—our way of walking and working through the day. Let's not live "waiting on Him" when He's wistfully watching for our permission to produce in us what we can't procure ourselves. Let's know that He never asked us to live *for* Him; He's always longed to live *with* us. Too many act like they're on a stage before Him and He's watching to see if they're going to perform right, proving their love for Him—but we aren't in an arena, and He has no appetite to be an audience to our attempts to act right. He is *in* every scene of every day *with* us wanting us to ask for His help constantly. When our self-control has taken flight, we can ask for *His* might—that He will choose right *with* us. When we simply *ask*, our will steps to the side, His strength surges forward, and the moment that could've been a mess becomes a *miracle*—every single time.

PART 4

The Habits

CHAPTER SEVEN

How to Grow in Relationship

"Are you weary, carrying a heavy burden? Come to Me. I will refresh your life, for I am your oasis. Simply join your life with Mine. Learn My ways, and you'll discover that I'm gentle, humble, easy to please. You will find refreshment and rest in Me. For all that I require of you will be pleasant and easy to bear."—
Matthew 11:28-30 (TPT)

Holy Habits

Draw near. This incredible invitation infuses the entirety of God's Word—and the whole of His heart. Jesus completely cleared the Way for us to *come* to Him and experience Him as **known** and **near**— to have the relationship with Him we were born to have. We are wanted and welcomed. The invitation is eagerly extended to *each* of us. Heed it here: *"Call to me and I will answer you. I'll tell you marvelous and wondrous things that you could never figure out on your own"* (Jeremiah 33:3 MSG), and, *"Look! I stand at the door and knock. If you hear my voice and open the door, I will come in, and we will share a meal together as friends"* (Revelation 3:20 NLT). He's daily at the door of both our lives and hearts asking to come in and become our Friend. As the gentleman He is and because of the free will that's ours, He does not force entry into any part of our lives. *We* must swing our lives wide open for Him to come in and *dwell* with us *daily*.

We've all witnessed those stand-out men and women of God—the ones who seem to know Him deeply, hear Him keenly, and live like Him powerfully. These are people who have learned to seek Him *diligently*. They have established a set of holy *habits* that daily transform their hearts and homes—and that cause health and happiness to hover over all they do even when hardship hits. These aren't hard, horrible habits. They aren't frustrating to follow. As Jesus said, they are light, pleasant, and easy to bear—and they bring *rest*. As we follow His habits, He fills and floods our whole lives with Him, and we firmly forge a true *friendship* with Him.

Spend Time Alone With Him

The most major move we can make to grow in relationship with Jesus is to spend time *alone* with Him. He encourages and invites our coming to Him personally in private all throughout His Word—and He will all throughout our lives, too. We see a glimpse of this even in the Old Testament when Moses would enter all alone into the Tent of Meeting, and *"the Lord would speak to Moses face to face, as one speaks to a friend"* (Exodus 33:11 NLT). Then, in Matthew 6:6 (NIV), Jesus instructed, *"But when you pray, go into your room, close the door and pray to your Father, who is unseen. Then your Father, who sees what is done in secret, will reward you."* Also, in Psalm 27:8 (NLT), we read of this incredible internal invitation spoken by the Holy Spirit to David: *"My heart has heard you say, 'Come and talk with me.' And my heart responds, 'Lord, I am coming.'"* In Matthew 11:28-30 (NIV), Jesus yet again encouraged our coming: *"Come to me, all you who are weary and burdened, and I will give you rest...learn from me...and you will find rest for your souls."* Then, here's the verse that spills the principal point: *"Draw near to Me, and I will draw near to you"* (James 4:8 ESV). We can be as close to Jesus as *we* want to be. We must *choose* to come close to Him. Out of anything else He longs for us to carry out, *this* is the most crucial.

This truth is captured clearly in the story of Jesus' visit to Mary and Martha's house in Luke 10. The two sisters had two separate responses to Jesus' presence in their home. One raced to *serve*; the other rushed to *sit*. Mary hustled to the kitchen to prepare something for Him to eat while Mary moved immediately to His feet to listen to Him speak. Eventually, Martha became stressed and scolded her sitting sister. Jesus responded with these wise words: *"My beloved Martha! Why are you upset and troubled, pulled away by all these many distractions? Mary has discovered the* **one thing most important** *by choosing to sit at My feet. She is undistracted, and I won't take this privilege from her"* (Luke 10:41-42 TPT). The "one thing *most* important"—according to the very words of our Jesus—is that we take the time to simply sit with Him. This isn't just a once-in-a-while need; this is an *everyday* essential.

In fact, spending time alone with Him is the way to truly know that we have a *true* relationship with Him. Soak in this sobering speech spoken by our Savior: *"Not everyone who calls out to me, 'Lord! Lord!' will enter the Kingdom of Heaven. Only those who actually do the will of my Father in Heaven will enter. On judgment day many will say to me, 'Lord! Lord! We prophesied in your name and cast out demons in your name and performed many miracles in your name.' But I will reply,* **'I never knew you'"** (Matthew 7:21-23 NLT). These are "church people" who didn't enter Heaven. These people served the church out in the open—even witnessing wonders happen in His Name—but they skipped being seated with Him in secret. They spoke about Him in public but never spoke with Him in private. They had a public reputation as being His but lacked the private relationship that made them *truly* His. Our serving Him cannot take the place of our seeking Him. He *expects* us to seek Him, sit with Him, speak with Him, secure direction from Him, and get up submitted to Him— serving Him in public in the ways *He* instructed us in private. There is nothing more vital than getting *this* right.

It's in His presence alone that we get to truly *know* Him, hear Him for ourselves, and become like Him. As we sit and speak with Him, listen to Him, find Him in His Word, and get led and loved on by His Spirit personally, our appetites shift, addictions break, and affections swell. It's *here* that we get set on fire with Heaven and freed from the chains of Hell—by the mighty power of the Holy Spirit. It's *here* that struggles end, the way ahead becomes clear, and we are made new again and again. Jesus longs for each of us to get into an unflinching, unending rhythm of sitting alone with Him—over and over, day after day. If we get in this flow, life will become better than we've ever known. If we aim to thrive *here*, we will thrive *everywhere*.

The Battle to Get There

Since spending time alone with Jesus is our most paramount

priority, Satan makes this his top target. We are at war with him, and our strategic enemy strikes at the part that would reduce us to rubble. He knows exactly what would weaken us, so he fights fiercely to keep us from the *private* presence of Jesus.

Even the Enemy knows what could and *does* happen in the life of one who spends time daily in the presence of God. He has watched in horror how a heart gets healed and filled—how power gets spilled and calling is revealed. The transformation terrifies him. The freedom, the peace, the joy, the *love* poured out—he loathes it all. Then, to watch the one who sat with Jesus get up and stand and speak like Jesus in public propelled by the power poured out in private—the miracles and ministry that manifest—*this* he *really* resents and reviles.

He first watched Jesus practice this pattern of private seeking and then public speaking and leaking of power. Some of the most monumental moments in the Gospels sound like this: *"Jesus often withdrew to lonely places and prayed"* (Luke 5:16 TPT, Mark 1:35, Matthew 14:35, Matthew 6:46, Luke 6:12, John 17:1). Before and after these significant sentences lay accounts of miracle after miracle—all the preaching and healing He's known for. Jesus demonstrated for us that the ability to walk and talk in obedience and under anointing in public flows straight out of our sitting, speaking, and soaking in His presence in private. Powerful public ministry pours out of persistent private intimacy.

The enemy despised this demonstration in Jesus' life, and he detests seeing it in *ours,* too. So, the enemy fights to foil this flow in every Jesus-follower's life. Satan whispers countless reasons and rationales to keep us from being alone with Jesus, and we must strive to shut down whatever is stopping us. The presence-prohibiting excuses most heavily heaved are these:

"I don't get to spend time with Him every day, but I do it when I can…" The suggestion that an every-once-in-awhile pursuit of Jesus is enough creates Christians who aren't *full* every day or always *fully* in-step with Him. We don't just eat physically occasionally; we eat constantly. We get hungry multiple times daily and need food to function. Our spirits need steady sustenance, too. Many times, our

messy moods, muddled thoughts, and mindless mistakes are really just spiritual hunger pangs. We *have* to "eat" spiritually. We must prioritize His presence *daily*. There is an amazing place of fullness, freedom, and fire that one finds and *lives* in when he or she sits with Jesus daily. "Most days" cannot be the goal. Let's get this deep down: the person who spends quality time with Jesus daily lives on a totally different level with Jesus than those who seek Him even "most days." He rewards those who seek Him *diligently* (Hebrews 11:6)—and our enemy knows this.

Next comes this one: *"I can't find time alone..."* Most people must *make* themselves rise early—before everyone else in the house, no matter how early it is—to sit with Jesus. Jesus Himself did this, too: *"Before daybreak the next morning, Jesus got up and went out to an isolated place to pray"* (Mark 1:35 NLT). He also lingered late when necessary: *"Jesus went out to a mountainside to pray, and spent the night praying to God"* (Luke 6:12 NIV). Jesus turned tired the same way we do, but He hungered for time with His Father—and He knew His spiritual appetite could not be satisfied by anything else. He faithfully fed His spirit, and we must, too. This miracle will happen: when we make ourselves get up or stay up to sit with Jesus, we will eventually become so hungry for more of it that the hour won't matter anymore. What begins feeling like a duty will become our *delight*. We truly can get to a place where even getting up extremely early to have this unrushed time with Jesus is a great *joy*—no matter how much we're not "morning people." Really, rearranging our bed time and entire schedule around this time is what's required. We *do* have the time. We must set it and let *nothing* steal it.

Others resonate with this rationale: *"I am one who talks to Him on the go..."* We *should* talk to Jesus on the go—*all* day long. However, there are treasures and truths we won't experience or hear unless we are willing to set aside *seated* and *still* time with Jesus. If we are only giving Him quick, short minutes *as* we have them, we are not really giving Him our best, and we are, therefore, missing *His* best. Things between us and Jesus won't reach the places His Blood bought for us if we only seek Him in the car on our way somewhere, but it *will* happen on the couch or in our literal closet where we've come *just* to be with Him.

Here's another one offered to overwhelmed people: *"I'm so tired and have too much to do..."* If life is this fatiguing and full, something has to go because it *can't* be our time alone with Jesus. If we are serving Him and people so much that we can't sit with Him, we haven't listened to Him and aren't really obeying Him—meaning we are doing more than *He* has asked us to do. Let's always remember this: just because a person requests that we do something, it doesn't mean that *Jesus* is requiring it of us. We must take each "extra thing" before the Lord and ask if it stemmed from Him. If He whispers, "No," *we* must unwaveringly say, "No," too. When we shape our lives around His "yes," we will *always* have space to say "yes" to time alone with Him.

At times, the enemy can point to our problems and push us to pull back from Jesus' presence: *"I'm just struggling with some things right now…"* So much of the Bible tells us to come boldly to His throne to be with Him and receive His help—*especially* when we are struggling (Hebrews 4:16-17, Ephesians 3:12). Let's never fall into an on-again-off-again flow of spending time with Jesus based on how we're doing. We can go to Jesus on our good, bad, *and* ugly days. Only *He* can heal our ailing bodies, renew our faltering faith, and free our fighting flesh. Jesus calls us to come boldly and bring it *all* because He has already borne the cost, and He alone can make us whole. He already knows it all, has covered it all, and *longs* to heal it all. Let's never hide or hold back from our holy *Healer.*

The examples could continue, but it's clear that even the enemy knows what would transpire if we treasured our time with Jesus daily. When we sit with Him in private, not only are our own hearts healed and helped, but we see Him work wonders in our public places, too—in our homes, offices, churches, and communities. Meeting with Him daily—in a planned, unrushed manner—is not something to do at our convenience but a choice to make out of obedience (Matthew 6:6). It is the most vital victory to get into a daily routine of spending unhurried time alone with Jesus, and *this* habit will cause us to walk and talk with Him and hear, experience, and share Him on a much higher level. This is key to developing the relationship with Him we were born to have. He cannot be deeply **known** if we do not daily draw **near.**

The Battle When We *Do* Get There

However, let's not think that when we *do* show up that the

Enemy is going to sigh and sink away in sheer defeat. No, he will then aim to distract and distort our time with Jesus *while* we're there. There are particular problems he'll present even as we're in the presence of Jesus that we have to alertly recognize and aggressively restrict.

First, let's know *this:* when we show up to meet with God, the Accuser arrives to blow us up with guilt. In Zechariah 3, Joshua, the high priest, stands before the Lord, and Satan, the Accuser, slips into the scene, too—to interrupt and corrupt their conversation. He begins to accuse Joshua—listing out his litany of offenses—surely aiming for him to feel unworthy and flee God's presence or to *waste* his time repenting for wrongs the Lord had already forgiven. However, the Lord arrests this attack of the Accuser—proclaiming that Joshua had been snatched from the fire, sanctified, and made worthy to stand in His presence. Satan goes for the same goal with *us.* He would love for us to spend our seated time with Jesus in shame—overly obsessing over our own sin. This is *not* the posture or practice Jesus intends for us or invites us to in His presence. If we need to confess something we've freshly done wrong and haven't dealt with, then let's do so, but we should not spend the entire time with Jesus listening to the accusing mouth of Satan. We must know that he, too, will appear to smear and steal our time with Jesus when *we* draw near—every single time. If we allow him to, he will bombard our time with Jesus, beating us down so that we don't get filled and lifted up by Jesus. We must shut Satan up swiftly and shout the same truths the Lord declared over Joshua: "*I,* too, have been snatched up and sanctified and made *worthy*—because of *Jesus*—to come into the presence of my God!"

So, at the very beginning of our meeting with Jesus every day, we must take authority over it. Begin by boldly declaring aloud that this time belongs to *Jesus*—that *no* accusations or distractions are allowed. Shut off all screens and phones and close doors; remove anything that would fray focus. Then, while praying, reading, and listening, we intentionally incline our minds only to Jesus. However, if and when it wanders, we just bring it back. This may be true, too: the very topics our thoughts turn to may be the very things we're to take time to pray through.

The enemy will also aim to get us to approach Jesus with our *own* agenda. Our prayer time should not consist of *us* voicing countless concerns and then closing it there. The enemy would have us believe that the longer we pray and the louder we speak, the greater our power before Jesus—but that's *not* true. We don't come to Him merely to be heard or to deliver a demand-driven list. We step into Jesus' presence sit before Him—and to *seek* Him. Yes, we draw near to pray—but also to listen, to receive, and to be shaped by His voice. We posture ourselves in His presence—physically and spiritually—like Mary: sitting at His feet, hungry to hear Him (Luke 10). She did speak, but she mostly *listened.* Our time with Him and hearing Him can be as radical and real as it was for her—even though He's not physically in our home. Satan will do anything to keep us from encountering Jesus—even by getting us to simply talk too much.

Satan will also work to have us *over-think* or *under-surrender.* The enemy delights in distraction and will discreetly draw our focus from Jesus and His goodness to doubts, questions, and fears—even while we are with Him. Our accuser will subtly, sneakily shift us from a place of worshipping and wonder to wondering and worry—and will make it whisper with a weight that feels real. Therefore, we must firmly fix our focus on Jesus and fend off the fog of confusion. We can't allow Satan to accomplish this either: to get us to go into God's presence holding back some part of our lives out of fear of what the Lord may require of us. We often cower over what He could call us to do or say—something that could cause discomfort. He certainly will when it's needed—*only* to take us to some place greater. We have to be a people who press into His presence wide open to whatever He would want—knowing that He is *good* through and through. We must welcome His whispers about what's wrong in our ways and trust that He works only to make us whole. We need to know this, too: the first steps of obedience in something stretching He tells us to stop or start can be painful, but the rest are peaceful—even *enjoyable*—because our lives level up. Let's hold *nothing* back. When we sit with Him, fully yielded in every area of our lives, He moves—bringing rightness and renewal to all that we are and all that we do. *This* is why Satan strives to steal our surrender. Even he knows that holding back our hearts or habits only halts Jesus' healing hand. So, a life surrendered in every seam and shadow is something Satan simply can't stand.

A Pattern for Time With Jesus

To avoid all of that attack, let's approach Jesus with the right agenda and aim. When we sit to spend time alone with Him, we're coming to *be* with Him—our Father, Friend, and Helper. We draw near as we are—even swimming in struggles—in full *honesty*. We arrive *hungry*. We approach Him excited and expectant—and completely confident in His compassionate care. His heart aches and burns with desire for us to come near to Him. Our simply sitting and speaking with Him satisfies and sings to His heart more than any other move we make. We should see His *smile* as we take a seat with Him. We are sitting right with the One who created us carefully and personally, sacrificed *Himself* for all our sins, and then consistently and intimately calls, "Come to Me!" As soon as we take a seat to meet with Him, He *gladly* does, too.

Sitting and spending time with Him like this can feel awkward the first few times—like struggling in conversation with someone we don't know well. It's especially uneasy because we can't *see* Him. However, we will *sense* Him—more and more strongly as we sit with Him again and again, day after day. It takes faith to sit with Someone we can't see. *This* kind of faith—that believes He exists and trusts that He'll be found if we draw near—is what most pleases Him. Hebrews 11:6 (AMP) says this succinctly: *"But without faith it is impossible to [walk with God and] please Him, for whoever comes [near] to God must [necessarily] believe that God exists and that He rewards those who [earnestly and diligently] seek Him."* Let's have the kind of faith that eagerly expresses, "If He can be known so closely that I can sit with Him, feel Him, and hear Him for myself—then I want to *know* Him! I will come—again and again, day after day—just to experience and know Him more and *more!*" We must trust that when we show up, *He* does, too. Then, as we keep coming, continue calling, and carry on in seeking Him, *He* will continually reveal and pour out more of Himself into our lives—over and over, again and again. More of *Him* is the reward for diligently seeking Him.

Let's always remember this: there's nothing else that will produce a *true* relationship with Jesus more than our own personal, private pursuit of Him. This alone-time with Him is powerful and peaceful, and it will become *the* time of day we pine for most. We can create a rhythm where Jesus becomes so increasingly real and our hearts so progressively free that we go to bed already longing for tomorrow's time with Him.

Here is a fundamental flow for our daily meetings with Him that we can follow: first, when taking a seat with Jesus, begin by taking *authority* over this time with Him. We should declare out loud that we are drawing near to Jesus, and these moments will be holy and wholly *His*. Speak with the authority that *Jesus* has given, and shut down any distraction planned by the devil—all in the peerless Name of Jesus. Then, *worship* Him. Worship in spoken-out-loud words, not silently. Psalm 100:4 (NLT) explains how to enter His presence: *"Enter his gates with thanksgiving; go into his courts with praise. Give thanks to him and praise his name."* We come close to Him with worship and gratitude, not requests. Concentrate on His character—on all His goodness and greatness. As we envision Him in our minds—aiming all our attention on how amazing He is—the Holy Spirit will shape what we see and surge into our spiritual senses, moving our mouths to give voice to His greatness. We should worship until we feel our way to Him. Worship until His nearness is *known*—until there's an acute awareness of His astounding presence. There's nothing like knowing and sensing His nearness *right there* personally—all around us, all over us, and within us. It's genuine worship that gets us to this wonderful place, so this is where we begin each time.

Then, open *the Bible*. Take time to soak in some Scripture while sitting with Jesus. This doesn't have to mean a radical amount of reading. We can always come back to the Word for more throughout the day. It's important to spend time studying it slowly—reflecting on each phrase and permitting the Holy Spirit to reveal all the wonders in the words. Opening the Bible like this as we visit with Jesus is vital. He uses it to teach and train us—just as Timothy wrote: *"All Scripture is breathed out by God and profitable for teaching, for reproof, for correction, and for training in righteousness, that the man of God may be complete, equipped for every good work"* (2 Timothy 3:16-17 ESV). It's a guide in our decisions—a "lamp" for our feet and a "light" for our path (Psalm 119:105). It's a living, breathing book brimming with anointed words that work on *us* while we work through them. Hebrews 4:12 (NLT) highlights this: *"For the Word of God is alive and powerful. It is sharper than the sharpest two-edged sword, cutting between soul and spirit, between joint and marrow. It exposes our innermost thoughts and desires."* Knowing the Word well and walking by it wholeheartedly is also what wraps blessing and success around our whole lives—just as the Lord spoke to Joshua: *"This Book of the Law shall not depart from your mouth, but you shall meditate on it day and night, so that you may be careful to do according to all that is written in it. For then you will make your way prosperous, and then you will have good success"* (Joshua 1:8 ESV). When we witness a person who walks, talks, thinks, lives, and loves *truly* like Jesus—we're watching someone who has been taught and transformed by the truth of the Word. We're seeing what Scripture *alone* can achieve in a human being.

It's even dangerous to spend time with Jesus without the Word open before us. He speaks foremostly through Scripture—and what He communicates in other ways will *always* be confirmed by and correspond to what is written in the Word. If we aren't in the Bible and progressively learning the points on its pages, our enemy can discreetly deceive us—even posing as God's voice in our heads, speaking words that may sound like Jesus but aren't from Him at all. Consistently studying the Bible both protects us from deception *and* propels us into perceiving the *true* voice of God. In fact, when we open the Word, it's like opening the mouth of Jesus and the heart of the Father—and the Holy Spirit makes it speak so personally and practically to each of us. Being in the Bible *is* being with Him. So, let's always study Scripture during our fellowship with the Father. It's one of the most crucial components of this time alone with Him.

After soaking in the Word, we speak out in *prayer.* We open our mouths *and* hearts and we *talk* to Jesus. Let's perceive prayer as first "bowing our hearts"—taking time to slowly and sincerely *surrender,* laying down *every* layer of our lives before Him at the start of the day. We submit our words, our bodies and habits, our thoughts and attitudes, our finances, and our work to Him—inviting the Holy Spirit to shape our minds with truth, temper our reactions with grace, and guide our every choice, conversation, and challenge according to His way rather than our own *all* day. From here, prayer then moves into simply "unloading our hearts." Our "worry list" *is* our "prayer list." Whatever is weighing on and burdening us—*that* is what we bring to Jesus. We voice to Him every question and impossibility, every fear and frustration, every wound and weakness—requesting His wisdom and strength and releasing it all into His sovereign care. As we sit with Him, we should get our hearts and heads completely unloaded so that we don't unload on people during the day. We leave nothing unspoken and nothing unsurrendered. Prayer—the *right* way—is power-releasing, purifying, and peace-making. As we sit and pour out what's piled up in our hearts, we rise freed and filled, emptied and empowered.

Remember that we are talking to a faithful Father and Friend who is unalterably *fond* of us. We can be confident that He cares and hears our every word (Psalm 66:19, Matthew 7:7, Jeremiah 29:12, 1 John 5:14, Psalm 34:17). He also does not require perfection in prayer. We can just *talk.* We can spill. We can be *real.* We speak to Him as if He's sitting *right there*—because He is. There's no need to mindlessly repeat ourselves or even overly explain our meaning (Matthew 6:7). He knows us better than we know ourselves. In fact, when we are so overwhelmed and unsure of what to pray, the Holy Spirit speaks up and prays *for* us. Romans 8:26 (NLT) reveals this: *"The Holy Spirit helps us in our weakness. For example, we don't know what God wants us to pray for. But the Holy Spirit prays for us with groanings that cannot be expressed in words."* When we run out of ways to word our worries, the Holy Spirit works on our behalf. When our words sputter out, it spurs *Him* to speak out— describing our deepest needs and desires to the Lord when we can't depict them ourselves. Even in prayer, we have His divine, holy *help.*

Then, after we've unloaded our hearts, we should allow the Holy Spirit to unpack *His* heart to us, too. Let's always linger at the end of our time with the Lord, listening for the Spirit to speak to us whatever He wishes. Get quiet and still and truly *listen.* Write down what's heard—each sentence, phrase, or single word. He may bring Scripture back up and teach. He may unveil the wisdom we wanted. He may address and adjust something unseen in our life or habits. He may impart special insight on a situation that we wouldn't have known on our own. He may bless us with a brilliant idea for our work or homes. He may point us to pray for particular people—or even an entire nation. He may reveal and heal a personal wound. He may choose to just love on and encourage us to our core. It's paramount to plan an amount of time for *this* part. Let's always end with *listening—*

letting Him reveal, heal, and deal with whatever *He* wants to. If we will pause and hush to hear, He *will* speak—and what He shares will utterly stun us. His words will shape, strengthen, sanctify, and shift us into an even deeper place of relationship and reality with Jesus—every single day, every single time. This is why our Savior said that *this*—just sitting, seeking, and listening at His feet—is *"the one thing most important"* (Luke 10:42 TPT). If we're missing *this*, we're missing *everything*.

How to Hear His Voice

We've surrendered to a saving, *speaking* Shepherd. He sticks close beside us and leads us along right paths; He gives us rest in green meadows along peaceful streams—even in the darkest valleys—and continually comforts and strengthens us (Psalm 23). Our shepherd's heart has always hungered to give all that is good for us even through all that looks bad to us. Let's understand that the way He leads us is by His *voice*. In John 10:27 (AMP), Jesus taught this: *"My sheep hear my voice…and they follow Me."* We cannot fully follow Him without fully hearing Him. Hearing His voice is not a capability that few have; it is a choice that we *all* have. One of the most necessary habits to hone is the ability to hear Him—not just when alone with Him but *all* day long. Not only will hearing Him totally redeem and rebuild our personal lives; it will also revolutionize our public ones. The most powerful people and influential leaders have ears that *hear* His voice.

Jesus makes His voice known and heard in an array of ways. First, He speaks through His *Word*. The Bible is the doorway to detecting His whisper—when first beginning this journey but also when commencing each day ever after. We will never out-grow our deep-seated need for Scripture. Any faithfully on-fire believer we've ever encountered is one who is consistently in the Word of God—one who has *continued* to feed on it daily for years. They have all discovered that He speaks *first* through the Bible—*always*. We will never reach a point where we've read enough of it to think we can hear Him enough *without* it. It's even reckless to try to hear the voice of God without being in the Word of God. The enemy can speak in a counterfeit voice of God—even hissing Scripture into our ears—to get us off Jesus' personal path for us. The only way to recognize this Scripture-using, God-sounding deception is to *know* the actual Word *well*—and not just from growing up but because we read it when we got up this morning. His Word prepares us to hear the Spirit in all His ways, and without it daily, our attempts to listen can easily go astray. Anything the Holy Spirit would say to us in any other way will always be backed up by the Bible. Also, sometimes when we ask Him for advice or direction and hear nothing, it's usually because the answer is *already* written in His Word, and He wants us to heed Him *there*. So, let's go there *first*—every single day—to hear Him.

The Lord also speaks through a *still, small voice*. This passage presents this phrase: I Kings 19:11-13. Elijah earnestly yearned to encounter the Lord and stood waiting for Him on a mountain. The Lord sent a series of loud, formidable forces—a windstorm, earthquake, and fire—but His presence did not show up in these. What ultimately presented the kind of power and glory that pushed Elijah to his knees was *this:* the sound of a "gentle whisper." Our massive, mighty God reveals Himself to us *most* in the quietest sound of all: a *whisper.* In our time alone with Jesus, we may endeavor to encounter Him in the "most exciting" ways possible, and we *will,* but let's know that hearing Him is the highest experience. There is no greater power or peace to partake in than what happens *to* us and *in* us when we perceive His voice personally. Anyone who has developed the ability to tune in to Him will testify of the times just hearing Him has healed, resurrected, protected, and guided them so precisely, personally, and powerfully. Remember we're hearing the same Voice that spoke all creation into existence (Genesis 1:1-26, Psalm 33:6,9). Nothing—not *one* thing—surpasses the awe of His words softly spoken straight to us, individually and intimately.

Here's what His gentle voice sounds like: His whispered words cross our minds like timely, touching *thoughts.* A thought from Jesus is bolder, more arresting than our natural thoughts. When we *hear* Him, we *feel* Him. When we receive a thought from the Lord, it's not something we would have told ourselves—and it usually interrupts our own musings. This "fruit" is also *felt* with it: peace, joy, clarity, comfort, empowerment, freedom, or encouragement. His voice is the most encouraging, loving voice we'll ever hear in our lives. If we think we've heard Jesus but feel discouraged, condemned, rushed, or panicked, that was *not* His voice. Even when He corrects commandingly, it's drenched in divine love. When He convicts, we will definitely feel *"godly sorrow"* over our sin (2 Corinthians 7:10), but the more deeply He deals with us, the more greatly He will gush His affection and affirmation on us. Remember that it's His *kindness* that leads us to repentance (Romans 2:4). Jesus never deals out discouragement, shame, or fear. His voice *always* breathes out life and brings us light.

Growing in detecting His whispers takes practice and patience. Pursue hearing Him in private *every* day. Ask Him to explain Bible passages after reading them. Ask Him questions about personal complications or *His* character and expectations. Then, linger and listen. Make moments in the car or on a walk about leaning into His whisper, too. Pinpoint pockets of time to pause and pursue His voice daily. This promise pertains to this pursuit: *"Keep on asking, and you will receive what you ask for. Keep on seeking, and you will find. Keep on knocking, and the door will be opened to you"* (Matthew 7:7 NLT). Hearing Him is essential, and it's something to exert effort in experiencing. As we commence a not-giving-up quest to hear Him, we *will* most certainly discover His voice. Then, as we learn to discern His voice in private, we'll detect it in public more easily and frequently. This ability—the privilege of hearing Him personally—changes *everything*. Even so, one final question calls for an answer: why would such a wondrous, world-shaking God *whisper*? He's that **near** and can be that closely **known**.

The Holy Spirit also speaks through *peace*. Colossians 3:15 (ESV) instructs us to *"let the peace of Christ rule in [our] hearts."* This means to allow His peace to act as an umpire in our decisions—calling the shots and the steps. We also know from John 14:26-27 that Jesus left us *His* peace as a gift. The Bible proclaims in so many places that we are to walk in the peace of the *Prince of Peace* at all times (Philippians 4:6-7, Isaiah 26:3, Romans 5:1, Romans 14:19, Galatians 5:22). So, one way He whispers to us without words is through a lucid sense of peace—*or* the absence of it. When we feel a deep assurance and quiet confidence about something that may not yet make sense to our minds, it is often the Holy Spirit gently urging us forward. The opposite is also true: when peace is wholly *absent*—even when a choice appears reasonable—it is the Spirit cautioning us away from something or even *someone*. This steady sense of sureness tends to remain until the Lord redirects us; still, we must take care not to confuse His leading with ordinary fatigue or the discomfort that sometimes accompanies obedience. In the same way, a lack of peace—an unsettled, uneasy stirring within—often lingers until we step back from what does not fit within God's design for us. We often land in messy places when we try to force peace where it doesn't exist—when we keep convincing ourselves that something is okay even though our hearts know deep down it *isn't*. If we keep having to replay the reasons that something—or someone—is "right" for us, we're still trying to create confidence and comfort where Jesus isn't giving it to us. He will never let us feel right about anything that's wrong for us: a relationship, a habit, or an opportunity. We must pay attention to *peace*.

We should also heed the Holy Spirit's *invitations* and *nudges*. Going back to those thoughts that cross our minds, we must know that the ones that return and repeat more than once—or that have to do with stopping what we're doing and turning our attention to something or someone else—are usually invitations and nudges from the Holy Spirit. If we are watching a show and this thought suddenly shows up: "Turn that off and talk with Me"—that's a Holy-Spirit invitation. If we are driving and listening to music and this thought turns up: "Turn off the radio and listen to Me for a few minutes"—that's a Holy-Spirit invitation, too. Let's be people inclined to immediately identify the Holy Spirit's summons and stop and give Him our attention. Any time the idea pops in our minds to stop and pray, get still and listen, or open the Word, it is never our *own* thought; it is always a holy invitation—and there's a reason it came. Likewise, if it *keeps* crossing our minds to check on or pray for a coworker, friend, or relative, that's a Holy-Spirit nudge. Let's be people who promptly move when we feel a prod towards a person. Any time we feel led to send a text, make a call, or stop and pray for someone at all, it is usually never our own idea; it is a holy nudge towards a need. These seemingly simple thoughts are actually spiritual and lead to some of the most powerful moments and miracles we'll ever experience in our lives. Let's incline our ears to His *invitations* because they always lead to miracle moments for ourselves, and let's notice His *nudges* because they always light the way to miracle moments for someone else.

Another way Jesus speaks without words is through open and closed *doors*. Revelation 3:7 declares that our God is He who opens doors no one else can open and closes doors no one else can close. When we become His children, our Father carefully controls the "doors" in our lives. This means that He alone will open the right opportunities for us and close those that are wrong for us. If we desire a "door" to unlock—of any kind—and it doesn't, we must decide not to decipher it as rejection. Here's a truth many have trumpeted: man's rejection is often God's protection. When an opportunity stays shut, we too quickly sink, thinking we aren't gifted enough, didn't work hard enough, haven't prayed enough, or just *aren't* enough—when it's really just not right for us altogether or it's just not the suitable *time*. When a door doesn't open up, we can't shut down. The proper response is to *trust* the One who's taken charge of the "doors" in our lives. This is also where we press into His peace. Not every possibility is His provision, and peace is the proof we pause for at the threshold. When peace is partial or missing, the path is either not from Him—or not for *now*. Let's learn to entrust ourselves to our divine Door-Opener *and* follow the peace He provides.

We can also hear Jesus' voice through *people*. Anytime we are in the presence of a person housing the Holy Spirit, we should open our spiritual ears. He can use any mouth to speak His Word at any time—in quick or slow conversations and through the old *or* the young. One conversation or comment leaving the lips of a person could actually be manifesting from the mouth of Jesus. We especially must force and firmly hold our ears wide open under the preaching of His Word. After years of walking with Jesus—if we aren't careful and intentional—we can get *too* used to hearing His Word, and we can let His words pass by unheeded—even those that were deeply needed. When we sit beneath the Word with open hearts and listening ears, leaning in on purpose, God never fails to give us something personal. We too often walk away from a moment of anointed preaching unimpacted. This often means we were distracted and didn't lean in and listen with *intent*. Let's remain hungry for fresh truth and just-in-time reminders each time His Word is shared. Let our hands sit still, our minds stand steady, and our ears stay eager to hear every word any messenger shares.

The most recognizable and resonant way He speaks to *all* may appear to be through the voices of His people. However, the preaching of the Word and seeking of a "word" from a person should never replace our time in His Word *ourselves*. A preacher or a podcast cannot supplant the Bible. A speaker or a sermon cannot supersede a personal prayer time. We cannot depend on discerning Him through others only; we must discover His voice directly for ourselves. When the Lord confronted Job with His complete sovereignty after Job's fed-up ranting, the humbled man tumbled to his face before the Lord and wailed these words: *"I admit I once lived by rumors of you; now I have it all firsthand—from my own eyes and ears!...I'll never again live on crusts of hearsay, crumbs of rumor"* (Job 42:6 MSG). When we just "eat" what others are sharing, we are consuming "crumbs" and "crusts"—what's left over from the full meal of the Bread of Life the speaker swallowed (John 6:35, 48, 51). That's all others can offer us off their plates. No person can physically survive on crumbs and crusts. No *faith* can thrive on that either. Let's be people who faithfully go straight to the Bread of Life and eat full meals *ourselves*. Jesus declared, *"I am the Bread of Life. Come* **every day** *to Me, and you will never be hungry"* (John 6:35 TPT). To live full—and fully *hearing*—we must meet with Jesus daily ourselves. However, let's also be people who are so hungry for more of Him that we ravenously want every "crumb" a person shares from his or her table, too.

Our Shepherd speaks—and He speaks *often* (Job 33:14). The highest height of relationship with Him happens when we *hear* Him. He whispers in the ways mentioned and in others—including dreams and visions, messages in spiritual scenes in the night or flashes of illuminating images that cross the mind during the day (Job 33:15, Numbers 12:6, Acts 2:17). He speaks with whispers and with peace. He invites and nudges. He opens and closes doors and directs us through His people. Still, the surest, shining light on our path remains His Word, already written and ready to guide. Drink from it. Draw from it. Then, all day long, listen for the Spirit's whispers—each one carrying power, each one bringing life, for each and every moment.

We never have to wonder "what we're supposed to do" when all we have to do is sit, ask, and *listen*. His voice will not only guide us with precision through every personal decision but will also give us specific solutions and statements for those surrounding us. People who sit and hear are the ones who will both walk in His will and talk with His words. Let's not be those who drive on fumes or survive on crumbs. Let's not just "do *our* best." Let's listen and know *His* best. Let's draw near—more and more, over and over—and *hear*. When we do, we'll live fueled with wisdom, filled with wonder, and finely tuned to His whispers—never wondering what to do *and* witnessing His words work wonders in others' lives, too.

All-Day Conversation

Another helpful, holy habit to develop is learning to walk and talk with Jesus *all* day long. The Bible challenges us to *"never stop praying"* (I Thessalonians 5:17 NLT), to not worry about anything but to *"pray about everything"* (Philippians 4:6 NLT), and to *"pray in the Spirit at all times and on every occasion"* (Ephesians 6:18 NLT). Jesus desires more than just sit-down visits with us; He delights in all-day, constant conversation with us, too. Jesus doesn't just sit with us; He *stands* and *steps* with us all day. Let's imagine Him—the unrivaled, Resurrected Jesus—walking beside us all day long. He's powerfully present in every activity and moment—and He does not wish to stand *silent*. Remember He's given us the Helper—the ever-present, ever-powerful Holy Spirit. Whether it's our melancholy mood, a maddening matter, or even a mind-bending math problem, our Helper constantly hungers to *help*.

So, let's invite Him into *every* activity. Getting ready in the morning, driving to work, walking from room to room, washing dishes, completing homework, practicing a sport, grocery shopping—He's present in *every* moment. His power can pour forth at any time—*as* we talk to Him. Comforting conversations with Him can calm us *whenever* needed. His heart can be heard in *any* moment. He can widen us with wisdom. His strength can surge into our spirits. Burdens can blow away and disappointments disappear. He can remind us of truths not remembered and ready us for rough roads ahead. Miraculous moments of meeting with Jesus can happen on our feet and on the spot minute by minute. Let's train ourselves to turn to Him in *all* moments. This habit makes Jesus so very **known** and **near** all day long.

A powerful part of our walking and talking with Him constantly is *casting our cares* to Him throughout the day, too. This command comes straight from our Father's affectionate heart: *"Pour out all your worries and stress upon Him and leave them there, for He always tenderly*

103

cares for you" (I Peter 5:7 TPT). Whatever weighs us down or wrecks our demeanor—worries, fears, pressure, stress, uncertainty—He says He wants it off our shoulders and in His hands. He sees *and* cares. In His kindness, He longs to lift off every load, and in His strength, He will seamlessly solve every situation surrendered to Him. We *get* to live like this all day: lifting our burdens to Him and then walking in the lightness this habit leaves. *This* is His will. It is not mature or godly to walk around burdened; it's actually unbiblical. He commands that we cast *every* care, believing that He cares. He's *there*—right beside us—and He *really* and *rightly* responds to our requests. He wants us to trust Him enough that we make it a habit to hand Him our hassles and hardships constantly. It is His joy to handle what's hard for the children He chose. We *get* to employ and enjoy this gift all day long.

Not only can we hand Him our worries; we can also offer Him our *offenses* throughout the day. Since He's so near us, the Lord fully knows when our hearts get hurt. Right along with ours, *His* eyes witness the faces that frown at us, the comments that cut us, and the moments that madden us. Jesus gets how it feels because *He* experienced this, too. He fought off the fire of offense with one weapon: *frequent forgiveness*. Jesus can help us forgive as quickly and fully as He did on the earth. We *all* make mistakes and messes and frequently need forgiveness. We know that Jesus forgives us fully every time—and we must understand that He expects us to give this same grace to others (Matthew 6:14-15, Ephesians 4:32, Matthew 18:21-22, Mark 11:25, Colossians 3:13). He wants to forge us into frequent *forgivers*. He desires that we constantly dispense negative feelings towards people into His hands and out of our hearts completely. When we hold hostages in our hearts, *we* are held captive, and *our* joy is murdered. We cannot walk closely with Jesus *and* hold grudges and judgements towards people. So, let's hone this habit: let's be quick to let things go. Let's be immediate in dealing with negative feelings towards people. This is another task our Helper aspires to assist us with *all* day long.

From start to finish, let's lean into the presence of Jesus *right there* with us all day. When we can't converse out loud, we can communicate in our hearts. In the middle of a moment with an audience or during a conversation that's a challenge, we can internally ask the Holy Spirit for help, and we'll have it right there on the spot without even opening our mouths. He is ever present and ever ready to *help*. So, as we have spare moments throughout the day, let's spend them with Him—more and more. At lunch, let's not let our phones have all our attention; let's *listen*. When resting at home, let's hurry our hearts to Him, not to headlines and other hang-ups. Even as we get into bed, let's turn our attention—and our affection—to Him once more. Let's *spend* the day with Him, and let's *end* the day with Him. Before closing our eyes, let's ask the Holy Spirit these questions and lean in to His answers: *Is there anything I need to confess? Is there anyone I need to forgive? Is there something I should celebrate? What final words do You want to say to me?* Imagine how our hearts would be healed, our minds un-muddled, and our spirits strengthened—even in those quiet moments before sleep. Imagine if we spent the *whole* day with Jesus—from sunrise to sunset—how fully we could lie down, truly rest, and rise again refreshed.

Careful Obedience

Just as a child must be taught to obey earthly parents, leaders, and laws, we do *spiritually* as well. When we surrender our lives to Jesus, He becomes our Savior and Friend, but He is also our Lord. We come under His lordship and leadership, and we must learn to loyally obey Him. It may feel limiting, even like liberty is lost—but in His Kingdom, our loving obedience leads to lasting freedom, profound peace, perfect protection, and overflowing joy. In fact, our *obedience* to Jesus is what both protects and progresses our relationship with Him.

Obedience to the Lord and His laws is what fenced and fortified Adam and Eve in Eden. Obedience was the shield that kept Satan from stealing, killing, and destroying anything about their God-blessed lives—including their relationship with Him. Consider the breaking and blighting that blasted forth from just the very first act of disobedience. That *one* bite of forbidden fruit fractured *all* of creation. That *one* act of disobedience destroyed their relationship with God and deposited their rulership of the earth into the hateful hands of Satan. Disobedience is deadly. Since this is true, obedience must become our *only* option.

The call to obedience overarches the Word. One passage

proclaims, *"If someone claims, 'I know God,' but doesn't obey God's commandments, that person is a liar and is not living in the truth"* (I John 2:4 NLT). We do not say a true "yes" to Jesus unless we say "yes" to *all* He says is right and wrong. Another sacred line shouts this: *"Look, today I am giving you the choice between a blessing and a curse! You will be blessed if you obey the commands of the Lord your God...But you will be cursed if you reject the commands"* (Deuteronomy 11:26-28 NLT). Obedience brings blessing; disobedience carries consequences. More than anything else, the Lord desires our obedience—*so that* His blessings can flow freely into our lives. Also, in the Old Testament, Samuel stated, *"What is more pleasing to the Lord: your burnt offerings and sacrifices or your obedience to his voice? Listen! Obedience is better than sacrifice, and submission is better than offering the fat of rams"* (I Samuel 15:22 NLT). Our Father desires a truly surrendered heart over showy service and sacrifice. Finally, our Savior spoke these words: *"If you [really] love Me, you will keep and obey My commandments"* (John 14:15 AMP). Anyone who truly loves Jesus will *obey* Him—even when it's awkward, anxious, or agonizing. We show Him the magnitude of our love by the measure of our obedience.

As His people, we should seek Jesus, not our culture or crowds, for direction on every detail in life—what's true or false, what's right or wrong, what's wise or unwise, what's healthy or unhealthy, what's holy or unholy. His ways are written in His Word, and His Spirit guides us into His truth, too. Let's study Scripture and seek His Spirit in *all* matters. Let's build our whole lives—all our opinions and habits— around what *He* says is healthy and holy. This applies to the practical pieces of our lives, too: our sleep schedule, eating and drinking habits, entertainment choices, time management, phone and media boundaries, spending patterns, and so on. We must do what is best—what is healthy and wise—in *every* area, even in the seemingly insignificant parts. The tiniest unhealthily, unwisely managed area of our lives can unfavorably ripple through the rest of it.

Honestly, we can too often think we have a spiritual problem when we just have a *practical* problem. We can think we're being attacked mentally and emotionally when we just aren't getting enough sleep. We can call off a "spirit of sickness" from our lives when—in many cases—we really just need to stop eating so much junk and drink way more water. We pray against financial attack and lack when we just need to ask the Holy Spirit for a spending plan and get it all back on track. Let's intentionally take every area of our lives to Jesus and begin to work through each one with Him—asking Him for *His* direction and dictation in literally every little thing. Remember, too, that He is the One who literally created fun and who gives joy, requires rest, and manifests freedom, so the way He would have us align each area will bring about these blissful blessings in more bountiful amounts than our own ways ever would.

Let's be vigilant against the enemy's veiled voice, tempting us toward disobedience. Too often we think a path apart from God's Word or the Spirit's direction will bring more bliss than the blessed obedience He calls us to. Too often we act like Adam and Eve, attending to the enemy as he artfully alters a God-given command, pointing out loopholes and presenting alternate meanings—all to allure us away from obedience. Focused, faithful obedience forms a fence around all that we have with Jesus and all that flows from Him to us. Adam and Eve were never happier than when they walked in perfect obedience. *We* will never be more content than when we walk in precise submission, too. There is *no* joy in compromise or partial compliance. Living in a constant cycle of, "Is this *okay*?" or, "How can I *justify* this?" drains and depletes us. Jesus will always prevent our hearts from resting in wrong. We cannot lean on verses to make peace with what Jesus will never bless. In disobedience, there is no rest—because nothing sinks us like sin. Nothing guts us like guilt. The Bible says it puts a literal weight on us, sapping us of all strength (Psalm 32:4). We will never be truly free until we *constantly* keep a clear conscience (Acts 23:1). The enemy knows this, so he prowls and pounces in the perfect moments, whispering lies to lure us into disobedience—just as he did with Eve. We must catch him and crush him habitually.

Let's understand why it's difficult to obey in so many moments—even when we *do* deeply love Jesus. Our spirit is alive to and adjoined with the Holy Spirit within us, and it longs for and leans into the ways of Jesus; however, our sinful nature that we are continuing to grow out of still remains within us, raging for its own way. Galatians 5:17 (AMP) describes this inner duel: *"For the sinful nature has its desire which is opposed to the Spirit, and the [desire of the] Spirit opposes the sinful nature; for these [two, the sinful nature and the Spirit] are in direct opposition to each other [continually in conflict], so that you [as believers] do not [always] do whatever [good things] you want to do."* Although we have been set free from the power of sin and have been filled with the Holy Spirit, we still carry remnants of our old nature. We are in a progressive transformation—day by day taking off our sinful nature and putting on our new nature (Ephesians 4:22-24, Colossians 3:9-10). We still have our free will and must *choose* to starve our flesh and feed our spirit. Nearly every choice becomes an opportunity to nurture one and murder the other. Do we lie or tell the truth? When faced with rudeness, do we fire back with meanness or mercy? Do we complete the task promptly or procrastinate *again*? Do we eat what's healthy or what's harmful? Do we get up early to sit with Jesus or snooze until the last second? These tiny but tremendous battles between our flesh and spirit bombard our every moment. Christlike change comes through consistent choices and courageous commitment to what is *right*.

Sometimes this feels impossible. This behavioral battle even baffled the Apostle Paul. He lamented his conflicted condition: *"Nothing good lives within the flesh of my fallen humanity. The longings to do what is right are within me, but willpower is not enough to accomplish it…So if my behavior contradictions my desires to do good, I must conclude that it's not my true identity doing it, but the unwelcome intruder of sin hindering me from being who I really am"* (Romans 7:18, 20 TPT). He declared that his *"true identity"* is a man who *"loves to do what pleases God,"* and he hates that it's hard to walk this out freely and fully (Romans 7:22-23 TPT). He finally cried out, *"Who has the power to rescue this miserable man from the unwelcome intruder of sin and death?"* (Romans 7:24 TPT). He then answered himself, attesting that God had *"provided a way out through Jesus, the Anointed One"* (Romans 7:25 TPT). Jesus *alone* is our way to obey. When we run out of willpower, we lean into *His* power—right there with us in the form of His very own Holy Spirit. When we can't choose right for ourselves, we ask *Him*—right then and there—to help choose right *with* us. The Holy Spirit alone can empower us to obey in any moment (1 Thessalonians 4:8 AMP).

Jesus, too, faced this war of wills in the Garden of Gethsemane before the crucifixion. In Luke 22:42 (NLT), a kneeling Jesus prayed this: *"Father, if you are willing, please take this cup of suffering away from me. Yet, I want your will to be done, not mine."* This passage describes Him as being in such distress that He sweat drops of blood. None of us have grappled with a battle of wills this grave, yet we give in to our flesh way too easily—to overeating, refusing a bad attitude, or wasting time on our phones. We can win over our will just as Jesus did if we do it as *He* did. The same scene is described in greater depth in Matthew 26:39-46. Here, Jesus didn't just pray and wrestle with His will *once*. He returned to His knees three times before becoming fully empowered by the Holy Spirit to lean all the way into obedience. As He said it the third time—"*Not my will but Yours be done*"—the Holy Spirit helped Him submit to it. If Jesus could concede to the most tortuous task in all history, we can accede to Him in *our* misery—using the same approach and by the same power. Instead of instantly indulging the flesh, we can pause, push back, and partner with the Spirit in the struggle. Like Jesus, let's speak out our submission until the Spirit's empowerment emerges. When we press into *His* help, we'll rise, not give in—victorious *every* time.

Finally, we must be fiercely vigilant against *deliberate* sin. Read this weighty warning: "*Dear friends, if we deliberately continue sinning after we have received knowledge of the truth, there is no longer any sacrifice that will cover these sins. There is only the terrible expectation of God's judgment and the raging fire that will consume his enemies*" (Hebrews 10:26-27 NLT). This message is meant for those who have processed and perhaps even professed Jesus—those who have *"received knowledge of the truth."* They have heard and understood the gospel yet persist in sin purposely and willfully. By choosing rebellion over obedience, they place themselves under God's judgment, facing the consuming fire reserved for His enemies. Deliberate, ongoing sin cannot be covered, and the price for pride is certain. While this is one of the Word's weightiest warnings, it is also a wake-up call—a blaring alarm beckoning us to *repentance* and *reverence*. This is not meant to shame a struggling believer—but to confront rigid, real rebellion. There is a difference between planned, sought-out sin and the unplanned mistakes of a humble heart. This passage does not condemn those who wrestle honestly with sin they hate; rather, it calls all of us to stay alert, humble, and obedient. Sin is severe, so our obedience must be sincere and *serious*. His grace—His full forgiveness for all sin—has not placed us on a playground but on *holy* ground, and we cannot toy with obedience or twist it to our convenience.

Let's remember that those closest to Jesus—those to whom He is most **known** and **near**—are those who are most *His*. We are most *His* when we are mindfully, carefully obedient. He desires surrender and obedience in *all* things—people whose whole beings and lives are yielded to Him and His leading, people who constantly ask for His will and way in everything. Remember this truth from Jesus' lips: *"The thief's purpose is to steal and kill and destroy. My purpose is to give them a rich and satisfying life"* (John 10:10 NLT). When we submit to Him in every way and want, there's no greater happiness and peace to experience. Simple joys and everyday fun flow even *more* when we've become *one* with Him. It's obedience to Jesus that opens the door to this overflowing, abundant life our hearts were made for.

Fasting

An additional holy habit to forge is *fasting*. Fasting is the voluntary abstaining from food for a period of time to humble oneself, seek Jesus' guidance, and grow closer to Him through a more serious manner of pursuing Him. While biblical fasting refers to refraining from food, fasting can also include forgoing other activities that distract us from the Lord as long as the time usually spent on *that* is given to *Him*—such as streaming shows, scrolling social media, savoring games, and similar distractions. The point is to withhold what we frequently feed on daily and feast more abundantly on Jesus instead. Whatever we fast must be felt. It must challenge and confront our fleshly cravings so that a deeper spiritual desire can rise. *True* fasting costs us something— but it also softens our hearts and sharpens our eyes.

We may fast for a myriad of reasons. The heart hungry for just simply *more* of Jesus—the one who wants to break through to the next level of intimacy and freedom in Him—may choose to forgo food and find *Him* instead. When we draw near to Him, *He* draws near to us (James 4:8), and fasting is a bold step closer to Him. When we fast to find Him, we flat-out *find* Him. We'll experience Him in ways we've never known—felt in the soul, heard in the heart, and encountered beyond expectation. When we press into His presence, His presence will press into us—stirring and shifting us into some place entirely new.

In *difficulty,* we may decide to fast, too. When facing a stormy situation, we can fast for protection and guidance (Ezra 8:21-23). When life gets windy and wild, we can wait on the Lord in the place of food, and we'll wind up wading in a pool of His presence and peace instead of the currents of confusion and concern. We'll also watch Him wield the winds of our storm and use it for good. We may also choose to fast when fighting our *flesh*. When the flesh flares and we're failing, a fast can help us find our faithful footing again. When temptation has us caught in a cycle of giving in, repenting, and getting up and doing it again, it's time for a fast. Focusing on Jesus over food will bring breakthrough to our battles. Jesus even modeled fasting *before* He faced impending fights (Matthew 4:1-4). Prior to stepping into public ministry, He fasted to prepare to preach and heal *and* to resist the temptation He knew was about to appear. When we are waging war through a ministry event or starting something new—even a new *year*— a fast can feed us the strength to step into it successfully and stand up to soon-coming snares. In short, fasting feeds us for any fight we face—*more* than any food we'd ever put on our plate.

Jesus gave us instructions on *how* to fast. First, He taught to fast with the right heart and motives. Here are His words: *"When you fast, don't make it obvious...Comb your hair and wash your face. Then no one will notice that you are fasting, except your Father, who knows what you do in private. And your Father, who sees everything, will reward you"* (Matthew 6:16-18 NLT). Notice fasting is not something to flaunt; we're to do it humbly and sincerely—even *secretly*. It also should include prayer and worship. The point of fasting is to replace the time we'd spend eating with meeting Jesus. When we would sit down to breakfast, lunch, or dinner, we take a seat with *Him* instead. *He* becomes our food—and we will certainly be fed in ways that go beyond our bellies.

Fasting can be done in different ways. A *complete* fast includes no food or drink for a set time (Esther 4:16). A *partial* fast can avoid particular types of foods or even just certain meals a day (Daniel 10:3). Scripture doesn't prescribe a strict length, and fasting should be done wisely and healthily, depending on our situations. The Bible also mentions both *corporate* and *individual* fasts (Nehemiah 1:4, Joel 2:15). If our entire church is doing a fast, let's press in and participate and partake of the corporate blessing fasting will foster. If we are struggling, breaking, or just aching for more of Him, we can fast individually any time. In fact, many people fast *regularly*—at the start of each month or the start of each week—just to find Him and be filled with more of Him. This kind of pressing in also preps and powers them up for all that's pending ahead.

Those that fast regularly find that they walk with Him more intimately and can even move in His authority more powerfully. In Mark 9, a boy bound by an evil spirit was brought to the disciples, but they prayed and could not cure him (v. 14-29). Once Jesus approached the boy and rebuked the spirit, it shrieked and scrammed. When the disciples asked why they were unsuccessful, Jesus responded with this: *"This kind can come out only by prayer and fasting"* (Mark 9:29 KJV). They didn't have time to see the need and then drop to their knees in prayer and fasting right then. Jesus meant *prior* prayer and fasting. He meant *regular* prayer and fasting would have prepared them to exert the power needed for *that* problem. When we live in an ongoing state of prayer and fasting, we cultivate a higher level of spiritual sensitivity and authority. A lifestyle of fasting—steadily seeking the Lord and His strength as the Spirit leads, week by week—releases His righteousness and rulership powerfully within us. It fills us fully with *His* power, and it's then poised to pour out the moment a need appears. Let's learn to faithfully fast like this so that we can powerfully pour out like *that*.

Let's open our hearts and ears and fully hear the call to grow in this holy habit. Let's feel the Holy Spirit faithfully prompting us to move beyond what is familiar and step into something fuller. If fasting is absent from our lives, we forfeit experiences with Jesus meant for us here on the earth. There are depths with Him—conversations we'd have, revelations that would flow—that we'll never know without fasting. So, when a leader calls a fast, let us respond without reluctance and without excuses. Also, when the Holy Spirit personally prompts us to fast—however He leads, for however long—let us be swift and surrendered in our obedience.

Let's also know this: fasting changes *everything*. Our most significant, soul-shifting breakthroughs are birthed while fasting. Battles that have burdened us for years can be broken in moments while fasting. Direction we have desperately desired will be drawn from His heart into ours as we sit with Him instead of at the table. As we fast,

His presence will settle over our families and hover in our homes with a nearness we have never known. Our ears will be finely tuned to His voice, and fresh anointing—new ability and authority—will be poured over us like oil. We will be more able to speak the exact words needed—at the precise moment—with power released and purpose fulfilled. Heaven will move, and Hell will be halted as we are able to hear Him clearly, speak boldly, and act immediately. The Father calls us to fast because He shifts us, shapes us, sharpens us, and shines through us when we obey. As we step into fasting personally, it will feel like leaving a dim, crowded, noise-filled room—where we could only partially perceive Jesus—and entering a brilliantly lit space where the clamor of the world is quieted, His presence is undeniable, and His voice is known with stunning clarity and keen intimacy. Fasting carries us forward into a deeper, stronger, more powerful way of living with Jesus. Because of what we encounter and gain when we fast, our cravings will change. Believe it or not, we will actually begin to hunger for Him *more* than for food—week after week—because He becomes more ***known*** and ***near*** than we ever thought He could.

The Sabbath

Arguably the most ignored and disobeyed of the Ten Commandments among God's people—especially in our culture—is this one: *"Remember the Sabbath (seventh) day to keep it holy (set apart, dedicated to God)"* (Exodus 20:8 AMP). That passage continues like this: *"Six days you shall labor and do all your work, but the seventh day is a Sabbath [a day of rest dedicated] to the Lord your God; on that day, you shall not do any work, you or your son, or your daughter"* (Exodus 20:9-10 AMP). It goes on to remind us that the Lord Himself worked for six days during creation but paused on the seventh (v. 11). He modeled a rhythm of work and renewal and mandated that His people follow the same pattern. Today, His call is not about legalism but about entering into the peace and *pace* of refreshment He offers. The principle of Sabbath still stands: God calls us to pause weekly, to be restored in His presence, and to embrace the life-giving rhythm of *rest* He designed for our good.

A true Sabbath day doesn't mean we have to sit still and pray all day. It *does* mean spending time in worship and reflection on Him, getting refilled and renewed—truly made ready for a whole new week.

This should definitely include extended time in the Word and prayer, but it can also include anything that stirs our affection, delight, and gratitude toward Him and the gifts He has given us. We set aside household chores and weekly tasks and reach for what brings rest and joy instead—like cooking with family, taking a walk, or enjoying a nap. All day, we should relish the goodness of God—thanking Him, listening for Him, loving on Him, *and* letting Him love on *us*. He calls us to sit, receive, decompress, and release all stress on our Sabbath day of rest.

A day like this—with no scrambling to finish chores or tasks before the work week begins again—will not happen without *planning*. This means grocery shopping and other prep for the next week may have to happen on Friday after school or work. Some keep Saturday as their Sabbath, the seventh day of rest, while others celebrate Sunday, the Lord's Day, as their Sabbath, centering the day on their church's worship service. Even if Saturday is our chosen Sabbath, we still aim to attend church on Sunday—but the Sabbath itself remains a day set apart from start to finish. Whichever day is chosen, all chores and errands should be done on the day that is not the Sabbath. This may sound easy, but our flesh will fight it. We are not used to stopping and resting. This is why the Lord commands it. Imagine the transformation a day of rest and worship—one we protect and *prepare* for weekly—could produce in our lives individually *and* in our families. The Lord will amply pour His anointing over this day dedicated to Him—and it'll become the day we delight in most. All week long, we'll carry extra hope in our hearts, knowing that the Sabbath is *coming*.

Our God knew we'd *need* this day of reset and refreshment. If we're not walking this out, we're missing out—restricting ourselves from more rest, renewal, and real joy than we realize. This is completely counter-culture, yet it's utterly God-commanded. This day meets one of our greatest needs, and we suffer more than we see when we stray from obedience in this. Observing the weekly Sabbath as He prescribes will renew and revolutionize our lives. Week after week, this day will be marked by miracles: deep refreshment, renewed vision, restored joy, and radical encounters with Jesus. When we faithfully honor Him in this, the God who is **known and near** meets us in ways we can see, feel, and carry with us all week long.

Right Community

As we cultivate our relationship with Jesus, it's crucial to do so in community, not in isolation. Even in Eden, the Lord said, *"It is not good for the man to be alone"* (Genesis 2:18 NLT). Although Adam enjoyed a perfect relationship with the Father, he was also created to have powerful relationships with other *people.* We were each divinely designed to experience love, connection, and partnership with one another. This reflects the Trinity—the Father, Son, and Holy Spirit. Even our God is not composed of *one* isolated being. He is comprised of three powerful parts who work together and are wound into One by love. Humanity was made in *His* image—to love and be loved by others. No one soars or succeeds in seclusion because we were literally created *for* community. If we want the kind of relationship with Jesus we were born to have, we won't gain it in solitude. We'll obtain it in the *right community.*

Beyond the first marriage between Adam and Eve, the Lord created families, tribes, nations, and—ultimately—the Body of Christ where everyone belongs and supports one another (Romans 12:4-9, I Corinthians 12:12-27). Of course, sin breaks our bond with each other like it blighted our relationship with God. So, through His death and resurrection, Jesus didn't just restore us to Himself; He also reconciled us to each other. We can witness the Blood of Jesus running its radical, redeeming repair through the first church in Acts. Here's the description of the first made-whole, united-by-Jesus community: *"All the believers devoted themselves to the apostles' teaching, and to fellowship, and to sharing in meals (including the Lord's Supper), and to prayer. A deep sense of awe came over them all"* (Acts 2:42-43 NLT). The depiction continues by saying that they *"met together in one place and shared everything they had,"* and they even *"sold their property and possessions and shared the money with those in need"* (v. 44-45 NLT). This account of this Christ-knit community concludes like this: *"They worshiped together at the Temple each day, met in homes for the Lord's Supper, and shared their meals with great joy and generosity— all the while praising God and enjoying the goodwill of all the people. And each day the Lord added to their fellowship those who were being saved"* (v. 46-47 NLT). None lived alone or in lack. Not one was unloved. *Together,* they listened and learned. They cared and shared. They met together, ate together, prayed together, and *grew* together—personally *and* corporately. This movement, this *miracle,* happened daily—and it still continues *today.*

For those in fractured families—those without parents, spouses, siblings, or children of their own—the Lord places people in *His* family. Psalm 68:5-6 (TPT) clearly commends His community-centered heart: *"To the fatherless, He is a Father. To the widow, He is a champion friend. The lonely He makes part of a family. The prisoners He leads into prosperity until they sing for joy. This is our Holy God in His Holy Place!"* Through our personal relationship with Him *and* through the church community, the Lord will give us all what and *whom* we need. Not only will *He* be our Father, but He gives us spiritual mothers and fathers—plus tons of brothers and sisters (1 Corinthians 4:15, Romans 8:29, Hebrews 2:11). Even the "prisoners"—those who enter His community caught in crushing circumstances, stuck in sin, or gripped by grief or fear—find a family who will help them find freedom. When we come close in healthy community, He fills and heals every hole in every life.

In fact, we won't become *whole* without our relationship with Him *and* with His people. Our lives only fully flourish and transform when lived in a Christ-centered, Spirit-filled community. In fact, there is some development we'll never experience in Jesus *without* people. Half the growth He'll grant us in Him will generate from our personal relationship with Him—the time we spend sitting with Him, studying His Word, and seeking to know Him ourselves. The other half will come straight from our relationships and service within the *body* of Christ. Scripture explains how as the apostles, prophets, evangelists, pastors, and teachers function in their gifts, they equip *all* of the body of Christ to build up the church with their gifts, and as this work weaves on, *"we will all come to such unity in our faith and knowledge of God's Son that we will be mature in the Lord, measuring up to the full and complete standard of Christ"* (Ephesians 4:11-13 NLT). Right community brings *maturity*—making us people no longer tossed around by tough trials and twisted teaching, people who can't be tricked by lies that sound like truth (Ephesians 4:14). Instead, we will continue *"growing in every way more and more like Christ, who is the head of his body, the Church"* (Ephesians 4:15 NLT). Our faith will flourish fully *only* in fellowship.

Each person matters, too. Jesus *"makes the whole body fit together perfectly,"* and *"as **each part** does its own special work, it helps the other parts grow, so that the whole body is healthy and growing and full of love"* (Ephesians 4:16 NLT). Each part—each *person*—is profoundly needed. We are many pieces that make up one body, and the eye can never deem the hand unneeded, and the head can't tell the feet, *"I don't need you,"* either (I Corinthians 12:20-21). Take in this truth: *"In fact, some parts of the body that seem weakest and least important are actually the most necessary"* (v. 22 NLT). Each person's gifts are essential—and each person *is*, essentially, a *gift*, too. When people don't connect in Christ's community, they forfeit the growth they'd gain through others—but they also block the blessing they'd *bring* to others. We can only reach full maturity—and even full joy—*together.*

Let's also not miss out on the day-to-day joy of having shoulder-to-shoulder *friends* who are filled with the Holy Spirit. When we lock arms and live life with the right people, life becomes more bearable and more beautiful. Like-hearted, Spirit-filled friends bolster us in battles and bear our burdens with us (Ecclesiastes 4:9-10, 12; Galatians 6:2). They spur us on to live and love right and spill life into us when we can't see light (Hebrews 10:24-25). They'll sharpen us like iron—speaking truth in love that leads us to more of Jesus (Proverbs 27:17). While *"unreliable friends"* soon bring us to ruin, our Jesus-given friends will *"stick closer than a brother"* (Proverbs 18:24 NIV). Instead of fighting *with* us, they will fight *for* us. Their prayers will even push and propel us to perfect freedom. The Word instructs us to do this: *"Confess your sins to each other so that you may be healed. The earnest prayer of a righteous person has great power and produces wonderful results"* (James 5:16 NLT). Some of our healing happens only through humble, honest conversations with friends who then hold our hands and *pray.* Their faithful prayers act as an added force that encircles and empowers our efforts and shoves us to the finish line of full freedom where we're fighting. Jesus-given friends—with their precious presence and prayers—are wonderful and powerful. Let's come close in a godly community and gain these *endearing* and *enduring* gifts of friendship.

Let's also *be* these powerful friends. The Word instructs us to value others above ourselves and to care about *their* interests, not just our own (Philippians 2:3-4). Jesus teaches that *"it's more blessed to give than to receive"* (Acts 20:35 NLT). Proverbs 11:25 (NLT) also adds this: *"The generous will prosper; those who refresh others will themselves be refreshed."* We live our best, most blessed life when we intentionally refresh our friends—with check-ins, encouragement, prayer, love, and laughter. In Jesus' Kingdom and community, when we pour out, we get filled up simultaneously. When we live connected to other Spirit-filled believers, our lives spill into each other. We are refreshed only *as* we refresh others. In this shared overflow, Jesus becomes more visible, more tangible—more **known** and **near.** However, when a fountain stands alone, its impact is limited. The Living Water may still flow, but the sound is subdued, the reach is restricted, and over time, even the joy may stall and still. We were never meant to flow—or *grow*—alone.

Holy Communion

At the Last Supper, our Savior established the custom of *communion.* Here's the account: *"And when He had taken bread and given thanks, He broke it and gave it to them, saying, 'This is My body which is given for you; do this in remembrance of Me.' And in the same way He took the cup after they had eaten, saying, 'This cup, which is poured out for you, is the new covenant [ratified] in My blood'"* (Luke 22:19-20 AMP). Jesus sat with His disciples, put symbolic bread and wine in their hands, and led them through not just a surface exercise but a spiritual *encounter.* He modeled this moment before returning to Heaven and meant for it to become a continued custom carried out by His people on earth.

We take communion *"in remembrance"* of our Savior and His sacrifice. The bit of bread in our hand embodies His broken body, and the deep-red wine or juice in our other hand depicts His delivering Blood. As we hold these physical elements, we enter into a spiritual encounter. His beaten and bleeding body becomes boldly real again. These radical revelations are renewed once more: He *truly* did come to this earth and die to deliver new life to us. He really does desire us *that* much. Jesus is truly and *radically* in love with us. As we grasp the bread and wine, we gasp over it *all* again. Our hearts re-center on the reality of it all. We become touched again—teeming with gratitude anew. We remember and relish what our God did to become **known and near.** With humbled hands, we hold the Body and the Blood that made the relationship with Jesus we were born to have possible.

Paul gave in-depth instruction on this holy habit. After retelling the story of the Last Supper—beautifully briefing them on Jesus' words—He then taught this: *"For as often as you eat this bread and drink the cup, you proclaim the Lord's death until he comes. Whoever, therefore, eats the bread or drinks the cup of the Lord in an unworthy manner will be guilty...Let a person examine himself, then, and so eat of the bread and drink of the cup"* (1 Corinthians 11:26–28 ESV). Paul points out that every time we partake in communion, we are "proclaiming"—both presenting and praising—that Jesus died, resurrected, and will return again. As we both reverently remember what's been done and powerfully proclaim what's ahead, we are worshipping Him with honor and holy awe. As we do, our hearts are humbled and awakened to Him afresh. However, Paul also gave a wise warning: he taught that none should take communion in an *"unworthy manner"* and emphasized that we must examine our hearts. As we clutch the bread and wine, we must cleanse our hearts of compromise and sin. Before consuming the elements, we should recognize and repent of wrong, recommit our lives to Jesus, and receive His forgiveness. We re-surrender our un-surrendered parts and reset our missteps with the Holy Spirit. As we realign our hearts and then partake of the bread and wine, a spiritual shift happens in areas that were out of line. We are set right and made new *again.*

Although we can partake of communion alone in our private time with Jesus, it is mostly participated in with our community to remind us of our unity. Paul declared this: *"And though we are many, we all eat from one loaf of bread, showing that we are one body"* (I Corinthians 10:17 NLT). During corporate communion, we eat from the same loaf, symbolizing that we all are saved by the same Body. Although there are differences in our biological blood, only *one* Blood brims within our spiritual beings. We are *all* His. We are *family.* We are brothers and sisters who belong to Jesus but also to each other. Corporate communion challenges draining division and creates uplifting unity.

Together, we celebrate the *next* time we will all sit with Jesus and eat around a table with Him as He did at the Last Supper. At His final feast, Jesus spoke of a future feast: *"But I say to you, I will not drink of this fruit of the vine from now on until that day when I drink it new with you in My Father's kingdom"* (Matthew 26:29 AMP). He anticipated—as *we* should, too, while taking communion—the promised banquet we'll have with Him in Heaven (Revelation 19:6-9, Isaiah 25:6, Luke 14:15, Matthew 22:2-4). When Jesus returns again, He will reveal His Kingdom fully and restore all things completely. Then, He'll hold a huge, heavenly celebration. He calls it The Wedding Feast of the Lamb. *Jesus* is the Groom, and *we* are His Bride—and this blissful banquet will celebrate our eternal union. Once more, His desire for deep, intimate relationship with us is demonstrated through His choice of titles. No one is more **known** and **near** to each other than a groom and his bride. He has *this* heart for *us*. So, as we take communion, we also anticipate this beautiful, unbreakable union we'll enjoy with our greatest Love for all eternity.

Giving

Another holy habit to establish concerns the thing that grips our hearts the hardest: *money*. Jesus taught that money and God would compete for the throne of our hearts. With tender care, He cautioned, *"No one can serve two masters. Either you will hate the one and love the other, or you will be devoted to the one and despise the other. You cannot serve both God and money"* (Matthew 6:24 NIV). We are servants, and our Master can either be money *or* Jesus. If money rules us—whether through materialism, wealth, possessions, or the false security they promise—it will demand our trust, time, and worship just as the Lord does. We'll devote ourselves to one and despise the other. If our focus is financial gain, we will neglect or resist God's way, which requires generosity and breaks the grip of greed. Ultimately, we *must* decide who holds the throne of our hearts: God or money.

The Lord established a sacred pattern that makes Him our true Master, keeps greed grounded, and opens the way for boundless blessing. Scripture calls it the *tithe*, which means "tenth." In the Old Testament, the tithe was the giving of one-tenth of income or produce back to God as an act of worship, obedience, and trust. We first see this pattern in Genesis 14:20, when Abraham freely gave a tenth of all he had to Melchizedek in honor of the Lord. Later, under the Law of Moses, tithing became a command for Israel, designed to support the priests, care for the poor, and sustain God's work among His people (Leviticus 27:30; Numbers 18:21; Deuteronomy 14:28–29). This portion was declared holy—set apart for the Lord—and within that covenant, withholding it was reckoned robbery (Malachi 3:8). Then, in the New Testament, Christ fulfilled the Law, and giving is now led by the Spirit—guided by generosity, priority, and willing obedience. It is no longer a matter of strict percentages but of the *heart*. Under the New Covenant, generosity is no longer governed by rules but by *relationship*—an ongoing conversation with the Holy Spirit, who lovingly leads us in how and when to give. God calls us to give as the Spirit leads—joyfully, cheerfully, and abundantly. Giving moves from something we *have* to do to something we *get* to do—no longer driven by fear or formula but by love and trust. Today, believers honor this biblical pattern of giving—set apart for God, led by the Spirit, and rooted in generosity—by giving regularly and proportionately to the "storehouse," the church or community where they are spiritually nourished and taught (Galatians 6:6). Through this, ministry, outreach, care, and mission continue to flow. This kind of giving is never coerced by the Lord nor meant to be forcefully demanded by leaders, yet it is joyfully encouraged; it is a tangible way we partner with God in His work and declare that He reigns over every area of our lives, including our finances.

Under the Old Covenant, the Lord even invited His people to test Him in their giving—a rare call rooted in covenant faithfulness. Stare at these daring words: *"'Test Me now in this,' says the Lord of hosts, 'if I will not open for you the windows of Heaven and pour out for you [so great] a blessing until there is no more room to receive it. Then I will rebuke the devourer…for your sake, and he will not destroy the fruits of the ground'"* (Malachi 3:10-11 AMP). When we give faithfully, Scripture assures us that God is faithful to protect, provide, and plentifully *bless*—not always in the way we expect but always with abundance. Proverbs 3:9–10 (NIV) affirms this same truth, calling us to honor the Lord with our wealth and "first fruits," trusting Him with the outcome. In the New Testament, Paul builds on this foundation—not commanding a specific fraction or amount but calling believers to give freely, generously, and *cheerfully*, assuring us that such giving reshapes both the heart of the giver and the good of the community (2 Corinthians 9:6–15). As we give in faith—through a rhythm of disciplined generosity that remains continually led by the Spirit—we receive a harvest that reaches far beyond material provision, touching our peace, joy, growth, and trust in God. In addition, *offerings*, given above and beyond regular giving, become an additional avenue of worship—supporting missions, ministries, and mercy wherever the Spirit leads. In all of our giving, generosity becomes a declaration: Jesus is King—not just of our worship but of our *whole* hearts and *whole* lives.

Additionally, one group that burns on the Lord's heart that should be branded into ours, too, is the *poor*. The Lord's heart hovers with the hopeless and helpless (Psalm 34:18). He is so one-hearted with those in lack that He receives any gift—no matter how minute—given to them like we gave it to *Him* (Proverbs 19:17). When we stand before Him one day, He'll even address anything we did—or *didn't* do—for the poor. In Matthew 25, Jesus explained that the Father will separate the "sheep from the goats" at the final judgement, and He will reward the sheep at His right hand for taking care of Him when He was hungry, thirsty, homeless, naked, sick, and imprisoned (Matthew 25:31-40). When the stumped sheep ask what He means, He'll say, *"I tell you the truth, when you did it to one of the least of these, my brothers and sisters, you were doing it to me!"* (v. 40 NLT). Then, He'll turn to the goats and condemn them for *not* taking care of "Him" in this way. The Lord takes our caring for the poor so personally that He will reward us for it in person one day (Matthew 19:21, Matthew 6:1-4, Luke 6:38). Let's be careful not to live our lives clinging to everything in our hands as ours. Let's share. Let's *give*. Let's even *look* for those who lack—both locally and globally—and love them like the Lord Himself *longs* to.

If we're struggling to give like this, we're grappling with greed—and we're wrestling to *trust*. We're challenged by control and choked with want. Putting our money in Jesus' hands is the truest test of our trust. We haven't fully opened our hearts to Him until we've fully widened our wallets to Him. When we give to Him regularly, He bountifully blesses the rest of our money—month after month. We'll experience His favor flowing into *all* facets of our lives. Often, when we've hit a wall in our walk with Him, the lost traction can be traced back to our giving. When He wholly holds even the financial space in our hearts, we experience endless expansion in our relationship with Him. When we withhold nothing from Him—not even our *money*—He becomes as **known and near** to us as He can possibly be.

PART 5

The Hurdles

CHAPTER EIGHT

Our Enemy

"Stay alert! Watch out for your great enemy, the devil. He prowls around like a roaring lion, looking for someone to devour. Stand firm against him, and be strong in your faith. Remember that your family of believers all over the world is going through the same kind of suffering you are."—I Peter 5:8-9 (NLT)

Our Battle With Satan

We live in a fallen world and fight a forsaken enemy—both of which hoist up *hurdles* to hold us back in our relationship with Jesus. We must know that we are at *war*. Satan knows our weaknesses well and does not take vacations from his violations against us. The Word wells with warnings about the war he wages. Revelation 12:17 (TPT) tells us that He specifically fights against those who *"follow the commands of God and have the testimony of Jesus."* Another verse reveals his relentless hunger to hurt: *"Be sober-minded; be watchful. Your adversary the devil prowls around like a roaring lion, seeking someone to devour"* (I Peter 5:8 ESV). Therefore, we are instructed to *"put on God's complete set of armor"* so that we can stand securely and safely against *"all evil strategies of the accuser"*—for our *"hand-to-hand combat is not with human beings but with the highest principalities and authorities operating in rebellion under the heavenly realms…a powerful class of demon-gods and evil spirits that hold this dark world in bondage"* (Ephesians 6:11-12 TPT). We deal daily with an enemy we cannot see. His purpose is to steal, kill, and destroy anything that's life-giving or God-given (John 10:10). He's after our peace, joy, freedom, purpose—and *especially* our intimacy with Jesus. His most noxious nightmare is the Lord's most

delighted-in dream: *any* of us experiencing Jesus as **known** and **near**—
any of us having the relationship with Jesus we were born to have.

While we live in this physical world, a spiritual realm looms
around us—one we can only view visually with special revelation
(Colossians 1:16). If our eyes were opened to it, we would behold
angels carrying out God's commands—protecting, strengthening, and
ministering to His people (Hebrews 1:7, 14; Psalm 103:20-21;
Revelation 10:1), and we'd also witness *fallen* angels working to deceive
and oppress us (Ephesians 6:12, Luke 10:18). Spiritual battles and
opposition between angels and demons transpire all around us tirelessly
(Daniel 10:12-13, Revelation 12:7). This ongoing opposition in the
spirit realm includes power struggles and skirmishes that even affect
earthly events (Daniel 10:12-13). Yet, in the midst of this spiritual war,
God surrounds His people with His protection (Psalm 34:7). In 2 Kings
6:15-17 (AMP), Elisha's servant fretted in fear over an enemy army
surrounding them, but Elisha replied and prayed: *"Do not be afraid! For
those who are with us are more than those who are with them.' Then Elisha prayed
and said, 'Lord, please open his eyes that he may see.' And the Lord opened the
servant's eyes, and he saw; and behold, the mountain was full of horses and chariots
of fire surrounding Elisha."* The servant witnessed a wonder that Jesus
wants us to waken to: though our eyes perceive the enemy's schemes,
we are encircled by an unseen Kingdom that reigns in unshakable *victory*.
No matter what visible chaos closes in, His invisible caring and covering
remain constant. We are always surrounded with supernatural safety;
we are *always* set up to subdue Satan.

In the middle of the battles that boom and bring doom around
us, our God is *always* in control (Colossians 1:16-17, Psalm 103:19,
Daniel 4:35, 1 Peter 3:22). He is not distant or disengaged. He is *"sitting
upon a throne, high and lifted up"* where he sees *all* (Isaiah 6:1 ESV,
Revelation 4:2). He reigns and rules from the highest place—
surrounded by wondrous worship, always in complete command. From
this seated position, He dispatches angels for protection, deliverance,
and endurance (Psalm 91:11, Psalm 34:7). Jesus, too, sits at His right
hand interceding for us, serving as our ardent Advocate and dedicated
Defender (Romans 8:34, Hebrews 7:25). Alongside that, here's a truth
that frees and relieves: the Lord sets limits on the activity in the spirit
realm—allowing only what can be redeemed (Job 1:12, Luke 22:31-

32). Anything He permits, He purposes to redeem—using it for our refinement rather than our ruin. Along with this promise, He's also given us power: He has filled us with His own Spirit who is *"greater than the one who is in the world"* (I John 4:4 NIV). His presence within us is stronger than *any* demonic attack that strikes and seeks to break us.

Still, why doesn't God just whisper a word that could wrap up the war? Here's why: He's merciful. He's patient. He's kind. He's giving *time*—even in the midst of evil—for more hearts to come home to Him (2 Peter 3:9). While He waits, He uses even evil to fulfill His redemptive plans in *all* lives (Romans 8:28, Genesis 50:20). His hands habitually hover even over hardship—employing it to *heal*, not harm, His people and allowing it to attract the aching and astray into His arms. He will not permit any weapon formed against us to prosper—but He *will* use it to prosper *us* (Isaiah 54:17). Every blow from the enemy will only become a brushstroke on the masterpiece of miracles God's manifesting in the lives of those who are *His*. Then, on the day He has planned, He'll send His Son *again*. Jesus will gallop to our groaning earth on a gorgeous white horse (Revelation 19:11). He'll halt the war and hurl our enemy into a forever-burning lake of fire (Revelation 20:10). Evil will end eternally. Know this: our Father's throne is secure. His justice is *sure*—and it's *perfectly* timed.

Until then, Satan does not have authority over us, but he *does* constantly seek access to us. Although we're saturated with the Holy Spirit and surrounded by supernatural back-up, the enemy can still seek us out. His approach is not as apparent as with Eve. To us, He slithers up silently and invisibly—shrouding himself in our own secret *thoughts*. Because we, too, are triune beings with a body (our physical part), soul (our mind, will, and emotions), and spirit (our inner, God-conscious part), we can interact with and be influenced by both the physical *and* spiritual realms (I Thessalonians 5:23). So, Satan can swindle our souls, influencing our thoughts, emotions, desires, and memories; he can also suggest fear, confusion, shame, and discouragement through deceptive thoughts and impressions. He can even prey and play on our physical senses and fleshly desires through our bodies—relentlessly tempting us. If we are not vested in truth and vigilant, he can perfidiously plant poison in our hearts. Scripture says Satan slipped the thought to betray Jesus into the heart of Judas (John

13:2) and dropped deception into the heart of Ananias (Acts 5:3). He blinds the minds of unbelievers (2 Corinthians 4:4) and launches "fiery darts" in the form of lies, doubts, temptations, and shameful thoughts at even solid believers (Ephesians 6:16). Though blocked from view, our enemy is bold and *busy*. We belong to Jesus yet are still bombed and bombarded by Satan's assaults, but we have been positioned and empowered to win—not just "someday" but *every day*.

Satan's daily aim is to destroy, but his angle is to *deceive*. Since he rejected God's truth, he became the embodiment of its opposite: *deception*. In fact, the devil is dubbed *"a liar and the father of lies"* (John 8:44 NLT). He is called *"the deceiver of the whole world"* (Revelation 12:9 ESV) and even *"disguises himself as an angel of light"* (2 Corinthians 11:14 ESV). Just as he deceived Eve—even essentially using Scripture—he *still* speaks lies dressed as truth to us, hoping to be believed. He spins and slips lies into our thoughts and hearts about *all* things—including who God is, how He feels about us, and what He will and won't do. He lies about our identity, too—bashing our appearance and ability, confusing our priorities, and accusing us of iniquity. He'll even take freedom-giving Scripture, twist it, and turn it into a trap that transfers us into bondage while sounding like truth. His lies—*if* listened to—will lead us to a loss of peace, joy, confidence, security, hope, love, faith, trust, and even time. He will weave us into wrong relationships, positions, and places. He'll both distract and discourage us all the way to full destruction—all the while detaining us from our divine destiny.

Since Satan's scheme is to deceive, we must learn to perceive him and achieve putting him in his proper place. Here's where to watch for him: he disguises his lies within our natural thoughts. All day long, we must stand like an authoritative guard over our thoughts and imprison intruders: *"We demolish arguments and every pretension that sets itself up against the knowledge of God, and we take captive every thought to make it obedient to Christ"* (2 Corinthians 10:5 NIV). When we think a thought that makes us sink—into worry, doubt, discouragement, offense, or temptation—we must take it captive before it takes *us* captive. We do this by literally spotting the lie and then speaking the *truth* aloud. For example, when we internally think, "Jesus isn't going to come through for me," we externally speak, "Jesus *will* come through for me!" We can't half-way do this; we have to *aggressively* lean out of the lie and totally into the truth. Also, here's the exciting part about the many moments when the enemy mouths a lie: in the very second he speaks a lie, the *opposite* is true. For instance, when we drive home from work or school thinking, "I'm not making a difference in peoples' lives," and we begin deflating in defeat—the opposite is actually the truth at *that* very moment. Otherwise, he wouldn't bother with the lies right then. So, we can both capture the lie and then celebrate the truth—all in one miraculous moment. With Jesus, even the devil's discouragement can instantly become encouragement. We can constantly beat the enemy at his *own* guileful game.

In order to have these swift victories all day long, we must do two things: know the Word well *and* watch vigilantly for thoughts from Hell. Increasing and deepening our understanding of the Word daily keeps the *truth* at the top of our consciousness. If we don't foreknow the truth, we won't know the lie on the spot. We must fill our minds so full of truth that a lie stands out like a shrill shriek in a serene room. We also must wake ourselves up *twice* in the mornings. When we open our physical eyes, we haven't necessarily opened our spiritual eyes. Before our feet even touch the ground at the start of the day, let's pray. In a quick prayer, let's awaken our spirits and dedicate our whole being and day to Jesus. If we don't submit to Jesus before standing, the enemy will begin his reminding and reprimanding. Across our barely awake minds, he'll parade yesterday's mistakes and today's possible heartaches and get us to break before we even make it to breakfast. He starts *early* every day. His aim is to take us captive in a lie first thing and make it *the* thing he chokes us with all day long. He'll succeed if we don't fully waken ourselves spiritually each morning. We must then *stay* spiritually alert, walking consciously in truth, countering every lie, and claiming victory throughout the day.

Every day—whether in a season of calm or calamity—we are in a spiritual *war*. The battle ground truly is the mind—and our battle plan is simple: *"Surrender to God. Stand up to the devil and resist him, and he will flee in agony"* (James 4:7 TPT). When we lean into Jesus and resist the lies, the enemy leaves. Whether the lie is about something trivial or critical—*this* is the way we war. *This* is the way we win.

Doubts & Disappointments

Our deceiver deals deeply in *doubt*. He'll aim to store it in our core beliefs first—raising questions about even the one true God's existence, God as Creator, God as sovereign, and God's Word as *the* Truth. Just as with Eve, Satan works subtly and strategically to plant seeds of doubt about Jesus in hearts. He does to *all* people exactly what he did with her: he aims to get us to question the authority, goodness, and truth of the Bible and to redirect our human longing for purpose, identity, and understanding toward false answers.

He does this because he knows that each person deeply desires to know the truth. He grasps that God has *"planted eternity [a sense of divine purpose] in the human heart [a mysterious longing which nothing under the sun can satisfy, except God]"* (Ecclesiastes 3:11 AMP). He also knows this truth: *"The truth of God is known instinctively, for God has embedded this knowledge inside every human heart,"* and from creation, He has made His invisible qualities—His eternal power and divine nature—clearly perceptible in the sky and earth all around us so that every heart can naturally recognize Him (Romans 1:19-20 TPT). In other words, we are each born innately wanting the true God and physically witnessing the proof of Him all around us. The enemy cannot delete this desire or erase the evidence of the Lord's existence, so he conjured up counterfeit truths—lies for people to latch their longings and their lives to *other* than the Lord.

The Word warns us to avoid this web of deceit: *"See to it that no one takes you captive through hollow and deceptive philosophy, which depends on human tradition and the elemental spiritual forces of this world rather than on Christ"* (Colossians 2:8 NIV). These philosophical lies and ideas sound intelligent, scientific, and even *spiritual*—like evolution, man-made theories, semi-religious organizations, and completely false religions. Satan wraps these in just enough logic and appeal to make them believable—even to well-meaning human beings. In filling peoples' minds with substitutes that seem to answer life's deepest questions and desires, Satan stops people from surrendering to Jesus. His counterfeit theories and truths keep people blind, confused, and separated from *the* Truth that could completely set them free (John 8:32).

One specific lie that Satan has cleverly erected and projected worldwide to cause people to doubt Jesus is this one: "*All* religions and roads lead to the same God." This lie is the opposite of what Christ claimed: *"I am the [only] Way [to God] and the [real] Truth and the [real] Life; no one comes to the Father but through Me"* (John 14:6 AMP). Satan proclaims there are *many* ways; Jesus maintains *He* is the *only* way. By promoting that *any* religion or set of spiritual beliefs leads to the same God, the devil dilutes the exclusive claims of Christ, making salvation seem like a matter of personal preference or cultural choice rather than a life-changing encounter with the One true Savior. This deception removes spiritual clarity and raises spiritual complacency as it declares, "Get to God however you want! It's all the same!" If we follow this, we can fabricate our own truth and fashion our own god. However, the Bible gives us this wise warning: *"There is a path before each person that seems right, but it ends in death"* (Proverbs 14:12 TPT). Jesus spoke of choosing the correct path, too: *"Enter through the narrow gate, because the wide gate and broad path is the way that leads to destruction—nearly everyone chooses that crowded road! The narrow gate and the difficult way leads to eternal life—so few even find it!"* (Matthew 7:13-14 TPT). It's easier—more *comfortable*—in a lot of ways to pick and choose which truths and paths to follow—but even though the narrow path looks like less liberty, it provides full freedom. There's only *one* path wrapped in divine protection—*one* single thread of Truth that weaves freedom and blessing into our days on earth and leads us straight into the perfection of eternity. That path has a name, and His Name is **Jesus**.

Although many other religions have well-known names attached to them, too, *none* of them are like Jesus. Christianity stands apart from all other theories and truths—and even all other world religions. While other faiths revolve around humanity reaching up to God through *their* own striving, Christianity is the only one focused on God reaching down to humanity through *His* own sacrificing. These belief systems center on self-effort to earn favor, enlightenment, or salvation while *only* Christianity proclaims that salvation is a free gift of grace through faith in Jesus. Many of them portray gods who are distant, impersonal, or conditional in their love. Christianity *alone* centers on the God who suffers for His creation out of love—to make a way for them to enjoy a real, loving *relationship* with Himself.

Let's understand why Satan *couldn't* create a religion that even compares to Christianity. Satan knows that rule-keeping would make people feel spiritual and stay busy but never *free*. Satan himself also knows that the false gods behind other religions are impotent idols or demonic deceptions that *can't* offer a personal relationship, because they are not the true, living God. He could not even make up another God who could have a real, walking-talking-and-experiencing relationship with people because there *isn't* another one. Satan's goal is to keep people from experiencing the transforming love, truth, and intimacy that *only* comes through Jesus. Remember that Satan experienced the beauty of God's presence and personal relationship with Him firsthand (Ezekiel 28:14-17). He has radically encountered the greatness of God's glory and goodness—and he recognizes that he couldn't possibly recreate *that* in a rigged religion. He realizes all other "gods" are deaf, blind, and dead (Psalm 115:4-8). Even he knows that only *one* God can be **known**. Only *one* God can be **near**. Only *one* God created all people for a real *relationship* with Him. He incites resistance against this intimacy with Jesus in people because he's jealous. He hates it with a fury unmatched. He knows that relational nearness with Jesus is the one and only thing that sets people free and defeats his deceit. Therefore, he *lies* about it all being true.

However, even after we *have* believed the verity and validity of the Gospel, he'll deluge new Christians with doubt in the early days of developing their new life with Him. He'll wickedly whisper, "You're not *really* saved"—digging for them to doubt their decision. He'll stir up shame over past mistakes and memories, sinisterly saying, "You've sinned *too* much for Jesus to *really* forgive and love you." He'll instigate impatience and unrealistic expectations by implying, "You're not changing very fast. You must be doing this *wrong*." He'll dump doubt in the form of discouragement and comparison, claiming, "Other people are more spiritual and better at this than *you*." He'll also drop doubts deeply and *daily* and declare that it disqualifies them: "Oh, you still have doubts? *Real* Christians don't doubt!" On and on the doubt-dumping will go until we know Jesus *well*. Doubt about Jesus is demolished by *experience* with Jesus. Many attend church weekly but still doubt Jesus daily—only because they don't spend time with Him alone *diligently*. Our faith is rendered fruitless and footless without real relationship with Him. Only intimate encounters that come from deliberate pursuit of Jesus destroy the doubt the deceiver aims to drive into us. The more we personally sit with Jesus, read the Word, learn to hear Him, and come *near* Him—the more we'll *know* Him. We will actually *feel* His presence wrap around us, unmistakable and alive. He will draw so near that we *cannot* doubt Him. In the quiet of meeting with Him, His voice will speak softly yet clearly, and we will know with unwavering certainty that He is good, fully present, and breathtakingly *real*. Our diligent seeking will eventually keep doubt from speaking anything that we'd believe over our own experiences with *Him*.

To those who do know Jesus well, the deceiver deals out doubt differently. He waits to draw near when *disappointments* appear. Those who know the Word know His promises—and when it seems that one has not been met or kept, it can shake a person's faith to its depth. Disappointment in the heart of a believer can become a door to doubt for our deceiver. One example of our God's many guarantees is this one: *"Delight yourself in the Lord, and He will give you the desires and petitions of your heart"* (Psalm 37:4 AMP). Many erroneously assume this means that when we walk with Jesus, He'll give us what *we* want. However, this promise pertains to a heart that has drawn near and delighted in Jesus so much that it has begun to beat like *His*. The hungers of this heart harmonize with *His*. He gave the person *right* desires—not the fulfillment of his or her own human hopes. Our desires and dreams may not have dawned because they aren't a part of *His* perfect plan. Our unfulfilled urge may even reflect His unseen protection. He's a perfect, protective Father with a powerful plan, and He *won't* break His promises—nor will He grant a request if it isn't His *best* (Numbers 23:19, Hebrews 10:23). So, when we feel let-down by a promise He made, we may have simply misinterpreted its meaning, or we may just need our desires more deeply aligned with *His* leaning.

We also must trust His *timing*. Dreams are often delayed until character is made. We may know the dream and destiny of the Lord for our lives but are still being shaped and seasoned so that we can succeed in it. He does with us as He did with Joseph: *"Until the time came to fulfill his dreams, the Lord tested Joseph's character"* (Psalm 105:19 NLT). We want our dreams to come true earlier; we often expect them way sooner than when He fulfills them. However, He often waits to release the most precious parts of His plans when we're older and wiser—and at the *time* and in a *way* that makes its fulfillment even sweeter. When a delayed dream delivers disappointment, if we'll lean our hearts into His, He'll reappoint it. He'll reset it to trust and believe, to see His best *still* on the way, and to *wait*—even with joy.

One of the experiences that can explode doubt into our hearts most extremely is *unanswered prayers.* The Bible boldly affirms—verse after verse—that the Lord both hears and answers when we pray (John 16:23-24, I John 5:14, Matthew 7:7-8, Psalm 34:15). He clearly says to ask, and He'll accomplish it. He truly *does* answer prayers powerfully and perfectly—every single time. However, what do we do when it seems that He *isn't* or *didn't?* First, we must know that He's not going to carry out what we ask if it isn't His best or the right course. Secondly, remember that the Lord reveals this: *"'My thoughts are nothing like your thoughts,' says the Lord. 'And my ways are far beyond anything you could imagine. For just as the heavens are higher than the earth, so my ways are higher than your ways and my thoughts higher than your thoughts'"* (Isaiah 55:8-9 NLT). His perspective, plans, and purposes rise and reside much higher than our human perceptions. Therefore, He will always answer, but, at times, it may *appear* to us that He did not.

For example, we may pray for our godly grandmother's cancer to completely disappear—knowing that healing is something God delights in doing and has made available in Christ (Matthew 8:16–17, I John 5:14-15)—and He *may* miraculously erase every trace of sickness. However, she may still *die* instead. When a long-term, faith-filled battle for a miracle ends in death, disappointment and doubt detonate like dynamite. Did He not listen or lean towards our need? Did we not pray correctly or enough? No, He clearly heard and dearly held us close. He also *answered.* We have to understand that what looks to us like the *worst* thing that could have happened can be to Jesus the *best* thing to allow. The believing grandmother who died *did* get healed. Standing on streets of gold, completely made whole—she couldn't be more healed or happier than *that.* He did answer—in the greatest way possible for that precious woman. Let's remember that we may not always witness the miracle we hoped for here, but God still heals fully and finally in eternity. Then, the Lord miraculously moves in *our* lives when we mourn. Jesus taught, *"Blessed are those who mourn, for they will be comforted"* (Matthew 5:4 NIV). When we need comfort, the

Father comes *so* close—cultivating even more tenderness and trust when we're crushed. What we take as a "bad" thing, He will always turn into a blessing. Even in our grieving, there is growing and a deeper knowing that the Lord is *near*. What looks like the worst to us, our loving God is quietly weaving into something rich with goodness and overflowing grace.

Consider this truth, too: *"Good people pass away; the godly often die before their time. But no one seems to care or wonder why. No one seems to understand that God is protecting them from the evil to come. For those who follow godly paths will rest in peace when they die"* (Isaiah 57:1-2 NLT). Remember that our Father is immeasurably merciful. Sometimes, when the righteous die—even those passing away "too early" in life—it may actually be His mercy. He sees the *full* span of a life—every part of a person's path—and He may spot unbearable sorrow, overwhelming hardship, or spiritual danger ahead and, in compassion, call him or her home early. When it seems something—or *someone*—is being "taken," mercy and protection are *always* being given. Our God *always* moves in goodness and kindness. With Him, even loss is laced with *grace*.

Let's also remember the power of human free will. Sometimes we intercede fervently for a person or situation, and the Lord truly does open doors—to salvation, freedom, or reconciliation—perhaps even more than once. He pours out His power, His presence, and His prompting. Yet, a person can still choose *not* to step into what God is offering. Jesus steers the hearts we pray for toward salvation. He showers freeing power on the addict we cry out to Him about. He brings the miracle needed to restore a broken marriage. Still, even when His power is present and His invitation is clear, people can sense it— and still turn away. The moment for the miracle may arrive, but it may not be received. Often, it's not that the Lord was unwilling; it's that the *person* was *self*-willing. Let's never doubt that He answers. He *always* moves when we pray. If the miracle didn't happen, it's not because the prayer went unheard—or because God was unmoved. It may simply be that what He lovingly rendered was, in that moment, refused. Yet, even then, His mercy keeps moving; He never stops pursuing these *same* people with the *same* goodness. So, let's keep praying without giving up (Luke 18:1, Colossians 4:2). Our persistent prayers for resistant people become a part of the unseen spiritual pressure drawing them to Jesus and *all* that He can do in their lives (John 6:44). The prayers of the righteous are powerful and effective—even when the answers take time (James 5:16). That's a truth we should *never* doubt.

When our enemy drops doubt, let's detect it and dump it out. Satan will persistently plant questions or thoughts that challenge truth and could weaken our trust if we let it take root. Let's rush to the Word, to the Holy Spirit, or to a mature believer and find the truth that hushes the doubt. If we deal with doubt in *this* way, we'll only keep deepening our faith and understanding of *His* ways. We'll beat the enemy at his own game *again*. Our questions can simply become quests into more understanding. Our doubts can become doors to deeper experience. Our enemy-given questions can just lead us to more God-given revelations. Let's take every doubt to Jesus. He's *real*. He's *good*. He's the *One* and *Only* God there is. Our enemy hates Him and hunts for opportunities to make us doubt that He really can be **known**, that He really is **near**—all to keep us from the relationship with Jesus we were born to have.

Church Hurt & Bad Examples

One of the enemy's most strategic hurdles is hurt—but not just any kind: *church hurt*. Countless people have abandoned the Church—and even *Christ*—because they were disappointed by a Christian. When people step into a Christian church, they expect to experience love, acceptance, truth, and healing—a great glimpse of Jesus through His people. They seek a refuge, a family, a place where grace greets them—a space where loads are lifted and chains are cast off. When they, instead, encounter judgement, hypocrisy, manipulation, or even just plain weirdness, it creates deep disillusionment. When they see a pastor slip into sin or a leader loathsomely abuse someone—or when church politics push them out, making them feel unseen and unimportant—the enemy begins his *deep* deception. He will point to the failed Christian and the flawed church to convince them of a false Christ. There may be no tool the enemy uses more tactically to turn hearts away from Jesus than a Christian who doesn't tend toward His likeness.

However, we *will* have run-ins with Christians who have short-comings (Romans 3:23, 1 John 1:8). When we come into a church, we hope to encounter the energy of Heaven—all love and no hate, all purity and no sin, all perfection and no perils, all joy and no sorrows. However, walking into a church is more like wandering into a spiritual *hospital* (Matthew 9:12-13, Mark 2:17). The church houses and helps the hurt, the injured, the sinful, the sick—people pursuing hope and healing from the inside out. If they stay, they *will* find it fully in Jesus. Still, each person is in process. We can *all* look like hypocrites in moments. We may be genuinely growing in grace and patience with people but still snap. We may be boldly breaking an addiction but still battle and lose here and there. We may have a heart headed towards full love for people, but it still trips into the trap of passing judgement. As people in process, we are still people with problems. No one should expect perfection in a church—or even an individual Christian.

When we *do* witness wrong in fellow believers, Jesus wants us to put forth patience and prayer—and polite correction when it's needed. He expects us to *"gently and humbly help [a] person back onto the right path"* when he or she falls into sin (Galatians 6:1 NLT). He exhorts us to clothe ourselves *"with tenderhearted mercy, kindness, humility, gentleness, and patience"* and to *"make allowance for each other's faults"* and to forgive anyone who offends us (Colossians 3:12-13 NLT). We are a family full of members with imperfections, and we are to love each other towards transformation. In fact, we prove to the world that we are fully Jesus' and that He is truly real by the way we *love* one another (John 13:34-35). In Jesus' view, every struggle and stumble we witness in a brother or sister is an opportunity to simply share His love and show him or her how to get back up and keep going and *growing*. Yes, stepping into a church is like entering a spiritual hospital, but it's filled with patients who should have patience with people at every stage of healing. Some are freshly wounded while some are finally healed—and *love* is the medicine that carries us through our mistakes and guides us toward wholeness.

Still, not every church, pastor, or congregation shines with this kind of light. Some are healthy and vibrant, overflowing with Jesus' presence in ways we can overwhelmingly feel. *Many* are led by truly Spirit-filled, integrity-rooted pastors and leaders. *Many* church buildings are basins fully filled with the presence and Spirit of God, and those who dive in find radical refreshment and life. However, others are like drained, dried-up cement pools, unfilled because of unholy stewardship—and those who jump in get *hurt*. It's *right* to seek out a healthy, holy community, a place pulsing with waves of genuine anointing, faith, and love. However, it's *wrong* to do this: to let the enemy use an egregious experience—or a few misguided ministers or corrupt churches—to force us away from the family Jesus longs for us to find. Too many have dashed out the doors of God's house, disillusioned by disappointing authority or damaging experiences, only to drift far from Jesus or even fashion a faith all their own. Let's refuse to let the deceiver drive us to these dead ends. Instead, let's keep searching—patiently, expectantly—until we *do* find a body of believers where we will blend and bloom.

Jesus clearly calls us to community, *not* to solitude—to belonging, *not* to isolation. It is the enemy who lures us away into loneliness—contesting that the Church cannot be counted on. He'll point to the organized Christian community and tell us it's outdated—and even full of out-and-out evil. He'll continue his not-true narrative by attacking the believability of the Bible—and he'll ultimately fog out our faith in Jesus Himself. However, when belief in Jesus is too deeply rooted to remove, the enemy rebrands the faith—offering a knockoff, at-home version wrapped in rituals and half-truths. It's close enough to comfort yet far enough to confuse and quietly corrupt, carrying us away from the core truths of Christ. So, let's stick close to the Body. The true Church is meant to be a gathering place where we grow *together*. When we isolate ourselves, the enemy's lies echo louder, and the *real* truth gets twisted. Apart from the Body, our faith fights to survive—but, *together*, we thrive.

Let's remember this, too: as Christians, the world reads *our* lives like a letter describing Jesus. We must live *so* carefully so that what others observe in us reflects our Lord lucidly. One of Satan's worst weapons isn't a lie from the outside but a life on the inside that doesn't line up. When a believer speaks of grace but spills out pride—or preaches love but practices hate—it blurs the true picture of Jesus, making faith look fake. The enemy slithers into these moments, spouting into searching hearts, "*See!* It's all a show!" This is why we must strive to stride carefully although we'll *never* step perfectly. When mistakes are made, let's confess to Jesus but also express our wrong to those who witnessed it. It's powerful to point out our pitfalls and to profess what *should* have been done—what *Jesus* would have chosen. This shows us to be real and authentic—people whose faith isn't fake but is forming day by day. Let's continue allowing the Holy Spirit to mold us into powerful, unmistakable mirrors reflecting the life and love of Jesus. Each word we speak and each choice we make holds the power to draw people to Jesus or to drive them away. In this world full of lost people looking for the truth—while being lured by lies—we may be the only glimpse of *the* Truth they see. Let's *purposefully* paint the full picture of Jesus before their eyes through our lives.

Temptation

The most common hurdle we'll have to overcome—over and over again—is *temptation*. Because of the sinful nature we're gradually growing out of, we'll constantly encounter enticement to disobey God. The Word makes it clear that these tests of our character do *not* come from Jesus: *"And remember, when you are being tempted, do not say, 'God is tempting me.' For God cannot be tempted by evil, nor does he tempt anyone. Temptation comes from our own desires, which entice us and drag us away. These desires give birth to sinful actions. And when sin is allowed to grow, it gives birth to death"* (James 1:13-15 NLT). Temptation surges because of the sinful nature we're still shedding, and Satan lurks in the shadow of our flesh—working through our weaknesses, whispering warped wants, and drawing us toward willful wrong. The war Satan wages with us rages *especially* in these moments of temptation when the clash between our cravings and our calling becomes most challenging.

Even Jesus knows this experience because He faced *all* of these tests Himself—but He never failed (Hebrews 4:15). In His understanding and unending mercy, He gives us this promise about temptation: *"Thet temptations in your life are no different from what others experience. And God is faithful. He will not allow the temptation to be more than you can stand. When you are tempted, He will show you a way out so that you can endure"* (I Corinthians 10:13 NLT). No temptation is uncommon *or* impossible to overcome. Our faithful Father places limits on the enemy's attempts to lure us. We'll never fight a temptation that He hasn't already equipped us to endure or escape. Every time temptation arises, a step of obedience appears, and when we remember that the power of the Holy Spirit is near, the test becomes a hurdle we *can* clear.

Through the power of the Holy Spirit—*that* is how we trump temptation *every* time. When we stand staring at a choice—feeling like a rope pulled powerfully by our flesh into sin on one end and our spirit into righteousness on the other side—we must open our mouths wide and invoke our Helper. When we run out of our own willpower, we have *His* power—the maximum might of the Holy Spirit, which can empower us to do *anything* (Philippians 4:13, Acts 1:8, 1 Thessalonians 4:8). In the exact moment of temptation, we must rush to Him and request this: "Holy Spirit, show me the way out, and empower me to take it *right now!*" He will reveal the way of escape *as* promised, and He'll give us supernatural strength to take it—if we *ask*.

Let's pair this promise with this powerful principle, too: Psalm 23:5 (NIV) says, *"You prepare a table before me in the presence of my enemies."* In the moment we battle opposition of any kind—including temptation—the Lord sets a table right *there* in the fight, right *then* in the face of our enemy. On this table, Jesus places victory, provision, peace, power—a bountiful buffet of *all* He gives. Notice that the verse says *"before me."* This is *personal* provision—a table set with care and a chair just for us individually for *that* "impossible" moment. Our God does not turn away from us when we're tempted. He doesn't just guard us from afar either. He rushes right in where the battle has launched and literally lays a table set with victory. Depending on the type of temptation, that victory may look like praying for an offending person, turning off the screen, deleting the app, putting down the junk food, worshiping instead of worrying, keeping our mouths shut, walking away from a situation, getting up to pray in the morning, and so on. We must simply ask the Holy Spirit to help us *see* the provided victory and *take* it—*every* time we're tested. In moments when our flesh is fiercely fighting—as in, we overwhelmingly want the wrong thing—we have to aggressively (even verbally) call on the Holy Spirit to charge into our hearts and choose right *with* us. In some moments, the victory is *easy* to trace and take; in other moments, even a tiny decision can roar like a wild war. In *all* of these tests, a table is set, and the help of His Spirit will jet right in. All we have to do is *ask*.

The *one* thing that makes this tireless tussle with temptation easier is, once again, what Jesus titled the *"one thing most important"*: spending time *sitting* with Him (Luke 10:42). Jesus passionately proclaimed this principle to Peter, James, and John in the garden of Gethsemane (Matthew 26:36-46). Just hours before His arrest, Jesus took these three friends into the garden to pray, deeply distressed about the suffering He was about to endure. He asked His disciples to stay awake and pray with Him, but they kept falling asleep. When He found them snoozing a third time, He declared this: *"Couldn't you watch with me even one hour? Keep watch and pray, so that you will not give in to temptation. For the spirit is willing, but the body is weak!"* (Matthew 26:40-41 NLT). He urged them in the same way He'd encourage us today: sit and *pray* every day. As we pray, our spirits swell with strength; they are filled with the power we'll need for the hour we face temptation. The more we *sit* with Jesus, the more we can *stand* up to temptation. The less time we spend at His feet, the more we'll experience defeat. In His presence, all that's present in Him pours into us—His desires, tastes, and abilities—which purges our fleshly urges. Therefore, building the daily discipline of devoted prayer delivers the power to defeat the daily hurdles of temptation.

Worldly Content

Since the enemy's top tactic is to strike through temptation, we must shut down spots where such schemes can sneak in. In Psalm 101, King David demonstrated taking such solid steps. Out of deep desire to *"walk in the way of integrity"*—even in the privacy of his *"own home"*—he set up brick-like boundaries against what would bring added temptation (Psalm 101:2 TPT). This king knew that God had planted godliness in the ground of his heart, and he knew that it could only grow in the right environment and under righteous influences. Some seeds won't grow in just any setting or surroundings. This is thoroughly true about what Jesus has planted in *our* lives, too. To flourish in our faith, we must uproot *anything* that stunts or stops our growth—weeding out *any* influence that keeps us from blooming strong and free and becoming who we were always meant to be.

King David first constructed walls around his *content*—what he would look at or listen to. He wrote, *"I will refuse to look at anything vile and vulgar…I will reject perverse ideas and stay away from every evil"* (Psalm 101:3-4 NLT). He made the definitive decision to stop beholding idolatrous images or practices, immoral behavior or scenes, ungodly speech or actions, and corrupt or dishonorable influences. In our time, these are the things he'd have blocked out: explicit or inappropriate media (pornography, graphic violence, or anything designed to arouse sinful desires or desensitize to cruelty) and immoral entertainment (movies, shows, music, or social media content that promotes profanity, sexual immorality, greed, hatred, or rebellion against God's principles). He understood—as *we* should—that what we consume, we become. Our hearts are cups that are filled by whatever our eyes and ears take in. That's why the Word warns, *"Above all else, guard your heart, for everything you do flows from it"* (Proverbs 4:23 NIV). Jesus even exclaimed: *"The words you speak come from the heart—that's what defiles you. For from the heart come evil thoughts, murder, adultery, all sexual immorality, theft, lying, and slander"* (Matthew 15:18-20 NLT). If we desire purity to flow freely from our lives, we must invite the Holy Spirit to cleanse us of every impurity—but at the same time, we can't keep pouring in what tempts and taints our hearts.

It's impossible to have a pure heart *and* consume impure media. We cannot ask Jesus to clean up our speech but then continue to absorb foul words through our ears in movies and shows. We cannot ask Jesus to remove lust from our hearts but *keep* watching sensual scenes on screens. Our hearts can't throw out what our eyes and ears take in. Our choices in shows become slim, but we shouldn't watch anything we wouldn't watch with *Him*. This includes content parading and praising sin, the occult, demonic spirits, excessive profanity, gruesome violence, crude humor and vulgarity, drug use, revenge and hatred, exploitation or objectification of human beings, and so on—*or* that promotes and pushes to normalize any truth that contradicts the Word. What we allow into our eyes and minds eventually settles in our hearts. So, guarding what we watch isn't just wise; it's essential to staying rooted in *right*, Jesus-like thinking, feeling, and believing. Let's be sensitive to the Holy Spirit about what we're watching; if we sense His conviction—even *slightly*—let's turn our eyes away.

The same truth applies to *music*. Let's remember that Satan *was* Lucifer—who was intensely involved with worship in Heaven. He *knows* the potent power of music—how it can stir the heart and steer the mind to want and worship whatever it emphasizes. Let's know this: he has *never* stopped leading worship. Whereas godly music carries the anointing to usher us into God's presence, make us feel His power, and help the health of our hearts, worldly music carries the anointing of a different kingdom. Secular music often glorifies sin or self. Over time, it normalizes in our minds things that God calls destructive—like sexual immorality, greed, violence, or pride. It may not *sound* sinister, but it quietly reshapes the heart. Just as anointed worship draws us into the places of God, worldly music can drag us into confusion, heaviness, sensuality, or spiritual dullness. Ephesians 2:2 (KJV) calls Satan *"the prince of the power of the air"*—and music moves through the air. He knows its power to deceive and influence, and he certainly uses it for his pernicious purposes. Not *all* non-Christian music is explicitly evil, but any melodies that move our minds away from Jesus may muddle His voice *and* muddy our thinking. Music is never neutral; it either draws us toward God or drives us away from Him. Again, let's allow the Holy Spirit to guide what we allow into our ears. We must pay attention to His direction; this is for our heart's protection.

Let's envision all the entertainment the world offers to us extended across a buffet. On the left side sits the darkest, dirtiest shows, songs, and stories. No true Christian feeds from there. There's *nothing* of Jesus in that section. In the middle lies "gray" options—media that's mostly "okay." Jesus' presence can be fairly felt and His voice halfway heard by those who feed from here. *Many* Christians daily fill their plates with this content. This is the *most*-eaten-from section of the buffet. However, on the right side sits the tiniest section, but it boasts the brightest choices on which to consume. In this petite—but *powerful* and *pure*—part of the buffet, one will find the Word, uplifting books and stories, pure music, some wholesome shows, and *time*. The line at this end echoes the list of its choices: short. Very few eat from here, but those who do are the most spiritually well-fed, filled-up, fired-up people on earth. These people *hear* Him. These people *feel* Him. They walk in *real* victory, clarity, and liberty. Their "diet" may look boring, but they live brimming with beautiful intimacy with Jesus. *He* becomes their food—filling them more fully than any fascinating meal featured anywhere else on the buffet. They sit with His Word, soak in His presence, savor His voice, sing His songs, and sense Him *clearly*. They eat *only* of the Bread of Life (John 6:35) and what brings them closer to Him—and they are the most joy-filled and healed people on the planet. They discovered—as we will, too—that the more they *at-first* forced themselves to feed from there, it eventually altered their appetites. They grew to *happily* only hunger for Him—and we can, too.

Wrong Crowds

King David continued safe-guarding his life from temptation by also choosing correct *crowds*. He resolved to remove people from his life who would not promote godly character or choices. He'd no longer have anything to do with those who *"deal crookedly,"* who *"slander their neighbors,"* who are full of *"conceit and pride,"* or who are liars or deceivers (Psalm 101:3, 5, 7 NLT). Instead, he would *"search for faithful people to be [his] companions"* and work closely only with those who were *"above reproach"* (Psalm 101:6 NLT). Like King David, we must know that only when we walk with the wise will we become wise (Proverbs 13:20). We must know that *"bad company corrupts good character"* (I Corinthians 15:33 NIV). The friends we allow around us *regularly* and *closely* either build us up in Jesus or break us down to pieces.

We are like sponges—soaking in whatever surrounds us. When we are *frequently* around people who make sinful choices, their habits, values, and mindset will leak onto us—and we soak it up without effort or even realizing it. We get wrapped into whatever water whirls around them, and we're pulled by its current in the direction it's taking them. This invisible influence that pours out of ungodly people is *dangerous*. The enemy rides this wave and uses it to get us to blow off our convictions, which will blow up our commitment to Christ. As we allow the wrong company to wrap around us *closely*, we'll gradually accept their values and worldview and adopt their unholy habits, and, without realizing it, we'll become increasingly distant from Jesus. When we're wound tightly with *them*, we won't feel right with *Him*. This happens because contaminating company doesn't just influence us; it truly does *corrupt* us. That word is *"phtheirō,"* which means to spoil, ruin, or destroy. It refers to ruthless spiritual decay. Let's remember that the enemy's fiercest weapon isn't a direct attack; it's the silent sabotage of steering the wrong souls into our lives, diluting our connection with

Jesus until intimacy with Him is completely washed away.

If unholy company crushes character, imagine what *holy* companions can do. The *right* friends will cleanse, refine, and sharpen us spiritually. Instead of being like rust feeding on a blade, their influence accomplishes this: *"As iron sharpens iron, so one man sharpens [and influences] another [through discussion]"* (Proverbs 27:17 AMP). This verse points to the process of two pieces of iron being rubbed together to remove rust, burrs, or dullness, resulting in a sharper, stronger blade. Similarly, when faith-filled friends live life together—engaging in honest conversation, giving encouragement *and* correction, and facing challenges *together*—they sharpen and refine each other's character and faith. Plus, our friends' fire for Jesus will feed and fuel our own. When fires burn side by side, their flames reach higher and spread wider than any could alone. In the same way, when we find godly friends and live closely with them, our faith catches fire from theirs, growing stronger and brighter together than we ever could on our own. Because of their influence, our *own* relationship with Jesus becomes a blazing bonfire that burns boldly, baffling the enemy's best attempts to blow it out.

How do we find and forge these friendships? We *ask* Jesus for them. We also gain them in godly circles. This is where connecting with Christian community becomes crucial *again*. We won't find these life-giving, life-changing friendships in isolation. Let's circle back to King David's wise words; he said he would ***"search** for faithful people"* to be his companions (Psalm 101:6 NLT). He knew—like *all* of us—that he needed friends, and he would *find* faithful ones. If we lack godly friends in our lives, let's not lose heart. Let's ask Jesus for them and start *searching* for them. Jesus doesn't want us to journey alone. He also doesn't want us to feel like there are *no* potential friends like this around us—like Elijah did after his victory at Mount Carmel when he then fled in fear from Queen Jezebel and believed that he was the only faithful one left (I Kings 19:10-18). As he cried and complained about his lack of godly company, the Lord corrected him, confirming that He had *thousands* of followers nearby (1 Kings 19:18). He would say the same to us. There *are* people near us who love Jesus and who are longing for the same kind of friendship we are. Let's ask Jesus to lead us to them. He delights in connecting hearts and creating community. We are *not* alone. Let's not be afraid to step into new circles—church, small groups, or faith-based gatherings. Our "faithful companions" might be just a sincere prayer and a step of courage away.

When Attachments Run Deep

Sometimes, it can feel so difficult—almost *impossible*—to cut off what or who brings temptation. In these situations, Jesus calls us to become radical. Jesus dramatically declared, *"If your right eye makes you stumble and leads you to sin, tear it out and throw it away [that is, remove yourself from the source of temptation]; for it is better for you to lose one of the parts of your body, than for your whole body to be thrown into Hell"* (Matthew 5:29 AMP). He followed that with another equally drastic example: *"If your right hand makes you stumble and leads you to sin, cut it off and throw it away [that is, remove yourself from the source of temptation]; for it is better for you to lose one of the parts of your body than for your whole body to go into Hell"* (v. 30 AMP). Jesus doesn't mean for us to literally gouge out eyes and saw off body parts. He used this strong, graphic language to stress the seriousness of severing what causes us to sin—even if it feels essential or valuable. If we don't, we could completely lose our souls eternally.

Just as it sounds, this is *painful.* The thought of voluntarily getting rid of an "eye" or an "arm"—something so obviously needed and depended on—seems unrealistic, even impossible. When Jesus says, *"Tear out your eye,"* or, *"Cut off your arm,"* he's urging us to get rid of anything or anyone—no matter how much it's valued—that causes us to sin. Today, these "eyes" and "arms" may come in the form of shows we've watched or artists we've listened to for years that now flood our hearts with wrong desires or our mouths with foul language. We may have to delete apps we've been addicted to or unfollow social media influencers we've faithfully followed. It might mean completely deleting social media accounts that feed comparison, lust, or pride—or turning down invitations to parties and places with people who provide temptation. We may even have to leave a job or friend group that pressures us to compromise our faith. It also may require that we detach ourselves from one who's been a close, faithful friend or a romantic relationship that we can't keep and *not* sin. We must tear ourselves away from what is tearing up our relationship with Jesus. *Nothing*—and *no* one—can stay that gets in Jesus' way.

Jesus *implores* us not to play around with sin. We can't manage it. We have to *murder* it. If something causes us to stumble—no matter how important it is to us—we must cut it out before it cuts us off from Him. Anyone who's dared to tear these treasured ties—be it a relationship, account, or job—to go all in with Jesus will tell you this: life on the other side is freer, fuller, and *far* better. Life is richer, deeper, and more alive with more of Jesus—even if it means losing an "eye" or "arm" to get there. Anyone who's literally lost an eye or arm endures the ache and grief of losing something once inseparable from them—but over time, they learn to live, adapt, and even thrive in a new rhythm without it. There *is* life on the other side of the severe severance. There is *the* Life. There is *so* much *more* of Jesus. There is *more* of His presence, *more* of His freedom, and *more* of His voice. Let's see these valuable yet violating things we cling to as nothing more than towering traps—tall walls that block our way to the true treasure: more of Jesus and a greater life with Him. Then, in radical trust and hunger for Him, let's tear them down.

In fact, Jesus wants us to passionately press our hearts into the place where *all* parts of us are *His*. Once we take *one* sacrificial step of surrender like this—and we experience the fulfilling fruit it fosters—it stirs our hearts to crave giving Him *all* parts of ourselves. Let's not live like the "rich young ruler" who asked Jesus how to inherit eternal life but then hated His answer. Jesus told him to keep the commandments and then to sell all his possessions and follow Him. The man walked away weighed down by wealth, his heart too tangled in treasure to trust the call to surrender (Matthew 19:16-22). Too many people do the same: they draw near to Jesus, hearts longing for Him—but then their grip slips because of other things they want more than they want Him. Too many live in a place of half-surrender—believing in Him but not giving *all* to Him—and they exist weighed down by restless misery. Let's remember these words from Jesus: *"Whoever wants to save their life will lose it, but whoever loses their life for me will find it"* (Matthew 16:25 NIV). Jesus taught that clinging tightly to our own desires, comfort, or control—essentially "saving" our lives for ourselves—ultimately leads to true loss. However, when we surrender *everything*—willing to "lose" our lives by following His purposes in every piece and part—we gain a deeper, richer life that *truly* fulfills—both now *and* in eternity. Let's understand that we won't have *His* all until we give Him *our* all.

Jesus longs to lead us from the chaos of self-choice into the peace of surrendering every part of our lives to Him. Perfectly good and endlessly kind, He alone sees the *best* choice for us in even the smallest details of our individual lives. He longs to track down and tear out even the tiniest traces of sin because He knows the broader, uglier effects of it even in microscopic amounts. Let's ask the Holy Spirit to move our hearts *here:* to a place where we are constantly sensitive to and running from the slightest wrong—always asking Jesus what pleases *Him.* If we aren't persistently pursuing what pleases *Him,* we are constantly choosing what *we* want—and this is what happens: we hear our own voice in our hearts most predominantly, not *His.* The danger in this is that we humans are experts at dressing up sin in fancy clothes, making it look harmless—even *sensible*—and blinding ourselves to the true transgression it is. We are talented at covering up what we want hidden or repainting reality into a better light than it really is. We must keep careful watch over our hearts—our minds, imaginations, appetites, and habits—because it's dangerously easy to belong to Jesus yet become so dulled to sin that we stop discerning the damage it's truly doing within.

This happens as a *slow* drift, not a sudden collapse. We can be the fabled frog put in room-temperature water in a pot—comfortable at first—until, degree by degree, the increasing heat boils it alive. It would have hopped out had boiling, bubbling water hit its skin immediately, so its killer started the slaughter subtly and stealthily. In the same way, our enemy does this to *us,* too. Because of that, a pivotal part of our spiritual life is to *daily* keep watch on ourselves—all of our thinking, wanting, and doing—and to keep open, honest conversation going with Jesus all day long. Then, if we detect a "slow-boil trap" in some part of our lives—an area where we've been discreetly drifting, dulling, and dying—we talk truthfully to Jesus and turn it over to Him *fully.* This vigilance is not merely defensive; it's deeply rewarding. There's so much more to feel, hear, and experience with Him every single day, and we have no idea how much our sensing Him and hearing Him gets dulled by defiled areas of our lives. This is the truth: the more our lives are cleared of sin, the more our ears can hear *Him.*

If we feel stuck or distant from Jesus, we've likely stalled—standing at the edge of a surrender we're struggling to make, staring down a sacrificial step we've not wanted to take. Quietly and personally, the Holy Spirit will whisper the step to us over and over, and the Word will spell it out, too. If we don't listen in private, He may even use people to speak it out in public—and if we don't obey what we hear, we stand *still.* We stand stopped by our lack of submission. To any person who ever says, "I haven't heard Jesus speak in a long time or haven't felt His presence in a while," we can ask, "What is the last thing He led you to do?" Usually, that's where the momentum halted: He was heard but not obeyed. We must lean in with reverent attentiveness, ready to catch even His quietest whisper—and respond with wholehearted obedience. Jesus' voice is not a person's voice—one we can choose to listen to or not. His directions are not suggestions. They are commands. They are from *God,* and they are for our *good.* In order to walk with Him, we must wait on and watch for even His quietest whisper and *willingly* obey anything He wants.

Even when what He wants hurts, let's not look at it as a loss. There will always be gain from this kind of pain. He promises: *"Everyone who has given up house or wife or brothers or parents or children, for the sake of the Kingdom of God, will be repaid many times over in this life, and will have eternal life in the world to come"* (Luke 18:29-30 NLT). He promises that *any* sacrifice we make to remove barriers or sin from our lives in order to follow Him fully will be repaid in full—not just in Heaven but *here,* too. Whatever "eye" or "arm" we must prune or purge will in no way parallel what He provides in its place. Let's listen to our Jesus and shut up the luring lies of our deceiver who aims to convince us—just as he did Eve—that there's anything better than *full* obedience to Jesus. Obedience brings blessing, not brokenness. It makes life better and won't leave us bitter. Obedience offers us *so* much more of Jesus— especially when it *hurts.*

Failure

What happens when a hurdle hurls us to the ground? What occurs when we try to clear it but it clips us—or even worse—when we *gladly* let it take us down? What do we do when we've completely faltered in our faith and fallen to the ground? We must know that right there in the dirt—right there in the pain, humiliation, and regret—*Jesus* can be found. The deceiver dashes there to be heard first though. He will exclaim and erupt in our ears that we're "done"—that "it's *over*," that we "*can't* go back," and it's time to "turn away and *hide*." He'll shame us and rush us to the bushes as he did Adam and Eve. However, let's remember that when they fell down, the Father came down— *still*. He personally pursued them *still*. When we've failed, His love for us does *not* fail. In fact, in our failures, He'll make Himself even more **known** and **near**. He can use our failures to forge—even *more* deeply—the relationship with Him we were born to have.

When we fail, we actually fall face-first at the feet of our Father—where we're met with *mercy*. The movement of His heart when we fail is to come *close*, not recoil and retreat. Take in Psalm 34:18 (AMP): *"The Lord is near to the heartbroken, and He saves those who are crushed in spirit (contrite in heart, truly sorry for their sin)."* Then, listen to His heart here: *"I dwell in high and holy places, but also with the bruised and lowly in spirit— those who are humble and quick to repent. I dwell with them to revive the spirit of the humble, to revive the heart of those who are broken over their sin"* (Isaiah 57:15 TPT). Our Father—who is exalted, holy, and far above all—*chooses* to come close to those who are crushed, humbled, and heartbroken over their sin. He doesn't just observe from afar, peering to see how *we* pick ourselves up. He literally draws even nearer to us. He "dwells" with us, pouring His presence into our pain—and He "revives" us, bringing life back to what got broken.

It's as if Eden echoes when we flat-out fail. As with Adam and Eve, the Father pursues *us* when we've fallen, too. Unlike many earthly fathers, He doesn't scold or shame or see us as "lame." Instead, as in Eden, He lovingly calls out our name without speaking blame. He will draw us up from the dirt again—like when he first made Adam—and lovingly remake us into something new. The first Fall wasn't final, and ours isn't either—*none* of them. The sacrifice for *each* sin has already been made. All debt is already paid. When we fail and then repent, we get to experience a re-creating, resurrecting transformation *every* time. Jesus' Blood bought this kind of mercy and miracle for us—one we *get* to experience every time we falter. Our falls become moments of being called and created *again*, resurrected into someone made new. His Blood has turned our every mistake into a *miracle* we get to experience even when we've messed up.

Here's His invitation to the fallen: *"Return to the Lord your God, for He is gracious and compassionate, slow to anger and abounding in love"* (Joel 2:13 NIV). Many in the Word experienced this kind of failure-to-closer-with-Jesus miracle—including Peter. Passionate Peter once proclaimed he'd *never* fall away from Jesus, but the Lord prophesied that before the rooster crowed that evening, Peter would deny knowing Him (Matthew 26:33-35). Not long after this, Jesus was arrested and taken to the high priest's courtyard, where Peter followed—but at a *distance*. Eventually, the heat of the hostile crowd, fear for his own safety, and the severe stress of the moment mauled Peter's broadcasted boldness. Despite his earlier faith, his fear forced him to deny knowing Jesus three times before the rooster's cry resounded. When the crow of the rooster rang in his ears, he immediately remembered Jesus' prediction of his contradiction. Filled with deep remorse and sorrow, Peter ran outside and cried bitterly (Matthew 26:75). He had disowned his greatest Love—and it devastated him for days to come. Yet, here's the most moving moment of this story: the Resurrected Jesus passionately pursued His forlorn, fallen friend. Before returning to the Father, Jesus sought out Peter *personally*. Through an unexpectedly loving conversation, Jesus restored Peter to Himself—*and* reaffirmed Peter's calling to shepherd His followers (John 21:15-19). Even when we fail and fall, Jesus neither forsakes nor forgets us. He *always* restores the repentant.

Amazingly, He even *rewards* the repentant. The Bible includes the beloved story of a brazen boy—one of two sons belonging to a benevolent father. The younger son demanded his inheritance early and left his father's home to live on his own terms, indicating no intention of returning. The father relinquished what the son requested, and the boy ran far from home with pockets full of inheritance and a heart full of pride, only to find himself starving in a pigpen of regret. When the son returned repentant—expecting only to be received now as a servant—the father ran to him, embraced him, clothed him with the *best* robe, put a ring on his finger and sandals on his feet, and threw a feast in his honor (Luke 15:11-32). The lavish love and gigantic grace of this father reflect *our* Father. No one is as *kind* as He is, and no one longs for us with the kind of love *He* does. He's not one who tolerates the repentant; He celebrates them. He rushes to the repentant with restoration *and* reward. He pulls them in closer, letting them feel His love like never before—and then He just keeps pouring out more and more. What makes Him respond to the repentant like this? It's His immeasurable mercy, His immutable love, and—once more—His irrevocable desire for *relationship*.

What makes Jesus' heart hurt when we've fallen is the fracture in our friendship with Him. What restores it is *repentance*—a move He hopes we make quickly. Like the father in Luke 15, our Father waits and watches for our return. He's always ready to restore—always *"good and ready to forgive"* (Psalm 86:5 AMP)—but we must *truly* repent. Repentance—according to the Bible—is a deeply chosen change of mind and direction, a full turning *away* from sin and *toward* Him. We first acknowledge our sin and feel sincere sorrow—a *"godly sorrow"* that *"brings repentance that leads to salvation and leaves no regret"* (2 Corinthians 7:10 NIV). We want to pursue this and not just *"worldly sorrow, which lacks repentance"* and *"results in spiritual death"* (2 Corinthians 7:10 NLT). When we mess up, we are even offered two "sorrows" to choose from—one from the Holy Spirit and the other from our eager enemy. We can surrender to Satan's sadness that smothers us in shame and makes us feel stuck—*or* we can seek the Spirit's sorrow that both shows us our sin clearly *and* summons us to our sympathetic Savior quickly. This kind of sorrow doesn't wear a frown and beat us down; it greets us with truth *and* grace and helps us get up, go back, and *grow*. It makes us eager to return to and to restore our *relationship* with Jesus.

Repentance doesn't stop at remorse. When it's *real*, it motivates us to *act*. Acts 3:19 (AMP) articulates this: *"Repent [change your inner self—your old way of thinking, regret past sins] and return [to God—seek His purpose for your life], so that your sins may be wiped away [blotted out, completely erased], so that times of refreshing may come from the presence of the Lord [restoring you like a cool wind on a hot day]."* True repentance involves turning. It includes removing wrong thinking and doing. It's returning to Jesus and *His* ways. *He* then brings refreshing. The wonderful wind of the Holy Spirit blows our sin away and breathes new life into broken places. He teaches us how to stand where we fell. He literally uses the fall to heal the way feel, which produces bold changes in our behavior that are real.

Yes, full repentance results in *fruit*. Matthew 3:8 (AMP) says that we should *"produce fruit that is consistent with repentance [demonstrating new behavior that proves a change of heart and a conscious decision to turn away from sin]."* We move from our failure to this fruit by first confessing our sin to Jesus (I John 1:9). We name our sin to Him. Then, we receive His forgiveness—right then and there. It's important to take time to truly take in His grace and His love—the healing hug He gives *right* when we're at our worst. When we confess our sin, it's *right* then that He *most* wants to be **known** and **near.** It's in *that* moment especially that He wants His unconditional love to become *so* real and deeply felt. In His *"kindness, He takes us firmly by the hand and leads us into a radical life change"* (Romans 2:4 MSG). It's important to Him that we lean into His love when we confess sin. *That* is what leads us into full repentance. Then, we daily submit the newly surrendered area to Him. We ask the Holy Spirit to continually guide, strengthen, and convict us (Galatians 5:22-23). Producing fruit in the area we've failed is often a process that involves ongoing dependence on the Holy Spirit—and let's remember that participating in this process is the Holy Spirit's *joy* (2 Corinthians 3:18, Galatians 5:22-23, Philippians 1:6).

However, if our private returning and repenting keeps *repeating* in the same area, it's time to pursue public accountability. This requires great honesty and humility, but it *will* result in liberty. Scripture teaches that when we are stuck in a cycle of sin—genuinely repenting but not walking in lasting change—one powerful, biblical step toward full freedom is to humbly confess our sin to a trusted believer. Through confession and prayer with this person, we will experience *healing* (James 5:16). When spinning in circles in private, that's our signal to seek support in public. Let's not let the enemy shame us into silence. He hates for us to get *real* and reach out to a praying person because he knows that *"tremendous power is released through the passionate, heartfelt prayer of a godly believer"* (James 5:16 TPT). So, he tells us not to trust, not to talk. He makes us fear judgement and rejection. He says keeping it secret is our protection—but it's actually our destruction. One of the most precious parts of a godly community is being able to be frankly, freely honest with a Christian brother or sister. One with the heart of our Father will respond as He does: smile, pull us close, affirm who we are, and—in the form of on-the-spot prayer and on-going friendship— break off the sin and walk us to our win.

What if we're *not* at the place of repentance? What if we know Jesus but we want our sin more? Let's be warned of this: when a Christian knowingly chooses sin over Jesus and refuses to repent, the relationship with Him becomes distanced, strained, and spiritually hindered—not because Jesus withdraws His love, but because unrepentant sin blocks intimacy and fellowship. Closeness with Jesus will crack and crumble. A grieved Holy Spirit—who *loves* us—will war for us, wielding clear conviction (Ephesians 4:30). If we cold-shoulder Him and continue, our consciences can be seared (I Timothy 4:2). Our joy will dim, our vision will blur, and our hunger for Jesus will die. Our devoted Father will deal out discipline, not to destroy but to draw us back (Hebrews 12:6). Our ongoing refusal to repent will race us to a dangerous place (1 John 3:6-8, Hebrews 10:26-27). If someone continually rejects repentance and clings to sin, it reveals a hardened heart and could even call into question the reality of his or her saving faith in the first place.

However, to the one who wants the sin but doesn't *want* to want it, at least begin praying this: *"Holy Spirit,* help me hate this and love you more!" Whisper these words—over and over—and *He* will begin His work. When our hearts have hardened, we cry out like David: *"Create in me a clean heart, O God. Renew a loyal spirit within me,"* and, *"Make me willing to obey you"* (Psalm 51:10, 12 NLT). David didn't pray this from a place of piety and purity; he sobbed these sentences on his face—after committing adultery, setting up a murder, and then being confronted by a prophet (2 Samuel 11-12). Even the *"man after God's own heart"* happened to sin and hardened his heart (I Samuel 13:14, Acts 13:22). We would think this descriptive phrase encased only David's dedication to the Lord—but it encompasses his *whole* life—his devotion *and* his repentance. A person "after God's own heart" is one who is faithful but also willing to *repent* when he or she falls.

Let's know this: no matter how much we love Jesus, we *will* fail Jesus. We *will* weaken and make mistakes in many moments. Yet, we must *keep* getting back up. Here's a verse to visualize when we veer off: *"A righteous man falls seven times and rises again"* (Proverbs 24:16 AMP). Righteousness isn't proven by never falling; it's shown in the getting back up. The righteous—those in right standing with Jesus— may stumble, but they keep rising. In Scripture, seven often symbolizes completion, which suggests that in the area we keep losing our footing but we continue to lift ourselves back up, we'll eventually lose our limp for good. One day, we'll step into strength where we wobbled in weakness. Where we once frequently failed, we'll become fully *free*.

So, let's see His hand extended to us even as we fall face-first in the dirt. *Still* smiling, our Father reaches for us. His love hasn't lessened. Our position with Him hasn't pivoted. Our calling hasn't crumbled. Let's just turn to Him, take His hand, say our sin, and stand again. Remember that in our *every* rising, resurrection power rushes through us, breaking chains and breathing life. When we stumble and then stand again, we're taught and transformed by Jesus—*each* time, a little more. We become more like Him than we were before. Our relationship with Him deepens and sweetens. He becomes even more **known** and **near** than He's ever been—all because we *failed*.

Condemnation

Another hurdle meant to hinder us is described in Romans 8:1 (MSG) as a *"continuous, low-lying black cloud."* This heavy, hanging haze is oppressive and ongoing—raining down reminders of our wrongs, making us feel wrong from the inside out. This cruel cumulous is called *condemnation,* and it blows in straight from Hell. It is our angry enemy who sends this sinister storm. These same churlish clouds cover his head, and he delights in dragging *us* into the same shame, misery, and distance from God that he lives in. So, the one condemned eternally condemns *us* perpetually.

Scripture labels Satan *"the accuser of our brothers and sisters, who accuses them before our God day and night"* (Revelation 12:10 NIV). Our enemy actively, endlessly accuses us. Inside our minds and hearts—*all* day and night—he persistently points out faults and failures and spotlights our sins and shortcomings. Even when we're living *right*, he aims to make us feel *wrong*. Without warning, he'll drag our past into our present, playing our lapses and losses on loop. He savors stirring up fresh shame for old mistakes—over and over again. He'll even just reach into one of yesterday's casual conversations, choose something simple we said or did, and shame us over *nothing*. All day long—in moments of rush *or* rest—he'll subtly send sentences like these across our minds: "You're *still* the same." "You didn't pray *enough*." "Your house is a *mess*." "Your kids *aren't* going to turn out right." "You're *so* awkward." "You're not even walking with Jesus *right*." "You *should* be in a different place spiritually." "You *should* be doing more." "You think you're doing okay, but you're *not*." "Jesus isn't going to do *that* for you." These bullying thoughts bombard us on and on all day long—and through the night, too. As we lay our heads down, we'll think: we got *this* wrong today, and we'll get *that* wrong tomorrow. One of these sinister thoughts might even seize us in sleep—our eyes flying open as our mind cries, "You *failed!*" The tormentor *never* tires of this tirade. He'll even talk and tuck this condemnation into us so deeply that it tightens our gut. Even when we're not hearing it, we're *feeling* it: a tightness in our shoulders and stomachs. This enemy-sent condemnation chokes out all peace—which is exactly his plan. This condemnation creates a barrier between Jesus and us—making Him feel distant and disappointed—which is precisely our deceiver's delight.

Satan especially sends this against those *succeeding* spiritually. He targets those walking more intimately with Jesus *more* intensely, not less. He fights to make those doing the most right feel the most wrong. His angriest accusations are aimed at those advancing in faith, living in obedience, bearing fruit, and threatening his kingdom. He unleashed this on Jesus on the earth, too. Jesus' much-talked-about temptation in the wilderness trailed His public baptism when the Father declared, *"This is My dearly loved Son!"* (Matthew 3:17 NLT). Then, in the wilderness, Satan's first words were, *"If* you are *really* the Son of God…" (Matthew 4:3). He attacked Jesus' identity and authority right after affirmation and victory—*just* as he does to us. Let's know that the closer we walk with Jesus, the *more* the enemy endeavors to undermine our intimacy, distort our identity, and smother us in condemnation. When this increases in our lives, it means *we're* advancing, and the enemy frantically fights to foil it.

Yet, Scripture hushes him with a higher truth: *"There is now **no condemnation** for those who are in Christ Jesus"* (Romans 8:1 NLT). The *absence* of condemnation should be our reality. In place of the false weight on our chests and the dark clouds in our skies, *this* should describe our daily existence: we open our eyes every morning to *Jesus.* We rise with lightness and brightness, and there is no dread as we get out of bed. As we take our first steps each day, we are greeted by Love, and His delight in us personally pours over us like power and peace. Inside, we are at rest. We deeply know that we are forgiven. Past mistakes don't move us, and the present morning manifests new mercy (Lamentations 3:22-23). *Nothing* stands between Jesus and us. In fact, His Spirit fully fills us, and we freely *feel* Him. There's no pressure to perform or be perfect—not even in our praying. We can just sit and sip our coffee with Him, speaking securely to Him. We can just *be*. We feel *free*. There's no panic or dread about the day ahead. Whatever the day holds, we know that *He* holds the *day*. He'll hear us and move in miracles—and He'll help us through every moment, every matter, and every mood. We'll have conversations without later replaying them. We'll pass people without fearing their judgement. We'll see our imperfections without spiraling. We'll make mistakes and simply make them right—without guilt, without falling apart. All day long, at every turn, we'll sense Him and His everlasting, empowering *love*. We'll hear Him and experience His *delight*—all the way from morning through the night. The *Son* shines in our skies, raining down *joy* even as we end the day and close our eyes.

This kind of peace *is* possible. Let's refuse to live under darkness when we can abide under light. Read the rest of Romans 8:1 (MSG): *"With the arrival of Jesus…that fateful dilemma is resolved. Those who enter into Christ's being-there-for-us no longer have to live under a continuous, low-lying black cloud. A new power is in operation. The Spirit…like a strong wind, magnificently cleared the air, freeing you from a fated lifetime of brutal tyranny at the hands of sin and death."* Jesus has *cleared* our skies of heaviness, dread, fear, and guilt. *No* condemnation comes from Him. So, what do we do when the skies shift above us and shame starts sprinkling down? We assert our *authority* over our accuser. As soon as Satan sends a thought that resurrects a failure, raises anxiety, rattles our confidence, or ruins our mood, we must open our mouths and shut him up. The thought can cross our mind, but it doesn't have to sink in and sink *us*. We have to catch it, take it captive, and cast it out (2 Corinthians 10:5). Full peace doesn't come without a fight. We must seize Satan's deceitful darts, send them back where they came from, and watch him retreat (Ephesians 6:16). We simply grab it, cast it, and *win* it.

We must live aware of this, too: as the Holy Spirit constantly helps and consistently loves, He also *corrects*. However, His correction comes as clear *conviction*—not as cruel condemnation. John 16:8 says this about the Holy Spirit: *"And He, when He comes, will convict the world about [the guilt of] sin [and the need for a Savior], and about righteousness, and about judgment"* (John 16:8 AMP). This conviction from the Holy Spirit comes in His gentle whisper and shines light on our sin—guiding us not into shame but back to our Savior. It's *clear;* there's no confusion. It's honest—but also *hopeful.* It affirms and declares, "This isn't *who you are*! You're a child of God, and righteousness is *yours*. You're *already* forgiven—and still wanted and loved. Let's make this *right.*" Conviction lovingly leads us straight to Jesus—to *more* of Him. Condemnation, however, shoves us *away* from Jesus. It's the harsh voice of the enemy—a cruel, vague accusation that drips with shame and hopelessness. It calls us a failure and claims that our Father is furious. It doesn't even make our "sin" clear; it just comes to smear. While conviction is straightforward and reminds of identity, invites repentance, and restores intimacy with Jesus, condemnation is confusing and uses guilt to gut us and get us to hide. One corrects in love; the other crushes with lies.

Let's discontinue this daily battle with the crushing weight of condemnation. That voice is not our Father's. It's our accuser's—our *enemy's.* He hates the freedom, the peace, the love, the deep delight we *get* to experience with Jesus. So, he fights to take away our light. However, living without condemnation is our spiritual right. Romans 8:1 isn't just a verse; it's our spiritual reality: *"no* condemnation." We are *not* on trial. We have been decidedly declared "not guilty." We are forgiven, redeemed, and loved—and we are forever surrounded and saturated by the very presence and Spirit of God. So, when condemning lies come, we trump them with *this* truth. The Cross has shut the mouth of the accuser and canceled every charge. So, let's lift our heads, shake off *all* dread, and walk in our Blood-bought freedom instead.

Adversity & Suffering

No matter how wholly we love Jesus, we will all have to handle hardship. We will all endure *adversity* and *suffering.* We are people with free will who live in a fallen world where people get sick, tires get flattened, death and disappointments happen, dreams die—*so* many things that make us cry. Our enemy also watches and waits for life to hurt us so that he can subvert our faith. In the depths of our suffering, the enemy spins his bleakest lies—but it's *there* that our faithful Father pours out His brightest grace. Right in the enemy's face, Jesus will arrive, avenge, and advance us in our darkest place.

A relationship with Jesus does not delete difficulty from our lives. In fact, Jesus said suffering *would* surface. In John 16:33 (AMP), Jesus foretold that we would face *"tribulation and distress and suffering,"* but He followed with this: *"'but be courageous [be confident, be undaunted, be filled with joy]; I have overcome the world.' [My conquest is accomplished, My victory abiding.]"* Scripture shows we'll tackle trials and tests, plow through persecution, pain, and pressure—but it always encases these warning words with encouragement. It declares that difficulty *will* dawn, but we will endure it without defeat. We will experience *His* victory—over and over. Hardship may hit, but *He* won't let it hollow us out. Peer at this promise: *"Even when bad things happen to the good and godly ones, the Lord will save them and not let them be defeated by what they face"* (Psalm 34:19 TPT). Our sympathetic, strong Shepherd especially surrounds His sheep in a storm. Jesus will *"gather the lambs in His arms"* and *"carry them in His bosom"* (Isaiah 40:11 AMP). He lifts us gently from the dangers descending upon us, and in His affectionate arms, we are carried calmly and completely through every threat, every storm—*every* time. Then, when the rain stops and the skies clear, the Shepherd is even more **known** and **near** to the held-tight sheep—their relationship deeper than it's ever been before.

We must know that *any* hard place we face was foreseen by our Father. Every day, He surreptitiously shields us from Satanic strikes meant to steal, kill, and destroy that we don't even know about (John 10:10). Daily, He protects us from mountains of misery that we never see (Psalm 91:3-4, Isaiah 52:12). Any adversity that *does* arrive in our lives has been wrapped in the warmth and wisdom of our Father. He doesn't bring the pain, but He fills it full of *purpose*. Anything horrible that happens to us—He intends to use it for *good* (Romans 8:28). In fact, if we could envision our entire lives like a street stretched before us, we'd witness changing weather along the way. We'd measure miles of road without rain—where the sun smiles through clear clouds and beautiful blue skies. However, we'd also spy sporadic spots of wild weather—places where rain and *pain* pour. Our Father foresaw these storms—and He's already foreordained them to pour *purpose,* too.

If we could zoom in and see into these storms, we'd witness Jesus wearing and wielding them. He doesn't cause heartbreak, but when it comes, He rushes into the storm, wraps Himself in its wildness, and wields the winds like a sword. In Psalm 18, a deeply distressed David calls upon the Lord, who then comes like a cyclone: *"He opened the heavens and came down; dark storm clouds were beneath his feet. Mounted on a mighty angelic being, he flew, soaring on the wings of the wind. He shrouded himself in darkness, veiling his approach with dark rain clouds. Thick clouds shielded the brightness around him and rained down hail and burning coals"* (Psalm 18:9-12 NLT). Thunder booms, lightning flashes, hail falls, and arrows assail his enemies, scattering and confusing them (v. 13-14). Then, David testified, *"He reached down from Heaven and rescued me; he drew me out of deep waters. He rescued me from my powerful enemies…He led me to a place of safety; he rescued me because he delights in me"* (v. 16-19 NLT). Our Savior rushes into our storms and *redeems* them—and He *rescues* us.

So, when adversity arrives, *He* does, too. He doesn't just watch us go through it; He'll walk, wade, and even *wash* us through it. Here's His promise: *"When you go through deep waters, I will be with you. When you go through rivers of difficulty, you will not drown. When you walk through the fire of oppression, you will not be burned up; the flames will not consume you…You are precious to me. You are honored, and I love you. Do not be afraid, for I am with you"* (Isaiah 43:2,4-5 NLT). Let's process how personal He promises to become in our pain. He truly presses into the brokenhearted, and the most powerful, precious moments we'll have with Him will happen in the rain, not the sunshine (Psalm 34:18, Isaiah 63:9). When our hurting hearts hear Him whisper, "You're Mine…," and we feel His nearly tangible touch and breath—this intense *intimacy* becomes the greatest gift in each gloomy gale. Our suffering shapes such a sacred closeness with Jesus. It's in our darkness that our devotion deepens. As we seek Him and sit with Him in our sorrow, we'll sense and see Him like never before.

We don't have to show up *strong* when we sit with Him in our suffering either. He mourns when we mourn (John 11:35). When we hurt, He'll hold us. When we cry, He won't scold us. He invites us to bring our fears and to cry our tears right there with Him. Psalm 56:8 (NLT) makes it clear that He cares about our tears: *"You keep track of all my sorrows. You have collected all my tears in your bottle. You have recorded each one in your book."* He comes so close and cares so much that our tears fall into His hands, and He *keeps* them. We are precious to Him, and our pain is personal to Him. We deeply matter, so He catches every tear before it can splatter. He does this so that there is *no* waste. Perhaps the bottles of our tears are poured back over us in future years—in the form of *anointing.* What once fell in sorrow will fall over us again in power. What once broke us may become the very thing that builds *others* around us (2 Corinthians 1:3-4). He stores our tears not just to preserve and ponder our pain—but to powerfully redeem and radically *use* it. In His hands, even grief becomes sacred gain. Even our weeping just waters something wonderful and new.

Our pain also makes *us* new. He never wastes a single storm; He'll use *each* trial to teach and transform (James 1:2-4). The same winds that shake us are the very winds He'll use to sift, shift, and shape us. As disappointment downpours, He washes away our pride. As heartbreak thunders, He heaves open hard places in our hearts and plants heaven-deep compassion. When loss lightnings, we're forced to cling to and hold Jesus in place of what—or *whom*—we've lost. Through our trials, He removes the rust of resentment, turns old fears into fresh faith, and supplants our self-reliance with surrender. The storm may boom and blow a while before it passes, but it always passes through His hands—and when it's over, we're *refined.* We walk, talk, think, live, and *love* so differently. We're steadier and softer—more surrendered and more shaped into *His* likeness. We've just been reshaped and readied to receive the blessing that comes *next.* In that picture of the personal path before us, after each storm comes promotion—a new place *spiritually.* Our paths elevate a level—right in the face of the devil. With Jesus, each storm just becomes a ship that drops us off on the shore of *more.*

This is why the Bible tells us to rejoice even in suffering (I Peter 4:13, Romans 3:3-5, Matthew 5:11-12, 2 Corinthians 12:9-10). With Jesus, our present plights are not wasted here *or* in Heaven. They are the ground where we grow *now*—but also where our eternal glory takes root. Every tear and trial we faithfully endure—they go as seeds into the ground of eternal soil, growing a heavenly harvest. Our Father will *greatly* reward us for remaining faithful. The pain we press through now is creating and shaping the *"crown of life"* He'll place on our heads in Heaven (James 1:12, Revelation 2:10, 2 Timothy 4:7-8, Hebrews 10:35-36). Our losses are glorious gains in disguise; our earthly affliction will one day turn into heavenly glory. In the hands of our Redeemer, none of our pain is ever pointless. He's weaving it all into a future where our sorrows fade like shadows—a future that will leave us breathless with absolute awe.

This is the kind of glory Jesus wants us to experience in pain. However, the enemy works to destroy this story. When life deeply wounds us, the enemy doesn't stay silent. He slithers into our sorrow and drops deception designed to devastate our faith. When picked on and persecuted for our faith, he hisses, "You're *foolish* for loving Jesus! Look what it brought you!" In moments of loss, he straight-up lies, "Jesus doesn't *really* love you. If He did, He'd have stopped this." When facing lack, he leaks more lies: "*You* don't matter that much to Him. He's not even providing for you." If a prayer seems to go unanswered, he twists it into, "He doesn't listen to *you*! Your voice doesn't reach Him!" When someone betrays us, Satan slyly says: "See! You can't trust people! Jesus will leave *you* next." Then, in moments when we can't perceive His presence, He'll convey the cruelest lie of all: "He's not here. He's left you all *alone.*" Every untruth is meant to undo our trust in Jesus. If listened to, His deception will drive us to doubt God's character and distance ourselves from our only Deliverer. This is why we must hold truth tightly when the storm howls heavily. Our Jesus is *always* near. He is *always* faithful—even when our toughest trials appear.

When hardship hits, let's aggressively shove Satan aside and rush to Jesus' side. He didn't take the person. He didn't cause the lack. He didn't send the sickness or the storm. Where is Jesus when the worst happens? He's right *there*. What is He going to do? He'll use it for *good*—so much more than we can imagine. He is the God who will take what people or the devil meant for evil and use it not only for *our* good—but for the benefit of *others*, too—and not just for a little while but for the rest of our lives (Genesis 50:20). He alone is our

Comforter in the most crushing circumstances—calming us and cheering us with hope-filled words as we lie crying pools of tears into our pillows. He alone is the Healer who can pick us up and put us back together when we're like crystal vases that crashed onto concrete. When we feel like we'll "never be the same," we're *right*. He'll restore us—more whole than we've ever been. He will renew our lives, richer and fuller than we ever dreamed. With Jesus, in loss, there is always lavish *gain*. There may be pain—and we may complain—but as His goodness emerges from what was meant for harm, we'll experience a gladness we can't contain—*even* in the rain.

Forgiveness

A final hurdle goes by the name of *forgiveness*. Forgiveness is not optional; it is an order from Jesus Himself. He boldly commanded, *"When you are praying, first forgive anyone you are holding a grudge against, so that your Father in Heaven will forgive your sins, too"* (Mark 11:25 NLT). He doesn't demand it because the wounds we've suffered were minor or meaningless. Some scars come from betrayal that broke trust, words that cut like a blade, abuse that shattered innocence, or abandonment that left us aching and alone. These things feel unforgivable—*impossible* to release. Yet, when we clutch our grudges, we chain our *own* souls. Unforgiveness festers like poison in the heart; it clouds our vision, chokes our prayers, and blocks the blessing of God's presence. That's why Jesus *mercifully* makes us let it go—so that we can move forward. He *lovingly* warned us, *"If you refuse to forgive others, your Father will not forgive your sins"* (Matthew 6:15 NLT). To withhold forgiveness is to wander in the wilderness of bitterness—while to extend it is to step into freedom. Forgiveness doesn't excuse evil; it expels its grip. It is the holy hinge on which healing swings, the gateway where grace rushes in, and the only path that keeps our hearts open to the One who has forgiven us most.

So, *how* do we forgive when the pain feels too deep, when the wound still bleeds, and when letting go seems impossible? We look to *Jesus*. When we remember the depths of what He has forgiven *us*—the shame He has erased, the sins He has carried, the debt He has canceled—we find strength to give that same gift to others. When hurt is heavy and hard to give up, we *lift* it up—along with our hearts—to the God who empowers us to do the impossible. The weight of unforgiveness is crushing, and the havoc of bitterness is cruel, so we cry out for *His* help. Practically, we begin by saying it to Him: "Lord, I want to forgive." Then, we ask Him to empower our hearts to *fully* let it go. We ask Him to strip away the anger, soothe the hurt, and soften what has been hardened. We verbally unload every thought, every loss, every broken thing into the Father's hands. Next, as we dare to then *pray* for the one who wronged us, a supernatural shift happens: His Spirit begins to *heal* our hearts (Matthew 5:44). He unwinds us from the wound and uses our mouths to intercede for our persecutors, and His power explodes like holy dynamite—destroying the grip on us, the grief in us, and even the ground where the enemy thought he *had* us.

Full forgiveness, though, does not always mean full reconciliation. Some relationships remain unsafe, unhealthy, or unwise to reenter—but we can still forgive completely from a distance, setting our hearts free even if the other person never apologizes or amends him or herself. Let's remember that when we cannot let go, *He* can—and whether reconciliation is possible or not, forgiveness is a hurdle we *must* clear. We cannot walk forward with Jesus while holding a heart full of hated hostages. One of the greatest miracles we will ever experience is Jesus releasing us from our hate and our hurt—yes, even the deepest, darkest kind. There is not a single thing He cannot help us forgive. Then, on the other side of that surrender stands *full* freedom. To withhold forgiveness—even from the *worst* offender—is to fall for one of the enemy's most subtle schemes: to keep us shackled in bitterness, stuck in the past, and starved of the abundant life Jesus died to give us. Forgiveness is not the enemy's idea; it is the *Father's*. When we refuse it, we forfeit *freedom*. However, when we release it, we ruin the devil's plan, we reclaim our peace, and we rise over this hurdle—*and* our hurt—into the wide-open life Jesus wonderfully won for us. We can continue walking with Jesus as **known and near**, enjoying the relationship with Him we were born to hold dear.

CHAPTER NINE

Our Hunger

"I thirst with deepest longings to love You more, with cravings in my heart that can't be described…I overflow with praise when I come before You, for the anointing of Your presence satisfies me like nothing else…I lie awake each night thinking of You…With passion, I pursue and cling to You. Because I feel Your grip on my life, I keep my soul close to Your heart."—Psalm 63:1, 5-8 (TPT)

Stir Up an Appetite

Our up-and-down *hunger* for Jesus can also be a hindering hurdle. It *is* possible to live with persistent passion for Him. As the body craves food and finds no satisfaction until fed, so our spirits can wholly hunger for Jesus—unsatisfied by anything but Him. We can rise each morning with bellies growling for breakfast and spirits groaning for Jesus. We can wake this way: *"I long to drink of You, O God, to drink deeply from the streams of pleasure flowing from your presence. My longings overwhelm me for more of you! My soul thirsts, pants, and longs for the living God. I want to come and see the face of God"* (Psalm 42:1-2 TPT). It can become our *pleasure* to rise early each morning just to sit with Jesus—to feel His presence, hear His voice, and read His Word. This morning meal with our Master deeply feeds us and fuels us with *joy*—a supernatural strength that will sustain us through whatever the day may hold.

Then, the conversation—the constant consuming of Jesus—continues all day long. Each spare moment becomes another meeting with Jesus. In the car, in the kitchen, in the quiet, we turn our thoughts toward Him and find He is already there—waiting and willing to satisfy us *again*. His presence becomes our primary pleasure—and His Word our dearest delight. Then, when the day dims and we head to bed, our hunger hasn't hushed; it hangs on *still*. We don't lie there replaying worries; we sigh and smile because our minds are still on *Him*. We're like David: *"I lie awake each night thinking of You and reflecting on how You help me like a father. I sing through the night under Your splendor-shadow, offering up to You my songs of delight and joy"* (Psalm 63:6–7 TPT). To crave Jesus like this is not only possible; it's what we were *made* for.

Even Jesus declared, *"Blessed are those who hunger and thirst for righteousness, for they shall be satisfied"* (Matthew 5:6 ESV). That word "blessed"—the Greek word *"makarios"*—means more than just "happy." It depicts a *deep,* spiritual well-being and favor with the Lord—a powerful *joy* that comes from being right with Him and near to Him, regardless of outward circumstances. It's similar to the wellness and gladness we experience physically from a delicious meal—but it's spiritual *and* more powerful. We were made to hunger and thirst for *righteousness*—to have a continuous craving for more and more of what's clean and correct in Jesus' eyes. When we continue to consume Christ, we are filled and satisfied inside to the fullest extent both now *and* eternally.

How do we arrive at this kind of avid spiritual appetite? We can *ask* for it, but we must also *eat*. Here's how it begins: *"Taste and see that the Lord [our God] is good!"* (Psalm 34:8 AMP). Our favorite foods began as a first bite. We sampled something new—not knowing what the bite would bring—and it made our taste buds sing. Then, the more we consumed it, the more we craved it. When we've tasted and seen that something is *good,* we'll want it again and again. This works similarly spiritually, too. It's when we get a taste of Jesus that we trigger an appetite for Him. When we sit and seek Him—and then *experience* Him—it deepens desire for Him. Then, the more we encounter Him, the more we hunger for Him. This isn't because He never truly satisfies; it's because He *does*—and each "bite" brings something *new*. We keep coming out of hunger—and *wonder*.

However, *competing* cravings crowd our table. Our spirits may hunger for Jesus, but our flesh features its own fierce appetites—demanding distractions in the form of entertainment and quick fixes. We can have a desire to read the Word, but our flesh will cry out for apps and screens—for scrolling, streaming, and shopping—*louder*. Bites from these mindless, meager meals only shallowly satisfy. Just as a body that only feeds on sweets and junk grows weak and tired, so our spirits grow famished and restless when we feed on fleeting pleasures instead of feasting on Jesus. We will not have healthy, strong spirits if we only eat spiritual junk food—and the switch from an unhealthy diet to a healthy one takes work. Appetites don't change automatically. When a person determines to transform his or her physical diet from junk food to what's healthy, it's *not* fun at first. We may want pizza and have to *make* ourselves eat grilled chicken and vegetables. We may crave donuts but have to *force* ourselves to forgo them for fruit. However, what starts as a duty will later become a delight. Appetites *can* be altered. We will hunger for whatever we feed on. After a while, the person begins to desire the salad, fruit, and lean protein and despise the donuts, pizza, and junk. This same principle is true spiritually, too.

When we struggle to *want* the Word—when we pine for our phone, for instance, more than His presence—it's time for some force-feeding. We must ask the Holy Spirit for help—to supernaturally transform our tastes—but we will also have to *make* ourselves consume meals of Jesus. When we really want to watch a show, we will have to tell ourselves, "No!" We'll have to remove the remote and move to a remote place to sit with Jesus and His Word. Whichever we feed most—our flesh or spirit—will become fiercest. When our spirits have sunk, we'll have to fight our flesh. We'll have to totally suppress it and starve it. It *will* die—actually more quickly than expected. When we tear our eyes off screens and stare at Scripture instead, our hearts immediately begin to warm and open wide. When we set our phones to the side and sit at Jesus' side, our spirits quickly begin to wake up. What felt like a difficult decision—to make ourselves sit with Him—then feels like a dumb dispute because *nothing* is better than Jesus. When we've lost our appetite for Him, we must wake up and return to Him—to our sitting and seeking, to all of our *tasting*. Each and every time, we'll find that He's still *good*. He's still what's *best*.

Let's know this about our Father: when we've lost our appetite for Him, He does *not* leave the table. He's the Father who remains— who watches and waits—even when our hunger wanes. Isaiah 42:3 (ESV) beautifully expresses, *"A bruised reed He will not break, and a faintly burning wick He will not quench."* A bruised reed—bent and brittle—could be easily broken by harsh hands, and a hardly-there breeze could extinguish a barely-burning flame. Yet, Jesus' heart is tender towards us even when our desire and fire have dwindled. He does not extinguish us in irritation or deaden our flame in disappointment. Instead, He quietly, gently keeps us *alive* spiritually. Even when our minds are far from Him, He keeps us close. His hand, His breath, His presence *remain*. The only way our flame could fully flicker out is if *we* intentionally force it out. *Jesus* won't. He keeps His protecting hand even over our faltering, barely-flickering faith and invites us over and over back to His presence and to His Word. He waits eagerly for us to come close to Him again—already planning to turn our tiny flame into a ferocious fire.

So, when we skimp on seeking Jesus, we'll discover that our desires for Him will droop and drain. If this happens, the right response to missed meals with Jesus is not guilt; we should feel *hunger*. He's not mad. He's simply a Dad watching His kids feed on junk that does not truly fulfill—even stuff that could kill. However, He keeps offering what *does* satisfy. Hear our Father's invitation to return to the right appetite: *"Listen! Are you thirsty for* more? *Come to the refreshing waters and drink. Even if you have no money, come, buy, and eat…It won't cost a thing! Why spend your hard-earned money on something that can't nourish you or work so hard for something to eat that can't satisfy?"* (Isaiah 55:1-2 TPT). He continues by calling His people to *listen*, promising that they'll enjoy *"a sumptuous feast, delighting in the finest food"* when they hear Him—and to come *closer* so that their *"total being may flourish!"* (Isaiah 55:2-3 TPT). These words pour from what He watches us do daily: tirelessly work for money and then foolishly spend it on what doesn't nourish. Too many of our minutes and too much of our money go to apps that feed wrong appetites. We watch the shows, scroll the accounts, shop the sales, and swipe through the games, but we're never satisfied. In fact, we feel empty—even truly *unhappy*. He knows this and calls us to come back close—to literally save money and feel fuller by returning to regular time—daily *meals*— with Him.

Let's know this, too: when we've settled into a season of shallow spiritual eating, it's been the *enemy*, quietly working to keep us from the soul-deep nourishment found in time with Jesus. Satan furtively fights to fill our plates with foul food. Without realizing it, we often chase the crumbs that our deceiver throws at our hunger. He tirelessly tempts us into tasting our way out of our appetite for Jesus. He'll do it one seemingly blameless bite at a time. He'll subtly talk us into shortening our time with Jesus one morning and then convince us to just be in the Word every other day, to spend more and more time on other tasks and apps—until he's zapped our right appetites. It will feel harmless along the way—until we wake up one day and realize how long it's been since we last prayed.

We will always face this hurdle that has to do with our *hunger*. Through the cravings of our flesh and our world's feast of distractions and pleasures, the enemy will tirelessly talk us out of time with Jesus. Even *he* knows that Jesus offers the only sustenance that truly satisfies—and it's all *free*. So, through our world, he lays out a feast of momentary pleasures—many with monetary consequences—but none can satisfy our deepest hunger. Only time with Jesus is the true bread that fills and the living water that quenches. Everything else leaves us empty again because *He* is the meal our hearts were made to consume. So, let's eat *well*. Let's eat *daily* and *diligently*. Then, we'll live not in a place of survival but in perpetual spiritual *revival*.

Slow Down

Another hurdle we'll have to handle that hits our hunger is the *pace* of our culture. Our world lives in too much of a wild hurry. We *have* to slow down. Although we're not literally running on the outside, we are almost always sprinting on the *inside*. Our minds race from one detail to the next regarding a current task while simultaneously hurdling ahead to the next several things on the to-do queue. Here's the truth: we too often overload ourselves simply because we live in a world and culture that calls the busy man "successful" and the woman wearing ten hats "impressive." Our culture—and our enemy behind it—pushes us to live in this pressed and rushed way, but *Jesus* doesn't.

Even during His quick time on this earth, Jesus lived at a

simple, *slow* pace. He moved from one moment to the next and truly *lived* in the moment. Faces and needs didn't get lost in the rush of His all-important agenda. He had the most massive mission of any person ever born—to reach and save a lost world—but His daily to-do list was not overloaded nor His pace over-rushed. He did not live in haste, nor did the hours slip through His hands like fast-moving sand. He didn't stay up all night analyzing data, making copies, or prepping meals. The only thing that we can see He ever lost sleep over was more time in prayer. He moved from one moment to the next taking the *time* to meet people, tell stories, teach truths, pray to the Father, heal the sick, and *love* each and every person in front of Him. He learned—as *we* can—to live *slowly* in a fast-paced world.

We cannot even hear the Holy Spirit's voice when we are frenzied and made crazy by a thousand details pouring off a mile-long list of things to do every day. We cannot even *be* like Him—full of peace, joy, patience, and love—when we are hurried and stressed. Think about how often we feel like we're going to snap at the next person, how overwhelmed we become by all we have to manage, how we struggle to stay asleep at night, and how we find it even hard to just sit and do *nothing*. This is *not* what life should be like. This is *not* the existence Jesus means for us to maintain. What's "normal" today isn't supposed to be typical. We *should* have time to stop and visit. We *should* have room—even when tackling a task or talking to people—to pause and hear Him, too. It's in those quiet, surrendered spaces *inside* that the Spirit breathes peace into our chaos, refills our weary hearts with joy, and pours out love that overflows into everything we do—and *onto* everyone we see. When we live slowed-down and *listening* inside, we begin to live *differently* outside. We're more like Jesus, more like the people God created us to be—and more empowered to do exactly what *He* has called us to do.

Let's remember that it's called "walking" with Jesus, not *running*. Just as two people could not have full conversations while racing at a full sprint, we can't in our spiritual lives either. We can talk while we *walk*—and we can walk *and* hear. When we run, however, we are moving too fast to catch His Words because we aren't traveling at *His* pace. He won't rush up to ours; He wants us to slow down to *His*. In order to experience Jesus as truly **known and near**—in order to literally walk in the relationship with Him we were born to have—we must *slow down*. This may mean scaling back—not just decluttering our schedules but also decelerating our hearts and minds. We must slow down—not just when we actually do sit down but even during on-our-feet moments. We must pull ourselves back to a "walk" on the inside—to the pace of Jesus—so that we can both step *and* speak with Him.

Jesus is constantly with us and wants us to continually hear Him. We just don't sense Him consistently because we're completely focused on doing, controlling, managing, and finishing. We have to force ourselves out of the frenzy our world lives in—where we are perpetually aware of a lot to get done but not persistently tuned-in to the presence of the Son. He is with us all day, longing for us to truly walk with Him—alertly hearing and acutely feeling Him, artlessly following His lead over and over again. This slow pace and sensitive place with Jesus—accomplishing what *really* matters while encountering Him all day long—is where He wants us to live on *purpose*. This is where He is *heard*—steady and clear. *This* is where He is **known** and **near**.

Get Still

A hurdle similar to hurrying is that we simply struggle to *get still*. This, too, sounds and feels so counter-culture, but stillness is a principle that peppers the Word: ***"Be still***, *and know that I am God"* (Psalm 46:10 NLT); *"The Lord will fight for you; you need only **be still**"* (Exodus 14:14 NIV); ***"Be still** in the presence of the Lord, and wait patiently for Him to act"* (Psalm 37:7 NLT); ***"Stand still** and see this great thing the Lord is about to before your eyes!"* (I Samuel 12:16 NIV). Verse after verse—even beyond these here—speak about stillness. There's no trick definition. "Still" means *still*. It is a full stop to all our grabbing and achieving. It is a complete ceasing of movement—a total pause before our heavenly Father. We must come to a full stop to see and sense Him, bowing before His reign, kneeling before the King who holds the whole world—and our *lives*—together. Remember, too, that He whispers—and when we are still and silent, we can clearly hear. It's when we get *still* that He becomes the most **known** and **near**.

He calls us into stillness so that our dulled senses can wake—to recognize His nearness and notice His hand at work all around us—

and what carries greater weight than this each day? To know Jesus deeply, to discern His movement within us and for us, we must make room for quiet. He could have directed us toward effort or urgency. Instead, He gives a gentler—but *harder*—instruction: be still. It's as if He beckons, "Stop striving. Stop reaching. Come and sit with Me. Be still and see. Draw near and hear." We live in an age of instant answers and endless motion—lightning-fast internet, drive-through meals, next-day delivery, and never-ending noise. Yet, Jesus has not moved with the times. He remains in *stillness*—and He waits for us there. As our world gets louder and faster, our efforts to "get still" will become harder. Yet, if we want Him, we must quiet the clamor, power down the pace, and turn aside from constant motion. We cannot expect to encounter Him as we run when He has told us plainly where He can be found: in stillness—where we stop and He is *known*.

Think of the last time all man-made sound was turned off and silence settled in, when the wind whispered, birds sang, and every rustle and ripple already present became unmistakable; this is how it is when all noise and distraction are quieted and stillness is shared with Jesus. What has been around us all along *spiritually*—the beauty, the movement, the life—can suddenly be felt and heard so clearly, and what He has already been speaking over our lives becomes evident and full of meaning. Space must be made for stillness; distractions and busyness must be dimmed on purpose. This cannot be reserved for the "end of the rope" or when we reach "empty" and require rescue. Stillness is meant for daily rhythm: to stop, sit, and sense His words, to pause and perceive His presence. When this practice becomes habitual, the rope never frays, emptiness is never known, and life is lived in *fullness* every day.

This truth will never taper off: our Father *expects* us to spend time sitting with Him and hearing Him daily. The *exact* life that Jesus shed His Blood for us to live will come out of *this* daily practice. Full life from Jesus flows more from "getting still" than from "getting things done," because He already accomplished what truly needed doing on the Cross. Now, He invites us to come, to sit, to receive—and all the anointing and ability we need will simply pour out onto us, and *through* us, into the lives around us. Let's not get this backwards: Jesus fills and uses us *most* powerfully when we take the time to *be still*. Our enemy knows this truth well. This is why he pushes and rushes the world, hoping to hush the very Voice that stills and heals every heart. Let's be people who draw near, get *still,* and let His words set us apart.

Don't Give Up

We will encounter many enemy-erected hurdles along our journey with Jesus. We'll hop over some hastily while others may hurl us to the ground. Even the steadiest Jesus-followers stumble at times—like Peter who miraculously walked on water one minute and then sank in human doubt the next (Matthew 14:29-31). All of us—no matter how lavishly we love Jesus—will have depleted days and doubting days. We'll even have some when we fall flat on our faces. Still, we never fall *alone* or *away* from Jesus. He's a Savior who sees every stumble and knows when we crumble. He doesn't flinch at our mess or frown at our failure. Even when we're faithless, He remains faithful (2 Timothy 2:13). When we're down, He doesn't turn around and count us out. He's a Savior who comes *close*—even as we cry a puddle of tears on our carpet. He won't stand by and wait for the wailing to end. He'll get down on the ground, lie eye-to-eye with us—with *His* face in *our* tears—wrap His arm around us, and whisper His *hope* into our hurt. He will stoop low to raise us high. He binds up the broken (Psalm 147:3), whispers to weary hearts, and strengthens feeble knees (Isaiah 35:3). When we've fallen, He will always reach out His hand and help us stand again.

It's nearly effortless to take His extended hand. It's easy to return when a hurdle has hurled us off track. We simply *come back* to our Father who watches and waits for us (Luke 15:20). He's still right there—always eager to embrace us in compassion. Remember that as the sun rises each morning, so does new mercy. With Jesus, any day can become a new beginning (Lamentations 3:22-23). We can *come back* at any moment in any place. We don't have to spend time reprimanding and repairing ourselves before we return. He extends a hand the very moment we fall—again, like He did with Peter who sank in doubt in the water. The very second Peter's sinking started, *"Jesus **immediately** reached out his hand and took hold of him"* (Matthew 14:31 ESV). Jesus didn't respond with delay or condemnation; He reached out at once in compassion and care. He *immediately* reaches to rescue when we've fallen. Let's always take His hand—and remember that it is offered without hesitation, and He hopes we grasp it without pause.

When we confront challenges that *we* didn't cause, let's always know that *Jesus* didn't create it either. Let's not let our difficulty make us doubt Him. Our problems aren't His punishment. They flow from our flaw-filled world and our fallen enemy. Jesus doesn't cause them, but He *does* come to calm them and carry us through. Here's the question many ask followed by the answer we *all* need: *"Does it mean he no longer loves us if we have trouble or calamity, or are persecuted, or hungry, or destitute, or in danger, or threatened with death?...No, despite all these things, overwhelming victory is ours through Christ, who loved us"* (Romans 8:35, 37 NLT). In all things—deception, doubt, disappointment, difficulty, distraction, disaster, and defeat—*Jesus* will help us overcome. In ways that only *He* can, He'll turn our every trial into a triumph.

No matter what deception or difficulty the devil deals out, our Savior will always shout out: "I *love* you, and *nothing* will make me stop!" Let's become as convinced as Paul of this truth: *"I am convinced that nothing can ever separate us from God's love. Neither death nor life, neither angels nor demons, neither our fears for today nor our worries about tomorrow—not even the powers of Hell can separate us from God's love"* (Romans 8:38 NLT). Not one bit of suffering, sin, or circumstance—no spiritual power in Heaven, Hell, or on earth—absolutely nothing in existence, which includes us and our own mistakes, could sever us from our Savior's love. His love for *each* of us is unbreakable, unconditional, and eternal. We stand secure in His love—not because we never fall but because Jesus paid for it all. His love *never* weakens. In fact, the harder we fall or the more heartbreaking life becomes, the *more* He pours it out.

So, when we get knocked down, let's take Jesus' hand and rise again. Let's brush off the dust and remain firm in our trust. Let's come *close* when we're crushed and lock eyes with the One who already overcame this world and all its woes (John 16:33). Our war is fierce, but His love is *far* stronger. Our hateful enemy may wield his hurdles, but our Jesus will always build our *hope*.

PART 6

The Fruit

CHAPTER TEN

He Changes Us Personally

"I am a true sprouting vine, and the farmer who tends the vine is My Father. He cares for the branches connected to Me by lifting and propping up the fruitless branches and pruning every fruitful branch to yield a greater harvest…As you live in union with Me as your source, fruitfulness will stream from you."—John 15:1-2, 5 (TPT)

A Healed Self-Image

As soon as we're born again, we're planted in new soil and begin to bear different fruit. Our Father tends to us with perfect care—knowing when we need propping up *or* pruning down (John 15:1-2). As we grow in relationship and yield to His Spirit within—learning to align and abide with Him more and more—we flourish with His fruit. Some of this fruit is *internal.* He works to re-root and reroute us from the inside out, including our *identity* and *self-view.*

The way we used to see ourselves—our self-image shaped by past pain, performance, and people's opinions—now becomes weeds. Our old view of ourselves must be ripped up by its roots and replaced with truth. As we spend time in His Word and His presence and allow Him to plant that truth, we begin to grow in the confidence, peace, and purpose that bloom and burst forth when our self-view syncs with Jesus' vision of us. Then, when His perspective settles in, deep healing rises within. We begin to embrace ourselves with the same genuine love *He* has for us. Comparison ceases as insecurity slips away, and we become people who no longer want to be anyone else—just our authentic, God-created selves.

One of Satan's greatest ongoing goals is to crush our *confidence*—and he starts in childhood. From the moment we're born, the enemy sees the face of God in each of our features and the power of God in each of our spirits, and he fears us. Therefore, he aims to gut us and get us on shaky feet. He's sneaky and strategic and has been throwing bombs at our confidence—aiming for full destruction—since we were children. We each went through hardship in our homes and teasing in our schools. Adults may have left us, hurt us, misguided us, or confused us, and kids called us "ugly," "fat," "stupid," "weird," and worse. We were each internally injured in many instances, and it's through these wounds that the enemy has whispered lies against our person: "See—you aren't *worth* sticking around for," "You're not like *other* people," "You'll always be *rejected*," "You look and sound *weird*," "You can't fully *trust* God"—on and on goes his litany of lies. The enemy aims in adulthood to not just protect but *widen* the web of lies he wound around and weaved into us in childhood. He becomes subtler and sneakier as we grow older and wiser, but he's always after the same aim: to cripple our confidence.

Even in adulthood, the enemy looks for every weak spot, ready to pick at our hearts and strike where he knows we are most vulnerable. He works through words—comments on our looks, our voice, or who we are—and through silent signals: demeaning glances, eye-rolls, and mocking laughter. Every interaction and every performance is a chance for him to sow doubt about who we are. He hopes we'll hold back, hurt, doubt, or even quit where we're *called*. His goal is to get us disheartened and discouraged—endlessly exasperated and exhausted. There's a world of difference between sheer physical exhaustion and being drained physically, emotionally, mentally, and spiritually all at once. Nothing is as grueling as pouring ourselves out fully, only to believe it wasn't good enough—or that *we* aren't enough— all because of the devil's deceit relentlessly playing across our minds and plaguing our hearts.

With the help of the Holy Spirit, we must do the work of recognizing and uprooting every lie. When these weighty weeds are wrenched from our hearts, we feel lightened and emboldened. We are filled with the kind of courage that caused diminutive David to take on giant Goliath (1 Samuel 17)—and the kind of joy that permeated Paul as he penned Scripture in prison (Philippians 1:12-14, 2 Timothy 2:9). We walk with full confidence in who we are and what Jesus is doing in us and through us—no matter *our* imperfections or the afflictions of each day. Truly, the only thing that ever steals this from us is the deceit Satan plants in our self-view. So, we don't just pull lies up to feel better; we pull them up to live *freer*. Freedom—along with *full* joy—takes root when we finally see ourselves how our Father does— and nothing frightens the enemy more.

To get *there*, we must understand *this:* within all of our hearts are wounds that aren't wholly healed. If they aren't washed and wrapped up by Jesus, the enemy will whisper through those wounds and wear us out—no matter how old we are. Some of us may wrestle with trusting Jesus because of a blow to our trust in Him from decades ago. Many live expecting rejection—seeing it when it's not even existent—because of the way they were passed over and pushed aside in their past. Some of us carry the scars of self-doubt—bruised by teen jeers that were echoed again in adult years. Others live under a cloak of shame, the kind that strikes after every conversation and interaction, making even innocent words or actions feel wrong. Some work without end, taking on more than they should, tirelessly trying to prove their worth. Others hold back and hide parts of their stories, hindered by heaviness from past hurt and humiliation. The examples of life lived through unhealed hurts are endless. Only when we identify these wounds and their whispers can we find full freedom, healing, and *confidence*—powerful fruit that flows out of a flourishing friendship with Jesus.

So, we must dig up every deeply-rooted deception. We start by recognizing every lie lurking and looping in our minds. Let's sit with the Holy Spirit and sift through the repeated patterns in our thoughts that bring shame, fear, defeat, or retreat. As He spotlights a lie, write it down. Then, record the *truth* next to each one. Search Scripture. Listen to Jesus. He'll supply the truth that will supplant each twisted tale of the enemy. Then, we take tight hold of those new certainties, and they become our response to the untruths when they uprise again. Over time—after many moments of thinking the lie but then speaking the truth—the lie will *die*. The truth will live and lead us where the lie lacerated us. Then, when truth takes root, freedom begins to bloom—not just in how we think, but in how we live, love, and look at ourselves through *His* eyes.

Some of us must journey back more deeply before we can move forward more freely. We may need to return to the beginnings of our stories, replaying each scene, searching for what still stirs *hurt*. We can sit with the Spirit and let our memories unfold like a slow-motion movie across our minds. When a scene stings, we press pause—and as painful as it is, we step back into that moment *with* Jesus. We ask Him to flood us with forgiveness for the offender in the scene, whether it's someone else or even ourselves. Wounds cannot be healed without full forgiveness—and when letting it go feels beyond reach, the Holy Spirit empowers us to release the seemingly unforgivable. One key to unlocking this healing is to ask where Jesus was in that moment. We can close our eyes and replay it again, looking for *Him*. He will show us that He was *there*—holding, helping, already weaving a path toward our healing. If we could turn up the volume on that scene, we'd hear perhaps the harsh words hurled at us—but layered over them, we'd perceive Jesus speaking *truth*. His words pierce the lies, shattering the power they try to hold. In that moment, the words that once wounded will be washed from our hearts, leaving only His voice—the One that restores and remains.

In some scenes, it may ache to realize Jesus was there but didn't thwart it. Yet, even then, He wasn't absent; He was anchoring us. He wasn't letting it break us; He was allowing it to *make* us. When we were being overly scolded, we were being molded. When we were rejected, we were *still* protected—and He would simply connect it to our calling. If we were abused, He intends for it to be used—for great, unfathomable glory. He invites us back into our stories—not to relive the pain—but to redeem and rebuild what wrecked us. Where hurt happened, *He* poured out purpose. We must revisit the scenes that still sting—to put down the hurt and pick up the healing. If we press pause and really press in, we'll spot the purpose He placed in our pain. Then, when we securely set these scenes in Jesus' hands, He'll replay the redeemed version of it. We'll watch it again across our minds—but the event will now have a new end. We'll watch these scenes not shatter us but simply shape us. We'll stand at the end—no longer bound by what broke us—but built by Jesus into someone with *special* purpose. We'll find we no longer wish to be anyone else—now that Jesus has reclaimed the severest scenes of our stories and surfaced our *true* selves.

Where we look at ourselves and see brokenness, Jesus sees *beauty*. He sees special *ability* and *possibility*. He's a creative, redemptive God—one who reshapes and reworks marred clay (Jeremiah 18:4). Even when life crushes us, we never fall off the Potter's wheel; we *never* leave His hands. We are held tightly and transformed into something even greater. Jesus longs to show us the beauty in our brokenness. *Because* we went through misery and misfortune, we carry *more*. Where holes were left in our lives, He filled them with *more*. When wicked words flooded us out of mean mouths, Jesus poured out *more*. The more fire we've fought through, the more anointing we've been filled with. Still, it's not just for us. It's for *others*, too. As we sit with the Holy Spirit and rewatch and rework the scenes of our stories— no matter how many sessions it takes—we'll eventually reach our present day, and when we arrive at the end, we'll no longer feel gloomy. We'll sense *glory*. What we've gone back and allowed Him to heal will reveal Jesus' care and our calling. We'll see the ministry that can come from our misery. We'll feel lighter, brighter—more relevant, more *confident*. When we let Jesus heal what hurt us, He helps us see even the damaged parts we once despised the way He always has: beautiful, purposeful, and full of potential in *His* hands.

Processing our pain like this with the Holy Spirit will change *everything*—how we wake up, how we show up, how we work, how we think, how we feel, how we love, and even how we sleep. Let's spend time sitting with the Holy Spirit and our stories. With pen and paper, let's ask Him to spotlight the lies still leading us. We may be surprised by what He shows us—shocked by how long we've heard it and let it hinder us, stunned by how well a bold-faced lie has blended into our daily thoughts. Let's ask Him to reveal which wounds aren't fully healed—and let's let Him make us *whole*. Let's fully receive His forgiveness and acceptance—and truly believe again in His goodness and trustworthiness. Let's let Him into all places and parts of our past— so deeply that the lies can't last.

Let's invite Jesus to make over the way we see ourselves in the *mirror*, too. Jesus calls us beautiful—wholly, wonderfully, even with every flaw—and He longs for us to see it as well. However, we live in a world that defines beauty far differently than the One who designed us. Satan has created and cast a *false*, glittering image of beauty across the earth—one that demands flawless faces, sculpted bodies, gleaming teeth, and poreless skin. He parades it across screens and pages of all types—through movies, shows, apps, advertisements, and magazines. He's even fabricated filters so that people can perfect their pictures—making their skin smoother, waists smaller, and hair shinier. He whispers it through endless ads that promise perfection in a bottle, a shot, a scalpel, or a starvation plan. Women are told they must shrink, smooth, and reshape every inch to be desirable. Men must bulk, chisel, and conquer to be admired. As people chase this image, their hearts grow emptier. Bank accounts bleed. Bodies suffer. Yet, the goal keeps shifting: body and beauty trends change—keeping "true beauty" always just out of reach. It's a race with no finish line, designed to keep us obsessed, insecure, and blind to the beauty we were *already* born with—the kind crafted by the hands of God, not the lies of a serpent.

We can drop out of that race and *rest*. We can stop and settle into this *truth:* we are *already* beautiful. Let's revisit Psalm 139, the passage that illustrates our Father knitting us together in our mothers' wombs, carefully choosing the details of each physical feature—our eye, hair, and skin color and even our height, shape, and voice tones. We are each one of His *masterpieces*—an intentional, artful, invaluable creation of our God (Ephesians 2:10). We can't even *"compare ourselves with each other as if one of us were better and another worse"* because *"each of us is an original"* (Galatians 5:25-26 MSG). In Psalm 139, this wasn't just information but *revelation* to David—so much so that he looked at his own body and exclaimed, *"I will give thanks and praise to You, for I am fearfully and wonderfully made; wonderful are your works, and my soul knows it very well"* (v.14 AMP). David beheld *himself* as one of God's uniquely crafted masterpieces—observing every intricate detail of his design and marveling that he was personally fashioned by God's own hand. As he looked at his hands, touched his hair, moved his arms—he saw it all as one *gift* from God after another and gushed with *gratitude*. He personally celebrated the one-of-kind way that his God crafted each part of him—

and this Scriptural scene invites *us* to do the same.

We can stop being so hateful towards ourselves by becoming *grateful* for ourselves. Hell has been behind all our self-hating. Satan can't stand the beauty and glory glowing on our faces, the way our hands mirror Jesus' both in physical form and in spiritual function, the way we stand and step with Spirit-strength and stirring power—each of us constantly revealing a unique portion of our Savior's splendor. He clearly sees the beauty we're often blind to, and he wages war on our self-image to hide our true beauty from *our* view. Through thoughts and peoples' comments, he's flagged down all our flaws and forced our focus to these features—parts that are "too big" or "too small," spots that are shaped or shaded "so *wrong*," and so on. Almost all of us abhor parts of ourselves—and this has come from Satan. So, let's break the grip of this hate.

Let's begin to truly *appreciate* what our God has given us—*personally*. Let's take a quiet moment and just stare at our hands. Before our mothers ever held them, they were formed by the Father's faithful hands. He shaped them with sincere care, then poured His own prayers over them, prophesying and proclaiming the unique works they would one day achieve. Now, let's lift our eyes to our faces and look for the traces of His touch. Every line, every curve, every freckle—it was all designed with *delight*. The color of our eyes, our skin, our hair—*all* of it was chosen with care. Let's lay down the lies and pick up the truth: *every* detail was divinely designed. Don't rush past this. Stare at *each* part. Let's look at the legs we've loathed and *thank* Jesus for them. Let's marvel at the marks we've wanted removed and *thank* Him for those, too. Let's wrap our arms around ourselves and dare to believe that we are embracing one of the most beautiful creations our Father ever designed and assigned to this earth. Let's ask the Holy Spirit to awaken this revelation in us—just as He did for David. Let's not stop asking—let's *persist* in pressing in—until this truth becomes so real that gratitude erupts from our lips as personal praise for the miracle that we *each* are.

Then, let's stop scrolling, staring, and comparing ourselves to false images. It's *okay* to have teeth a little crooked, a waistline a bit wide, eyebrows a tad thin, and wrinkles setting in. We are *more* than our skin. We are filled with *Him*—and the more authentic we are, the more *anointed* we are. Even our God gazes at us and is endlessly enthralled by our beauty (Psalm 45:11). In fact, with each second that passes, He's thinking an adoring, admiring thought about each of us. David's revelation of the Lord's view of him personally in Psalm 139 includes this truth: *"How precious are your thoughts about me, O God. They cannot be numbered! I can't even count them; they outnumber the grains of sand!"* (v. 17-18 NLT). If His thoughts outnumber the grains of sand on the earth, we can conclude that with each breath we take—both while sleeping and awake—a brand-new, beautiful thought about us bounds across our Father's mind. If we ask the Holy Spirit, He'll let us *hear* them. As *His* words wash over us, what we hear will heal us. *This* is the pathway to a fully restored self-view and the freedom it forges. We anchor our worth no longer in fickle fashions or our world's warped standards but in the unfailing, ever-flowing love and delight of our Creator—who crafts only cherished *masterpieces* that are fully **known** and fondly held **near.**

Changed Character

The Holy Spirit also plants and produces new fruit in our *character*. We may have stepped into our relationship with Jesus impatient, short-tempered, lazy, lustful, deceitful, envious, and selfish—but our old fruit will fade as we flourish in friendship with Him. The moment we became born-again, our spirits awakened *full* of Jesus' exact spiritual DNA. This means *we* possess the potential to become as patient, compassionate, obedient, truthful, faithful, joyful, gracious, gentle, humble, bold, and holy as *Jesus* is. Peer at 2 Peter 1:3 (NLT): *"God has given us everything we need for living a godly life. We have received all of this by coming to know him."* The very next verse reveals that His promises enable us to *"share his divine nature and escape the world's corruption caused by human desires"* (v.4 NLT). When we belong to Jesus, we can grow in *His* nature—a powerful, lifelong process propelled by the Holy Spirit.

The Holy Spirit *plants* Himself within us, ready to grow a garden of Heaven's own character in the soil of our hearts. *His* fruit is life-giving and life-changing—both to us *and* those around us. Look at this list: *"The Holy Spirit produces this kind of fruit in our lives: love, joy, peace, patience, kindness, goodness, faithfulness, gentleness, and self-control"* (Galatians 5:22-23 NLT). The more we walk and work with Him, He'll produce love that doesn't quit, joy that shines in sorrow, peace that calms in chaos, patience that waits without complaint, and kindness that disarms hardness. He'll cultivate goodness in our actions, faithfulness in our commitments, gentleness in our demeanor, and self-control in our decisions. The Holy Spirit reshapes us from the inside out—making us into people who think, speak, respond, live, and *love* like Jesus. Gradually, we will bear less of the world's lesser crops and more of the flawless fruit that comes from our Father. The potential is already planted in the soil of our spirits. Day by day, we now allow the Holy Spirit to nurture it, bringing it above the surface to boldly bloom in *all* our behaviors.

How do we let the Holy Spirit guide this growth? We *ask* Him. Let's endlessly *ask* that He uses each moment to manifest more and more of the character of Christ in us. We also avidly study Scripture. Hebrews 4:12 (NLT) says this: *"For the word of God is alive and powerful. It is sharper than the sharpest two-edged sword, cutting between soul and spirit, between joint and marrow. It exposes our innermost thoughts and desires."* Our time in the Word tills the soil and waters the spiritual seeds in our hearts. Page after page presents and projects God's nature—and it points out what behaviors we need to get out. As we sit with Scripture, the Holy Spirit serves as a surgeon—surfacing and severing sin and replacing it with more of *Him*. So, our time in His Word offers ongoing opportunities for the Holy Spirit to cultivate His character within us. The Word doesn't just inform us; it *transforms* us. By revealing truth and exposing hidden places, the Word and the Spirit lovingly shape our hearts to reflect Christ more fully. Still, as we dig in daily, we must also become *doers* of the Word—determined to walk out what we read (James 1:22-25). As we study Scripture, we must also *act* on it daily. Then, we change and become carriers of His *character*.

In fact, in our quest to quicken Christlikeness within us, we can begin to see our daily lives as a spiritual *gym*. Committed, muscular gym-goers once began with a desire to get in shape and grow muscle. The early days of showing up included great discipline, pain, commitment, and push-through. Once growth became obvious, motivation swelled, and the trip to the gym became more of a delight than a duty. Even as committed gym-goers hit plateaus, they continue to show up and switch up parts of their routine to continue to grow and make physical gains. This is because committed gym-goers became *addicted* to *growth*.

As Jesus-followers, we must become like gym-goers: obsessed with progress—but *spiritually*. Just as someone training the body knows which muscles need the most work and which reps will strengthen them, we must discern which parts of our character need building and what spiritual "reps" will help us grow. Let's live in a place of intentionally identifying which parts of our character need the most work, and let's get out of bed and head to our God's "gym" every single day. The beauty is that His gym isn't confined to a building or a schedule; it opens wherever we are, woven into every circumstance and opportunity of our daily lives. Each moment becomes a chance to exercise faith, build strength, and grow closer to Him.

All around us each day are life's "work-out machines" and spiritual "reps" waiting to strengthen us. Most arrive disguised as *frustrations* and *challenges*. No muscle grows without resistance—physical or spiritual. Instead of resenting difficulties, we can relish them, seeing each as a "work-out bench" for weak spots in our character. Rather than despising struggles, we can delight in them, knowing they are part of the daily routine that develops us. Opportunities for growth surround us constantly; those who crave progress embrace the grind while those who resist it *resent* the resistance. Scripture tells us to deem every difficulty *"an invaluable opportunity to experience the greatest joy [we] can,"* and it continues by pointing out *how* we can see a trial as a joy: *"You know that when your faith is tested, it stirs up in you the power of endurance. And then as your endurance grows even stronger, it will release perfection into every part of your being until there is nothing missing and nothing lacking"* (James 1:2-4 TPT). Our greatest growth springs from what makes us groan. Depending on the depth of our desire to grow in Jesus' likeness, daily difficulties can either simply irritate us or ignite us toward transformation. Only those addicted to growth discover purpose—and even *joy*—woven into the challenges that confront them each day.

Gym-goers also don't show up without a *plan*. They know which muscles to move, which reps will build strength, and how to tone and train. Likewise, we must detect daily where our spirits need growth, then remain alert throughout the day, spotting every opportunity to stretch, strengthen, and grow in these areas. Maybe it's practicing patience in a confounding conversation, responding with kindness to someone who's repeatedly rash, or telling the truth when staying silent would be smoother. Perhaps it's jousting jealousy and, instead, celebrating the coworker or teammate receiving the promotion we pined for. It could be standing strong against the temptation that tripped us yesterday, seeing a financial struggle as a test to *rest* while we trust, or choosing to deal with doubt deeply each time it dawns throughout the day. Every *planned* step like this—each *rep*—compounds and creates the character of our Jesus in us. Let's live daily knowing where growth is needed and constantly catching opportunities to *do* it.

Let's know this, too: where we need to blossom next will never be blurry. The Holy Spirit works in clarity where He's bringing liberty. Whatever habit keeps wreaking havoc, whatever tendency keeps turning up tiresomely—wherever it seems the Spirit is shining light on sin—*that* is where we're to dig in. If we could observe His hand healing our hearts, maybe we'd see a hammer and a chisel. We'd see the section—perhaps all the way to the left—He's made new. That corner glows like glittering gold while the rest remains covered in rough, rugged rock. Where He applies pressure with His chisel, He desires to work. We know where the chisel is charged when the same struggle keeps surfacing, voices around us echo it, conviction keeps knocking, and every sermon and Scripture seems to spotlight the *same* spot. Be aware of this: if we don't yield to His direction—surrendering to the chisel in that section—He'll pause the progression. We don't get to choose where He chisels. He works through our hearts in an ordained order. If we refuse His movement in an area, He won't just maneuver around it and move on to the next. Where we don't surrender, we cycle. We'll spin in circles without moving forward until we surrender what He's surfaced.

So, let's always *yield*. Let's constantly concede to the careful, care-filled work of the Holy Spirit. Bearing fresh fruit is wonderful, but it's sometimes work. Even under the ground, natural seeds struggle quietly in darkness, stretching and straining to break through the weight of the heavy earth. Without giving up, it persistently pushes upward towards the light it longs for. In the same way, we Christians often fight resistance when the fruit of Jesus forces towards the surface. Fruit like peace, love, and joy don't always come easily; they must press through doubts, fears, and old habits. Yet, just as an earthly seed's struggle eventually births new life above ground, our spiritual pushing-through (and *working-out*) brings a harvest of right-living that makes every battle worth winning. Let's never give up or let up. Let's *want* the Holy Spirit to work. He'll continually cultivate His fruit in us, fostering freedom and joy as we flourish into lives that fully reflect Jesus—*the* life we were born to have, a life we will love to live.

Finding Our Freedom

When Jesus is **known and near**, everything—even the bad habits that have held us hostage our whole lives—can be *totally* transformed. Beyond what we've dared to dream, abundant breakthrough, triumph, and joy are possible. Through relationship with Him, the Holy Spirit can empower us to completely conquer *the* flesh battle we've fought and lost our whole lives. Jesus' Blood bought total victory; every chain is breakable and every struggle beatable. If we believe this and ruthlessly press into victory without quitting, we will overcome what used to overthrow *us*.

It's never too late for a total *turnaround*. No matter our age, Jesus can completely rewrite and rearrange our rhythms from the inside out. He can even change our cravings and create a love for nourishing food and daily movement. He can wean us off too much screen time and awaken us to the joy of real presence in down moments. He can make any of us who have been senseless spenders into some of the wisest stewards who have ever lived. He can give us the gift of godly, healthy sleep. He can slow us down and make us calm and focused— and satisfied with a slower, simpler life. He can cause us—our homes, spaces, and minds—to become completely uncluttered. Even our most hated habits can be healed and honed, lifting us into a life flowing from a fresh height of freedom and joy.

Since we have the all-powerful help of the Holy Spirit, let's aggressively throw aside excuses. Let's *fully* find our freedom—every drop of it bought with the Blood. Let's be willing to be uncomfortable as we cross out of where we've always been and head to where we never thought we could reach. Let's be willing to do what we've deemed impossible. Remember the lame man by the pool at Bethesda (John 5:1-15). He had been stuck in an unhealthy state for years. When Jesus approached him, He asked, *"Do you **want** to get well?"* (John 5:6

AMP). Let's hear Jesus passionately posing us the same question. Let's desire full health in every part of lives, especially the corners we've battled longest and felt trapped deepest.

Still, here's the most powerful part of that story: Jesus told the man to do the very thing he'd *never* been able to do. He told him to take the very step that had been impossible, the one that had kept him from living fully and wholly. He boldly instructed, *"Stand up, pick up your mat, and walk!"* (John 5:8 NLT). When Jesus *declared* it, the man *did* it. This can happen for us, too. If we will get still and listen, Jesus can speak straight into the space of our lives that has felt most immovable, and our miracle can manifest, too. When Jesus proclaims a command to us, He also pours over us the power to *do* it. If we lay that impossible area at Jesus' feet, He'll speak the life-soaked, power-drenched words that activate change: "Get up, and *walk!*" "Follow *this* spending plan!" "Here's how to reshape your time on your *phone…*" "Eat like *this…*" "Slow your soul down *this* way…" "Break the addiction with *these* steps…" Whatever our stuck place is, He knows *exactly* what to say—and we'll hear it as we pray. Let's sit and surrender our harmful habits and messy mindsets to Jesus—and let's *listen* to Him. Power— and never-before-found *freedom*—flows where His voice is heard.

This is encouraging, too: experiencing victory in a practical area will bring breakthroughs in spiritual areas. Let's consider every corner of our lives—even natural components—as *spiritual.* Jesus wants us whole—completely right and healthy in *all* areas—even down to what we eat and drink. These practical parts are spiritual because they impact our bodies—His *temple* (1 Corinthians 6:19-20)—as well as our minds, emotions, confidence, energy, awareness of Him, and ability to walk in spiritual authority. These areas affect everything—every single day. They're not small or shallow; they ripple through the whole ocean of our lives. When we sleep well, our minds clear, and even our prayers sharpen. When we eat to nourish, we feel lighter, stronger, happier— more *alive.* When we exercise and move our bodies, confidence soars, and our joy dances. When we tightly and *rightly* rule ourselves, we're better equipped to stand in sure authority over darkness. Surrender in the natural swings open new doors in the supernatural. So, let's lay these everyday areas before Jesus and humbly and hungrily invite Him to reshape what's out of shape. If we do, we'll walk in higher levels of health—and our joy and freedom will flourish like a garden in full bloom after a long winter.

All of this might sound like an invitation to climb a massive mountain—but let's remember that Jesus is in the *moving* of mountains (Matthew 17:20, Mark 11:23). Maybe we've been calling our mountains "a lack of confidence" or "anxiety" or a "personality quirk"—yet it really might be our out-of-whack natural habits causing what feels like spiritual lack. However, *"everything we could ever need for life and godliness has already been deposited in us by His divine power,"* so we have *no* spiritual lack (2 Peter 1:3 TPT). Our natural habits can be the mountains blocking the miracles that are *already* ours. It all streams down to *surrender*—allowing each section of our lives to be steered by Jesus. Let's let Him have our eating, drinking, sleeping, spending, and even keeping or giving of things. Let's ask Him for *His* way in even the practical pieces of our lives, and let's walk it out with the power He pours out when He speaks it out. Our mountains—the ones that have long felt immovable—*can* move. We *can* break free. We can thrive in areas we've *never* felt alive—as we grow in closeness and cooperation with Jesus and allow His power to flow everywhere it wants to go.

So, let's let Jesus lead—even in our *physical* parts. Remember this verse that is proclaimed with poignant passion: *"Don't you realize that your body is the temple of the Holy Spirit, who lives in you and was given to you by God? You do not belong to yourself"* (1 Corinthians 6:19 NLT). Our bodies don't belong to us. They are *His*. We must feed, water, rest, protect, and care for them *His* way. We have not fully surrendered *all* our lives if we have not also submitted our bodies to Him. Not giving Him all of ourselves—even physically—can block us from His *full* peace, joy, and freedom. Let's imagine Jesus appearing to us in person and giving each of us a physical building—about which He requests, "I want you *personally* to keep this building clean and in good shape for Me because this is where I am going to pour out My presence and do some of My greatest miracles on earth!" We would faithfully tend that space— swept clean, polished, arranged with care, and kept ready for *His* use and purposes. Well, He *has* said this—about our *bodies*. Our bodies are sacred sanctuaries entrusted to us for special care—living temples where He *chooses* to dwell and to fulfill some of His most monumental miracles in the world.

So, in gratitude and worship, let's take holy care of ourselves physically. Let's *eat* well. Much confusing and even conflicting information about this runs rampant, but let's keep it simple: eat fruits and vegetables, lean protein, some healthy fats, and whole grains daily. Get rid of the junk, break the sugar addiction, and stop eating so much processed, "easy" food. Let's treat ourselves with something sweet here and there, but let's eat mostly for nourishment, not entertainment. Let's also drink *water.* Set a daily goal for water intake, and make it happen. This is easy to do and will exponentially change how we feel. As we're making these modifications, let's remember this: we'll hunger for whatever we feed ourselves. Once we start eating what's healthy, we'll soon begin wanting it. Our tastes and appetites will alter and adjust to whatever we feed on. Our flesh will cry and defy our efforts at first, but we must deny ourselves, and, eventually, right eating will lead to right craving. Eating right will make us *feel* right. When we eat well, anxiety fades, sluggishness lifts, and energy flows freely—bringing balance and beauty to body, soul, *and* spirit.

Let's also *move* our bodies—even if it's simply a daily walk, stepping into more healing and health one stride at a time. Literally, in the words of Jesus, let's, "Get up, and *walk!*" Simply start by setting a daily "step goal"—and once that endeavor is solid, incorporate some safe strength exercises several times a week and build muscle. If we lower our daily calories—but keep our protein up—and raise our daily steps, we'll *enjoy* the effects of this. Not only will this change us outwardly, but this will transform us inwardly. Obedience in caring for our bodies overflows us with deeper spiritual confidence and joy. We don't have to chase quick fixes or pour money into injections and medications to change what Jesus can transform through simple, *daily* decisions. Small shifts in our habits—fueling our bodies with life-giving food and moving with intention—can lead to profound change. As we honor Him even with our health, He'll *heal* us—more than just physically—and *fill* us with vibrant joy and a new depth of relationship with Him to enjoy.

Jesus also wants to give us godly *sleep.* Psalm 127:2 says that restful sleep is a sacred gift from a loving God—His gentle way of renewing those He cherishes. One translation of this verse even adds this: He will *"provide for His devoted lovers even while they sleep"* (Psalm 127:2

TPT). In Psalm 4:8 (TPT), the psalmist proclaims, *"I will lie down in sleep, and sleep comes to me at once"*—and then he testifies of the peace trusting God brings. In Proverbs 3:24 (TPT), we are promised that our sleep will be *"sweet and secure."* Through these and various other verses, it's clear that rest isn't random. Deep, restoring sleep is a gracious gift from Jesus Himself. Even science—study after study—echoes the same truth: we thrive on seven to nine hours of sleep each night. As people of Jesus, we're called to set up our lives in a way that makes room for His gifts—including *sleep*. He mentions it multiple times in His Word because He knows our deep need for it—and He longs to meet us even in *rest*.

So, let's not laugh about how little sleep we get—or proclaim to be people who "don't need much of it." The *kind* of—and *amount* of—sleep we're getting affects our awake time more than we're aware. If we're unable to sleep, let's ask Jesus *why*. This is an area that actually may need His *healing* as well. Restless nights often come wrapped in stress, worries, or the glow of late-night screens—habits that secretly steal our peace. Some may struggle with age or physical challenges that disrupt deep sleep's rhythm—but *hope* remains. Even as our bodies change, simple shifts—like calming routines, nourishing habits, lessening caffeine, and surrendering anxieties to Jesus—can restore restful nights. Let's also *unload* at night. Let's empty each regret, concern, offense, hurt, or fear from our hearts before we lie down. Pray all the way to *full* peace. It's even helpful—and *powerful*—to pick a verse to rehearse in our minds as we fall asleep. The Holy Spirit can take that truth and strengthen us spiritually *while* soothing us to sleep night after night. Deep, steady sleep is more than physical repair; it's spiritual renewal—and it's deeply needed. Physical sleep strengthens us *spiritually*, too. It renews our bodies *and* puts resilience in our spirits to face each day. Without it, we're fragile and live far from flourishing in the fruit the Holy Spirit faithfully fosters within us.

Let's also move our *money* more fully into Jesus' hands. Jesus can give us full freedom in our finances. No matter how out-of-control we've lived—or how much lack looms over our lives—Jesus can personally provide us a pattern to practice with our money that produces peace. Nothing else both blesses *and* stresses us like money—and we desperately need Jesus' methods for it. *He* can move each of us into a monthly plan for our money that will bring monumental change to our lives. As always with Him, He'll keep it simple and *doable*. No matter how much we make, His plan will look something like this: we set aside what we've decided to give to the church first; then, we cover bills; next, we set aside an amount to bless someone as the need arises or as the Holy Spirit leads us (which is *fun*—even if it's only a little); after that, we determine how much we can put into savings; and, finally, what remains goes to groceries and miscellaneous spending. If sticking to a plan means less dining out, then we trade takeout for the table. If it means fewer shopping sprees, we embrace simplicity. If it means packing lunches instead of buying them, we do it with purpose. When money feels tight, the answer isn't always making *more*. It's usually just spending *less*. There's always something we can live without, and the very thing we cling to most may be *the* thing Jesus is inviting us to release. Sometimes, what feels like sacrifice is really freedom in disguise. We'll actually find more happiness with less. We often think doing and having more increases our smile—but it actually makes us more stressed and strapped. With Jesus' help, we can gut our greed and grow into a God-honoring place of gratitude—and *contentment*. Our culture claims, "*More* is better!" while our wise Savior says, "*Less* is best!" He even said to the disciples as He sent them out, *"You won't need a lot of money"* (Matthew 10:9 TPT). Let's lean in and listen to Jesus, pursuing *His* plan for our personal money. When we follow Him and forgo spending that sparks regret, freedom blooms in our finances—and from there, it flows into *every* corner of life.

Another surprising yet sacred step to take towards spiritual breakthrough is this: *declutter* every space and place. A habit that harbors heaviness and robs joy—more than we realize—is to keep piles, bags, and boxes of things everywhere we can fit them. This task will topple the tallest weight off of our lives and provide more peace than we'd think: go room by room, closet by closet, drawer by drawer, and give away what's not being used—and throw away what *no* one would want. The clothes that don't fit and haven't been worn in a long time would bring the biggest smiles to faces who have hardly anything to wear. The dishes never used would be the greatest blessing to a family who doesn't have a full set. There are so many things in a lot of our homes that have had their day with us and are now supposed to belong to someone else. Clean out. Give things away. Let's bless others with all the extra overflowing in our homes. Let's also clear the stacks of papers and clutter on counters, in drawers, and across closet floors. As we undertake this, the unexpected will unfold: when we declutter our homes, Jesus will declutter our *hearts*. Subconsciously, piles, excess, and mess *stress* us. The opposite is true, too: decluttering—even our physical places—*frees* us. As we take time to go room by room like this in our spaces—filling both donation and trash bags—the whole atmosphere changes. *We* change. Even this very *natural* move will bring spiritual breakthroughs we didn't know we needed.

We'll find further freedom at our very fingertips—by putting down our *phones*. Phone addiction has evolved into an egregious epidemic—and not just among teens. Even adults cling to their screens—scrolling mindlessly in spare moments, tapping and texting while talking, and taking it to the bathroom like a trusted companion. Nearly every down moment is dedicated to it, and many of our faces stay lit by its glow until we shut our eyes at night. The phone funnels our focus, keeping us from recognizing what *really* matters in moments, enjoying the people around us, and—worst of all—communing with the Holy Spirit *constantly*. For way too many of us, the phone stands in the way of the Holy Spirit. Let's make this switch: in spare moments, before touching the phone, turn to the Holy Spirit. Let's ask Him if there's anything He wants to say or show us— anything He wants us to pray for. *Every* time we turn to Him, He'll touch us. This "high" from Him will always trump any "hit" from a phone. All day long, He stands by our side—*waiting* to speak, direct, encourage, heal, inspire, and fill us at *any* moment. *He* must become our go-to, not our phones. Let's limit our social media scrolling and posting and all our email-checking—and let's not take our phones to bed. This horrible habit hinders many moments of divine exchange and intimacy with the Holy Spirit. Let's see our phones as "stop signs" we unknowingly raise in the face of the Holy Spirit—signals that say "not now" to the very One who *longs* to lead, speak, and move in our lives constantly. When we lower those "stop signs" by setting our phones aside, we open the way for the Spirit's powerful presence to flow freely—turning *many* ordinary moments into extraordinary encounters.

Some of our struggles may seem less surface and more stuck deeply in us like roots. It can feel as if we were born with some battles. The truth is that we actually *were*. The Bible speaks of *generational curses*—patterns of sin, brokenness, and consequence passed from one generation of a family to the next. Exodus 20:5 addresses *"the iniquity of the fathers"* affecting future generations—not in the way of punishment for someone else's sin but because unrepented-for patterns persist and repeat. Just like we inherit our physical DNA from generations before us—the shade of our eyes, shapes of our bodies, and shifts in our health—we also carry the imprint of spiritual and emotional patterns, too. Issues such as fear, addiction, abuse, anger, insecurity, control, poverty, rebellion, divorce, and more can pass from one generation to the next—choking chains passed down like cherished heirlooms. However, we *don't* have to keep them. Jesus' Blood broke *every* curse—breaking us free to birth brand-new legacies. Galatians 3:13 (NIV) testifies, *"Christ redeemed us from the curse of the law by becoming a curse for us."* When we place these passed-down patterns and problems at Jesus' feet—by saying the sin, *really* repenting, and giving it *all* to Him— the cycle ceases. What ran rampantly in our family runs into His Blood, and it's both resolved *and* dissolved. It downright *disappears*. What generations before us started stops with us. Then, we have the powerful privilege to sow fresh seeds of strength and grace—planting holy habits that will bloom in the generations yet to come.

Let's bear down on breakthroughs in *every* broken pattern. Where have we been circling the same maddening mountain? Where have we been fettered but want to be free? Breakthrough isn't up to Jesus; it's up to *us*. That doesn't seem encouraging, but it *is*. Jesus has already finished the work that makes us free. He's already bought *all* our breakthroughs with His Blood. We just have to go get it. Here's how: first, let's be wholly and humbly honest with ourselves. What in our lives is not *healthy* or *holy?* The things we've justified or accepted repeatedly, the things we've known weren't quite right but have just tolerated and accelerated, the things we've wrestled with for years—*those* are what Jesus wants to *thoroughly* mend. Whether it's a habit that needs healing, a real hurt that needs releasing, or a higher level of love and patience that needs reaching, *anything* can happen. There's not one area that Jesus can't *completely* change. There's not one battle we can't *boldly* beat.

The Enemy has lied to many of us and told us things like this:

"That's just your *personality!*" "The *Lord* has put this on you!" "You'll *always* fight with this!" "It's too *late* to change this!" "This isn't *that* big of a deal!" "*Not* caring about this is freedom!" (He often tells us that something is "freedom"—like not truly caring about ourselves physically—when it's really *disobedience*.) Let's ask the Holy Spirit to be our "lie detector" and spotlight every lie that has fenced off freedom. Permit Him to be deeply honest. Let's *want* this. Then, let's pursue personal miracles. Ask the Holy Spirit what steps to take towards transformation, and take them bravely and obediently. Those steps may be painful at first, but we must push through to *full* breakthrough. There is *always* transformation on the other side of obedience—and the more difficult the steps, the more dramatic the miracle. Let's also not get tired of getting back up and doing it *again* daily. Spiritual deliverance is immediate, but walking it completely out in our natural reality takes diligence and discipline. This is because a drastic change involves rewiring brain pathways and revising deeply entrenched habits and patterns we've followed for years. This requires *determined* repetition. When we persevere, we'll reap a rich harvest of healing that will totally transform our lives.

So, let's not give up. Let's force our way to *full* freedom. We'll find that as we fight this fully in even one part of our lives, other places begin to shift as well. *Every* area we get aligned with His will and ways will open up windows through which supernatural peace, power, healing, and joy will pour in like light all over the place. Even a single, shining victory will set off a ripple of transformation. So, let's pursue healing in our hardest-to-change, most-stuck areas. These mountains *can* move and be removed. Let's lean into the Holy Spirit, listen, and let go of even long-lived, loved habits. Let's also recognize the recurring flaws of our relatives we're reliving, and let's repent. Let's shatter strongholds and fight for *full* freedom in every area—so that we bear His fruit all over our lives. *Anything* can change when Jesus is **known and near**, full victory keeps flowing as we keep growing in *relationship* with Him year after year.

Life is Lighter

Jesus wants us to *enjoy* our lives. His principal passion has always been—and will always be—to heal us and to fill us with His fruit—including His *joy*. He communicated it clearly: *"The thief comes only in order to steal and kill and destroy. I came that they may have and enjoy life, and have it in abundance [to the full, until it overflows]"* (John 10:10 AMP). He declares it again here: *"I have told you these things so that My joy and delight may be in you, and that your joy may be made full and complete and overflowing"* (John 15:11 AMP). Then, Romans 14:17 (NIV) reveals that the Kingdom of God is not defined by external rituals but by living a life of *"righteousness, peace, and joy in the Holy Spirit."* That means the life Jesus releases in us through relationship with Him not only refashions how we behave—but also revolutionizes how we *feel*. Our Savior doesn't just offer us survival. He came to dress us in a *"garment of praise"* in place of a *"spirit of heaviness"* (Isaiah 61:3 KJV). He came to flood our lives with uncommon *joy* and unexplainable *peace* that doesn't disappear even when difficulty appears. He came to make our lives *lighter*.

Look at Jesus' invitation to a lighter life: *"Are you tired? Worn out? Burned out on religion? Come to me. Get away with me and you'll recover your life. I'll show you how to take a real rest. Walk with me and work with me—watch how I do it. Learn the unforced rhythms of grace. I won't lay anything heavy or ill-fitting on you. Keep company with me, and you'll learn to* **live freely and lightly***"* (Matthew 11:28-30 MSG). When we draw near to Jesus—when we pause to simply be with Him, to know Him, and then rise to live life alongside Him—our hearts begin to move in the bright and light rhythms of His grace. Suddenly, people, problems, our past, and even the path ahead take on new clarity and perspective. From the depths of our spirits flow *His* joy, *His* peace, *His* strength—the very life that pulses in *Him*.

Jesus continually whispers, "Come to Me." He invites us to *sit* with Him sunrise after sunrise. As we do, our entire beings find *real* rest, renewal, and refreshment—day after day. As we unload our hearts and lovingly linger with Him and listen, He removes every weight, reminds us of truth, and refills us with His presence. Every time we sit down with Him, we rise up with *more* of Him. It's also in this sitting and seeking time that we find out what *He* wants us to do with the rest of our time. It's our culture that crowds our plate with too much to control or carry, *not* our Jesus. He doesn't put anything *"heavy"* or *"ill-fitting"* on us. People do—or *we* do. People have plans for us, and we often say "yes" to it all because we don't know our clear *call* from

Christ. So, we say yes to every request—not from choice but to dodge letting others down or to earn our worth through constant approval. However, as Jesus deepens our understanding of our standing with Him, He prunes our need to prove ourselves to people. We *know* who we are. We are *His*. We are *enough*—and we follow *His* plan. We no longer have to work to prove our worth to the world. We are freed up to say "no" to people and become fired up to say "yes" only to what *Jesus* reveals is right for us. This leads us to a life that is *light* and feels just *right*.

Then, we get up and walk with Him—doing *only* what He's directed—inviting His leadership and enjoying His love all day long. We lean in, listen to Him, and *love* Him moment after moment. His presence pours in like a running faucet—anointing us to handle the day with *direction* and *delight*. With our heads and hearts caught up in Him, we handle life like *He* would. We are anointed to have patience with problematic people, to opt out of offenses that could become obstacles, and to trust Him in trying trials and tests. When we make mistakes, we don't melt into a puddle of guilt and grief. We rise to our feet, receive His grace, and resume our going and growing. Not even bad news breaks us down to our shoes. We stand. We *trust*. We lean in and listen *again*. Encouragement rushes in like rain, washing away every reason to complain. We *know* He'll only use unforeseen trials to bring us growth and glory beyond what He could explain. All day long—even when things go wrong—we turn and talk to Him, and then encouragement and empowerment trickles from Him. We are still standing when we should have been knocked down—and still weightless with peace when we should be heavy with panic. Constant, on-our-feet relationship with Jesus helps us handle life right—and keeps us lastingly *light*.

We also enjoy the gifts He gives us throughout the day—*guilt-free*. We are no longer pained by our past—no longer crazed by constant condemnation. When guilt creeps in, we can crush it. We have been freed to receive the gift of His grace, sense the ceaseless smile on His face, and savor the delights He dispenses all over the place. We have been gutted of guilt—and in its place, He's planted *gratitude*. Our Father enjoys giving good gifts to His children. He endlessly blesses us—just to make us smile. He *"richly provides us with everything to enjoy"* (I Timothy

6:17 ESV). James 1:17 (AMP) echoes this: *"Every good thing given and every perfect gift is from above; it comes down from the Father."* Our lives should be lived *relishing* every good thing given—the first breath in the morning, the food we eat, the fun we have, the fellowship with Him that never falters—down to the final moment of the day. Every bit and spot of joy that pops up in our lives is a present from our Father. Every sunrise, every sip of coffee, every smile from a friend, every Sunday church service—each birthday party, each dinner date, each needed nap, each baseball game, each early-morning hunt—they're *all* gifts given from Him. We are to *enjoy* it all—expressing praise and thanks. With Jesus, we *get* to live with gratitude, which is a gift in itself. Living in constant thankfulness is like flipping on an inner light switch. It shines in every shadowed corner of our existence, casts a glow over our circumstances—literally both lightening *and* lighting up our very lives.

We also live free from heavy *regret*. Our Redeemer redeems even our remorse. We may glance back at our past and cringe at our sin—or we may look back on time missed with people and wish to have it again. Jesus wants to tenderly turn our focus forward. Even Paul—who had many *real* regrets—expressed this: *"I focus on this one thing: Forgetting the past and looking forward to what lies ahead. I press on to reach the end of the race and receive the heavenly prize for which God, through Christ Jesus, is calling us"* (Philippians 3:13-14 NLT). When regret continues to weigh on us, Jesus wants to lift it off of us. If we'll place our regrets in His hands—what we missed and lost in the past—He'll replant them like seeds in our future and grow something *more*. It may sprout up as more sensitive and spot-on behavior in an area—a lesson learned that leads us to radical righteousness (2 Corinthians 7:11). It may grow up from the ground as a past moment rewound—a chance to do it again and, *this* time, win. It may also bloom endlessly in eternity—especially if it has to do with the loss of a loved one. There's more *there* than we'll ever have here. In Heaven, everything deepens, widens, and brightens—even in relationships. We'll know our believing loved ones again, only more fully—with *greater* joy and closeness than earth ever allowed. Together, we'll make richer memories that never fade, relishing moments that'll never end. What felt lost will be found—redeemed, restored, and *richer* than before. So, we don't have to cling to regret or fret over what we lost. We move forward with freeing hope. The relationships we cherished most aren't gone; they're just ahead, *waiting*—and there will be more to the story. For loved ones who died without knowing Him, our grief is *real*—but He can *still* turn it into comfort, and their lives can compel us to live *more* fully for Jesus, carrying their memory. So, let's hand our heavy regrets to the Redeemer, and He'll trade them for lightness. With Him, even regret gets rolled into *glory*.

A life lived in this rhythm—of sitting and walking with Jesus, expressing gratitude, and handing over our regrets—becomes a melody, and its sound is *joy*. Jesus' joy is a deep, inner gladness that radiates through the understanding that our sins are forgiven, our burdens have been lifted, our lives lie in His loving hands, and our Jesus delights in constant relationship with us. This gladness remains even in grief. His joy isn't fleeting—only flowing on perfect, peaceful days. It's a fruit deeply rooted in our spirits—flowing and flourishing even when it rains and storms. That's because He *never* leaves, and this joy comes from Jesus: in His presence is *"fullness of joy"* (Psalm 16:11 NLT). This joy doesn't ignore our pain; it outlasts it. Even when life is heavy, His joy lifts our spirits—and when our tears fall, they just water joy's roots. That's why Paul could pen, *"Always be joyful,"* even from prison (1 Thessalonians 5:16 NLT). The Bible explains that this joy is our strength (Nehemiah 8:10). When life gets heavy—like it did for Paul— Jesus' joy keeps us *light*. It gives us the power to endure, persevere, and live boldly—even when life is going badly. His joy jolts us with strength, resilience, and hope. This is what makes people praise persistently—even in illness, loss, and devastation. This joy is powerful—and *perpetual*.

That's because it's the same joy that flows from Heaven. Psalms 46:4 (TPT) reveals this: *"God has a constantly flowing river whose sparkling streams bring joy and delight to His people; His river flows right through the city of God Most High into His holy dwelling places."* We are those *"holy dwelling places"* (I Corinthians 3:16, Ephesians 2:22, John 7:38). The same joy that rushes through the rivers and veins of those in Heaven races right into the spirits of those who are Heaven-bound on earth, too. This means we don't have to walk weighed down by the melancholy moods of our world. We get to live *lifted* by the actual atmosphere of Heaven—right here on earth. We have joy when there should be sorrow, peace when there should be panic, and hope when most would give up. Heaven isn't just our future home; it's the source of our present strength.

His *peace* pours out right alongside His joy, too. These are two of the greatest gifts and most fascinating fruits Jesus produces in His people. Like His joy, the peace Jesus gives isn't fragile or fleeting; it's a gift, not earned or manufactured, but given from His own heart to those who walk in close relationship with Him. He referred to this in John 14:27 (NLT): *"I am leaving you with a gift—peace of mind and heart. And the peace I give is a gift the world cannot give. So don't be troubled or afraid."* His peace is steady and sustaining—even in uncertainty. He keeps His people in *"perfect peace"* as they trust in Him and fix their thoughts on Him (Isaiah 26:3 NLT). This is a peace that comes as we pray; it *"exceeds anything we can understand"* and guards our hearts and minds (Philippians 4:6-7 NLT). His peace makes us steady and strong on the inside—even as chaos swirls outside. It feels like His arms wrapped fully around us—holding us securely—in the middle of a storm. We see the wind stirring, but it doesn't shake us; His presence wraps us in a stillness, and *that* is what we feel. Without His presence, we live in inner unrest—blown by the wind and bombarded with fear, anxiety, and pressure to hold it all together ourselves. With Him, life feels lighter—lifted by a joy and a peace that free us to walk confidently and cheerfully even when the world feels heavy.

We are also lightened and lifted by sharing in His *strength*. Beyond filling us with joy and peace, Jesus also strengthens us supernaturally—totally empowering us to rise above life's challenges. Without Jesus, life is *a lot*. Towering to-do lists, crying kids, terrible traffic, unforeseen uproars, money matters, challenging careers or classes, rough relationships, harrowing health issues—we have to handle *a lot*. Life can often feel like *too* much. This is because we were never meant to live life by our own might. We were *always* meant to live with a strength that makes us soar. Isaiah 40:28-29 (TPT) describes our Creator as One who *"never gets weary or worn out,"* whose *"intelligence is unlimited,"* and who *"empowers the feeble and infuses the powerless with increasing strength."* The next verse points out how tired and exhausted even young and fit people can become because of life, and then it expresses this extraordinary truth: *"But those who entwine their hearts with Yahweh will experience divine strength. They will rise up on soaring wings and fly like eagles, run their races without growing weary, and walk through life without giving up"* (Isaiah 40:30-31 TPT). When we constantly expect, look for, hope in, and include Him in all our endeavors, we will encounter Him—*and* experience His empowering strength. When we reach the end of *our* ability, creativity, productivity, and even stability—He still stands *full* of possibility.

This strength isn't reserved for crisis or catastrophe; it meets us in the repeated rhythms of *ordinary* days, too. We experience it when we still surging panic and breathe in prayer—when we pause to seek Him instead of spinning in our own sinking strength throughout the day. His power slips into the smallest, most strained corners of our lives, saturating our places of pressure and giving us the lift to rise, run, and remain resilient without wearing out. It shows up in the simplest, seemingly insignificant moments, too—like tackling a towering to-do list with patience, listening attentively to a tired child, folding yet another pile of laundry with peace, handling hours of homework without wavering, or offering kindness to someone who frustrates us. When we invite Jesus into these everyday efforts, He doesn't merely help us endure; He empowers us to excel in finding joy and gladness in even the most mundane moments of life.

As we deepen in relationship with Jesus, He develops powerful, *internal* fruit within us. Through gentle tending and necessary pruning, He heals the way we see ourselves, reshapes our character, and brings breakthrough where we were broken and stuck. He forms healthier rhythms and holier habits—and from deep within us begins to flow a steady joy, a settled peace, and a resilient strength that lifts the weight from everyday life. With Him close and faithfully forming us day by day, the road feels freer, our burdens less binding, each breath more restful, because life is lighter when Jesus is truly **known and near**—and the fruit He plants within us blooms and thrives, touching and transforming *every* part of our lives.

CHAPTER ELEVEN

He Uses Us Publicly

"Each believer has received grace gifts, so use them to serve one another as faithful stewards of the many-colored tapestry of God's grace…If you have a speaking gift, speak as though God were speaking His words through you. If you have the gift of serving, do it passionately with the strength God gives you so that in everything God alone will be glorified through Jesus Christ."—1 Peter 4:10-11 (TPT)

A Heart for People

As we progress in relationship with Jesus, He doesn't just grow grace quietly in the corners of our hearts; He bears fruit *through* our lives—fruit that spills outward, shaping and shining in the lives of those around us as well. Matthew 5:16 (NIV) mandates active, visible faith that impacts people: *"Let your light shine before others, that they may see your good deeds and glorify your Father in Heaven."* Jesus doesn't merely make us like Him on the inside; He moves through us to reveal Him on the outside. However, before this fruit can flourish and flow, He must *deeply* till the soil, pull up weeds, and plant new seeds in another area: how we see and feel about *people*.

People are our Father's *heart*. Let's remember that *all* people first existed in His heart before they entered their mothers' wombs. He dreamed up and designed *every* face. He held every hand and knew each heart before it beat—prophesying destiny even before conception. What He spoke to Jeremiah, He'd say to us all: *"Before I shaped you in the womb, **I knew you intimately.** I had divine plans for you* *before I gave you life, and I set you apart and chose you to be mine"* (Jeremiah 1:5 TPT). *Every* person matters. Our Father's heart longs for *every* life to come close in relationship with Him—even the *most* ungodly. He *"does not want any to perish but all to come to repentance"* (2 Peter 3:9 TPT). The Father that watches and waits for the lost ones to come home—He's *that* Father for *every* person (Luke 15:20). He's the Shepherd who would leave the ninety-nine sheep and sprint in search of the *one* who has strayed—and who would frantically forage for the *one* concealed coin until it's finally found (Luke 15:1-10). Our Father doesn't see crowds; He sees individuals. His love longs to make *each* one His—and *each* one healed. If our hearts are wholly His, *we* will, too.

Both Jesus *and* His Word teach and preach this clearly and consistently. Even when asked which was *"the most important commandment in the law,"* Jesus responded with this: *"'You must love the Lord your God with all your heart, all your soul, and all your mind.' This is the first and greatest commandment. A second is* **equally important***: 'Love your neighbor as yourself.' The entire law and all the demands of the prophets are based on these two commands"* (Matthew 22:36-40 NLT). Genuine love for Jesus—and for *others*—is the foundation of everything He desires of us. It's just as important to the Father that we truly love *others* as it is that we fully love *Him.* He even proclaims this plainspoken point: *"If anyone says, 'I love God,' and hates (works against) his [Christian] brother, he is a liar; for the one who does not love his brother whom he has seen, cannot love God whom he has not seen"* (I John 4:20 AMP). Genuine love for our God will *always* grow into God-like love for *people.*

As the Holy Spirit works this wonder in our hearts, He'll withdraw us from warring *with* people and weave us into warring *for* them. Instead of eye-balling people as our enemies, we'll realize our true battle isn't against *"flesh and blood"* but against the powers of darkness (Ephesians 6:12 AMP). Instead of living in irritation against people, we'll live with compassion for people. Instead of seeing the surface, we'll see souls. Apart from Jesus, we misunderstand, measure, and mock people. With Jesus, we notice, nurture, and naturally *love* people. We will no longer see people as problems or projects. We'll see them as *precious.* We'll see them through eyes like we would have had in Eden. Before the Fall, we would have naturally noticed each divine detail and the unique portion of God's glory poured into each person. We would have *only* admired one another in awe. In our fallen state, however, we focus on flaws and frigidly *judge*. Jesus even restores *this*—gives us Eden-eyes that see beneath the surface and spot splendor and significance instead. We'll lay eyes on people—even the *messiest* ones—and our hearts will well up with the Father's love. With hearts awakened like this by the Spirit, we become reflections of God's own love—seeing, valuing, and fighting for others as *cherished* treasures. Our hearts are restored to the place He intended in Eden: pulsing and pouring with love for both Him *and* the people He made in His image.

With hearts healed toward people, we will move into Jesus' *mission* for mankind. He's called us to cherish people so much that we go into all the world in search of who's lost and bring them to Him no matter the cost (Matthew 28:19-20, Mark 16:15, Luke 19:10, I Corinthians 9:22). He even shared a story that shines light on exactly what He meant—one that flowed from a question asked by a religious scholar fishing for answers. Jesus had just quoted the love-your-neighbor-as-yourself commandment, and the man joltingly questioned: *"What do you mean by 'my neighbor'?"* (Luke 10:29 TPT). Jesus shared the story of a stranger who is badly beaten and then abandoned in a ditch—bleeding and left to breathe his last (Luke 10:30-37). Two religious leaders in a row see him from the road but rush to the other side and ride away. A Samaritan—a man of a reviled race—then spots the suffering man. Immediately, he rushes to *rescue* him. As he beholds the bleeding man, his heart, too, begins to bleed with boundless compassion. He stoops down to stop the seeping blood—pouring out oil and wine over his wounds and wrapping him with both bandages and *love*. He carries him to an inn, secures a room, pays his way, and promises to return. This simple story shows us still today that our "neighbor" is *anyone* in *need*—whether we know them or not, whether they're *like* us or not. True love doesn't just feel pity; it purposely *acts*. It unselfishly sacrifices. To love like Jesus is to live like the Samaritan—with eyes that see, hearts that break, and hands that reach.

We live and love wide open—everywhere we go, to everyone we meet. We don't just pay attention to our own interests *"but also to the interests of others"* (Philippians 2:4 ESV). We don't step into a store and rush and push past people—aiming to stick to our schedule. When we see a need, we have feet that *stop*. We help the perturbed person pick up dropped items, and we empathize with the emotional employee. We have ears that *listen*. We chat with the crying child and halt to hear the falling-apart friend. We have mouths that *pray*. We grab the hands of the waitress under the weight of heartache and lift her load to the Lord even mid-meal. We also have wallets that *pay*. We hand over dollars to the man counting his too-few coins at the checkout counter; we give generously to the girl who's going on a mission abroad. We become *people*-lovers and *need*-meeters. No one is unimportant, no need insignificant. *Each* is worth our time and every dime. The Holy Spirit will lead us to live and love *this* boldly—seeing, stopping, giving— turning every moment into a chance to change a life for eternity.

So, let's ask the Holy Spirit to make this love bloom within us bountifully. As He responds and reworks the ground of our hearts, let's know that He'll have to pull up the weeds of *prejudice,* too. The Samaritan did not see *race*; he just saw a bleeding face. We, too, must see people as *people*—in every nation and neighborhood. We must tear up our prejudices and tear down our barriers. It is evil to turn up our noses at differences in skin color, addresses, or even denominations. It's the devil who divides. He paints our minds with lies and even tells us that it's "wise" to keep to our kind and shut off new ties. Yet, Jesus calls us beyond these walls—in schools, neighborhoods, workplaces, churches, and cities alike. Let's be people who crush cliques, share stories with foreign-born neighbors over fences and around our tables, build relationships across skin colors at school and work, and welcome believers from every denomination with open arms. It is only by His grace and the Spirit's power that we become *one*. Only *Jesus* can make us convinced that the same blood flows through all our veins. Only *He* can make us committed to loving *every* neighbor equally. When He unfolds this unity within us, His heart is demonstrated to a divided world. Jesus loves without division, and when His love flows through *us*, it breaks barriers, heals hearts, and ignites hope—in *every* neighbor and even *entire* neighborhoods.

Jesus takes this deeper *still*. He leads us to love *all* people— even the ones who agitate, anger, and appall us—without excusing sin or giving cold judgment, with hearts willing to remain *warm* while praying and interceding for them. A variety of verses implore us to be deeply, *uncommonly* merciful, patient, kind, and forgiving. Colossians 3:13 (TPT) clearly calls us to *this* kind of character: to be merciful as we *"endeavor to understand others,"* to be compassionate as we show *"kindness to all,"* to be gentle and humble—even *"unoffendable"* in our patience with others—to tolerate the weak and to forgive peoples' faults. This passage then proclaims, *"Love becomes the mark of true maturity"* (Colossians 3:14 TPT). These next verses also describe the very deep, mature love the Lord lavishes on us *and* that He expects us to lend to others: *"Love is patient and kind. Love is not jealous or boastful or proud or rude. It does not demand its own way. It is not irritable, and it keeps no record of being wronged…Love never gives up, never loses faith, is always hopeful, and endures through every circumstance"* (I Corinthians 13:4-7 NLT). Both of these passages point our hearts to the kind of love that has *patience* with problematic people. We will know when the Holy Spirit fully floods our hearts with Jesus' love for people when we can genuinely embrace—even pray for and intercede on behalf of—the most irritating, annoying—and even *appalling*—ones around us. When we are moved to compassion and patience with them, we are loving more like *Him.* We have grown into a greater maturity.

Yet, Jesus dared to take it even deeper. We aren't just to love annoying people; we are to lavish love on *offending* people. The ones that spread the rumors, start the fights, steal our stuff, and strip our confidence—even *these* Jesus says to love with *ease*. Heed His words in Matthew 5:44-45 (TPT): *"I say to you, **love your enemy**, bless the one who curses you, do something wonderful for the one who hates you, and respond to the very ones who persecute you by praying for them. For that will reveal your identity as children of your heavenly Father."* If we *ask* and *allow* Him to, the Holy Spirit can shape our hearts so fully into the form of the Father's that our response to hurt is no longer to hit back, snap back, and *get* back the one who harmed us. Though we may feel human hurt, out of our hearts will *flow* the Lord's love—and we will bless, pray, and *care* about even our offenders. This kind of freedom and maturity is possible. It's a wonderful work of the Holy Spirit—one we should *seek*. He can heal our hearts so wholly that it can hold no hate, not even towards those who hate and hurt *us.*

We will even resist *revenge*. Here's Jesus' view on vengeance: *"I say to you, do not resist an evil person [who insults you or violates your rights]; but whoever slaps you on the right cheek, turn the other toward him also [simply ignore insignificant insults or trivial losses and do not bother to retaliate—maintain your dignity, your self-respect, and your poise]"* (Matthew 5:39 AMP). Jesus calls His people to pause and stay in peace even when verbally or physically smacked. We are to rise above retaliation. It is *easy* to hit back or shout back when struck. It is *holy* to stand in grace—*real* strength—and trust in Jesus' justice. When we are humiliated, we don't retaliate; we don't drop down to the offender's low level and fight. We stand in a supernatural inner strength—in *His* might—and we trust Jesus to make it right.

Romans 12:14-19 lays this out unmistakably: the Lord commands us to bless those who persecute us, pray for them, and never repay evil with evil. He then explains what to do instead: *"Leave that to the righteous anger of God. For the Scriptures say, 'I will take revenge; I will pay them back,' says the Lord. Instead, 'If your enemies are hungry, feed them. If they are thirsty, give them something to drink. In doing this, you will heap burning coals of shame on their heads.' Don't let evil conquer you, but conquer evil by doing good"* (Romans 12:19-21 NLT). We are clearly called to bless, not blast. When people pain us, we don't respond with payback but with patience—showing uncommon, unexpected *kindness*. Even when let down, we let *love* lead—leaving justice to Jesus, who promises to repay on our behalf. We will never overcome evil by matching it; instead, we outshine it with *good*.

How is it possible for *anyone* to answer aggression with such grace? When betrayed, berated, lied about, or let down, we will *always* feel fury. Anger will *always* be the signal that wrong has been wrought. However, the Word warns not to *sin* or to *stay* in our anger: *"Be angry [at sin—at immorality, at injustice, at ungodly behavior], yet do not sin; do not let your anger [cause you shame, nor allow it to] last until the sun goes down"* (Ephesians 4:26 AMP). In our anger, we can't let sin win. Our flesh will *want* to yield to yelling and rebelling, but—by the power of the Holy Spirit—we *can* stand firm in His strength and not give in. On the spot, we turn our whole selves to the Spirit inside, imploring His strength to swell within us and quell the fight around us. We pause and pray—right there inside—and patience arrives. We say something soothing to stop the spat—remembering that *"a soft answer turns away wrath, but a harsh word stirs up anger"* (Proverbs 15:1 ESV). If the offender offers additional arguments, we turn and walk away without wavering—withdrawing from the would-be *war*.

Then—later—when left alone with our anger—we *finish* the fight before it becomes night. We do *not* take our offenses to bed (Ephesians 4:26). We obey by pressing in to *pray* for our offenders instead (Romans 12:14, Matthew 5:44). We take our temper and torment to the Throne. We speak their names and tell our offenses, and we take on Jesus' heart that graciously blesses. We wholeheartedly ask *Him* to help *them*—and we don't stop praying until our seething anger softens into sympathy. We may come to Him mad, but we will end up *moved*. He performs a miracle when we obey and pray for those who hurt us: He clears our hearts of destroying offense and charges it with compassion—with mountains *more* of His love even for the one who dealt out the "shove." *Each* time we pray for those who pained us, we unlock Heaven's power to soften hearts and shut down Satan. Remember that our true war is *not* with people but with our spiritual enemy (Ephesians 6:12). People's attacks are really Satan's assaults—meant to wound and weigh us down, to heavy our hearts with overrunning offense. When we pray our offenses away, we dismantle one dark scheme after another—closing the gates to Hell's campaigns and causing a flood of Heaven's love that breaks chains.

Then, we give feet to this freedom—and this part becomes *fun*. Jesus directs us to pray for our persecutors in private but then to provide for them in public. He said to *give* to them when seen hungry or thirsty, to *"do something wonderful for the one who hates [us]"* (Romans 12:20, Matthew 5:44 TPT). He reminds us that our Father shines the sun and releases rain on both the just *and* unjust—and when we do good even to those who do wrong, we are *"acting as true children of [our] Father in Heaven"* (Matthew 5:45 NLT). When the way we war with those who do wrong becomes giving *gifts*—we will know that our hearts truly *do* beat like our Father's. Our world flings insults when fighting, and it kills, steals, and destroys. In God's Kingdom, we war with powerful praying and wonderful giving, and it awakens, convicts, and saves. When we pray over our offenders, we open a door to the Holy Spirit in their lives, and then our "doing good" does even *more*. As we verbally give compliments, intentionally cheer them on, and even unexpectedly give them gifts, we *"heap burning coals of shame on their heads"*

(Romans 12:20 NLT). This metaphor means our kindness could lead to their deep *conviction,* which could cause them to reflect and repent. It's a picture of the powerful, purifying effect of genuine, godly *love.* As we do this, delight ignites in our hearts. There is *fun* in this kind of *freedom.* We can become people who trade hating for healing—who walk in a power so pure it pours unexpected goodness like rain on even the ones who've caused pain. In loving like this, we stand unshaken—flooded with a joy that Hell itself can't weaken.

In short, here's our plan for *peace* and *power* when offended: first, we respond to rudeness with kindness. When someone insults us, we don't fire back. We stay grounded in grace. Then, we pray regularly for the people who hurt us. This prayer both softens *our* hearts and opens the door for the Lord to work in *theirs.* Next, we do something kind on purpose. When someone wrongs us at work, scorns us at school, or even humiliates us at home, we write an encouraging note or do something unexpectedly helpful or thoughtful—not because it's deserved but because we're living out of His love and fighting the *right* war. We also speak well of them behind their backs. We don't join in on gossip or criticism. When their names come up, we compliment. We cover the one who criticized us—and we let Jesus deal out justice. Vengeance is *His* (Romans 12:19). We let Him handle what's unfair while our hearts live free from harbored hate. When we love like this, it transforms lives. Through our private prayer and public kindness to our persecutors, He will open blind eyes, soften hardened hearts, and change deeply-set minds. When we allow an outpouring of Jesus' love on the scene of our offense like this, it becomes an *opportunity* for Him to make Himself **known** and **near.** They will look at us and see *Him*—and *that* is an eternal win.

However, let this be clear: this kind of forgiveness and kindness does not mean we enable *abuse.* We can show grace while walking in wisdom and setting limits. We can build boundaries and set up space between our offenders and ourselves—but *still* without hatred in our hearts. Proverbs 22:3 (ESV) encourages wisdom and self-protection: *"The prudent sees danger and hides himself, but the simple go on and suffer for it."* We are not to passively endure harm. Jesus calls us to love and forgive our enemies, but He never calls us to remain in abusive or destructive situations. Whether we are teens or adults, we seek shelter and support in situations like these. Yet, as we wisely get away, we *still* send hate on its way. We *always* heed His words about hatred: *"But now put away and rid yourselves [completely] of all these things: anger, rage, **bad feeling toward others**, curses and slander, and foulmouthed abuse and shameful utterances from your lips!"* (Colossians 3:8 AMPC). Why would he request this of us even when abused? A heart that holds hate can't *heal*. So, even about those who harm us the harshest, He says, "Give them to Me—along with your hate!" He *still* says to pray for them—and we pray until our hate gives way to *hope*. When needed, we talk it out with one who can give *true*, healing, godly counsel, too. Sometimes, this takes *time*, but we don't give up. We don't stop until we heal and experience the most moving miracle of all: a heart that *still* beats with love for the one who hurt us *most*.

To love even our greatest offender means we've taken root in the very depths of our Father's heart. When we become grounded *there*—in that place where love flows freely to *all*, no matter what they've done—we are *truly* free. Life after life will be touched and transformed by experiencing Jesus' love through us so unexpectedly, so unmistakably. We'll be the kind of people they'll see and say, "Jesus *must* be as real as He claimed to be!" He'll become beautifully, powerfully **known** and **near** through us—drawing others toward the relationship with Him *they* were born to have, too.

He Uses Our Gifts

Inside each of us, Jesus has also planted *talent*. Just as He'll water, grow, and produce fruit in our character, He'll do likewise in our *creativity*. Each of us is born with multiple natural gifts. We're born inherently with abilities such as an athlete, artist, or arborist—with talent for writing, singing, drawing, teaching, leading, cooking, counseling, planning, decorating, organizing, analyzing, designing, building, or even fixing. The list of human crafts and capabilities is nearly endless. Our creative God has given *each* of us our own outlets of originality—gifts He desires to develop and deploy for *His* glory. These talents aren't random; they're heaven-assigned and purpose-filled. These gifts aren't unimportant either; they're meant to be recognized, refined, and released—*not* to impress people for a moment but to *impact* them for *eternity*.

Let's identify our inherent abilities. What do we enjoy doing? What gifts bring both us *and* others joy when we employ them? Let's not see them as "small." The enemy always downplays gifts of great anointing. He can perceive the power of our potential even when *we* can't. We'll pen a poem on a page during class, and he'll put it down, calling it "pointless." We'll strum and sing in solitude, but he'll say, "This would be pathetic in *public!*" That business idea burning in our hearts—he'll douse it with doubt before it ever sees daylight. He'll say we're "without gifts," even when every space we touch turns serene and pristine—each shelf, each hanger, each drawer organized with brilliance. He'll title us "talentless" while we're quietly solving what breaks at our job—when we're the very ones who patch what's torn, untangle what's knotted, and make the impossible run smoothly again. We *each* brim with brilliant gifts from our God. None of them are small, and each carries His call. Each one is *sacred*—even the ones that *scare* us. Let's ask the Spirit to awaken each one, and watch as what the enemy mercilessly mocked becomes what God miraculously multiplies.

The Bible even says to use these gifts boldly: *"God has given each of you a gift from his great variety of spiritual gifts. Use them well to serve one another. Do you have the gift of speaking? Then speak as though God himself were speaking through you. Do you have the gift of helping others? Do it with all the strength and energy that God supplies. Then everything you do will bring glory to God through Jesus Christ"* (1 Peter 4:10-11 NLT). He encourages us to use our gifts as if God *Himself* were doing it. That's because He desires to put His hands, mouth, and power into *our* gifts and touch the world around us. It's obvious and undeniable how a yielded voice—singing *or* speaking His truth—can become the vessel through which He stirs souls awake to His presence. It's also plain how a writer's pen can be picked up by the hand of God and pour words onto a page that will propel healing into a heart. However, He desires to use *all* gifts. Not as obvious, yet just as real, His hands move through the party-planner, too—lifting burdens, weaving joy, and crafting unforgettable moments that linger long after the last guest leaves. Our coffee shop could become His sanctuary—a haven steeped in His presence, where conversations spark life-changing moments and the warmth of rest replenishes weary souls. Our lawn-cutting business could become a ministry of mercy—lifting burdens from those who struggle and cultivating moments where interactions with us become encounters with Jesus. On and on these examples could go. Whatever is in our hands and hearts—even if just two fish and a loaf of bread—Jesus desires to take it in His hands and multiply it into *much* (John 6:1-14). He longs to use each of *our* gifts for *His* glory.

So, let's uncover our gifts and nurture them into *full* bloom. Practice really does make perfect; it both prepares us and propels our *potential*. Wherever we're gifted, we have the responsibility to *grow* it. So, if it's writing, then let's work with words—week after week. If it's preaching, let's scribble down scriptures and sermons and practice sharing them—rehearsing in private before ever stepping on a stage. If it's design and decorating, we can experiment and elevate— room by room, right within our own homes. Let's research and refine our crafts. Let's explore what's possible—what *we* are capable of. Let's do it *daily*. Let's be like David—the young, pre-king shepherd playing his harp in the pasture. Before David ever performed for a person, he practiced in front of sheep. As he poured out more and more notes over the grass, the Lord poured out more and more anointing on the gift. As he practiced—not to be seen in front of people—he grew in both ability *and* anointing. Years later, when a harpist was requested in the palace, David was fetched (1 Samuel 16:14-21). During the years he practiced in the pasture, he was preparing for the palace—without even knowing it. It was a seemingly "small" ability—but one that He faithfully fostered to the point of flourishing—that first brought him to the place of his destiny. It was this natural talent that he had diligently developed—and the Lord had anointed—that transferred him from a pasture to a palace. Fully sharpened, *our* gifts will direct us through doors to *our* destiny, too.

Let's let Jesus have and hone all our abilities. Let's also remember that when our gifts put us on platforms, it's never for *our* fame; it's so that we can proclaim *His* Name. Through a booming business, a thriving teaching position, or an ascending athletic career— wherever our name is known and our voice is heard, we're to point to *Jesus*. If our talents take us to the spotlight, it's so that we can shine it on *Him*. Wherever we're seen or heard, we speak for Him and act like Him—giving others a glimpse of our great and gracious God. When our hearts stay humble and we remain *His* when our talent is seen, He'll *keep* us on the scene—because He's not just looking at our talent; He's looking for a heart He can trust. He craves *character* that He can count on—that will completely convey who *He* is. When He finds both gifting *and* integrity in us, He'll amplify our influence and anchor it in eternity. If we live learning and leveraging our talents, leaning them into Him, and letting Him use them *His* way, we'll thrive in success and in *purpose*. He will use our surrendered gifts to touch hearts and take territory for His Kingdom. Talents grown and given back to Him will not just produce personal achievements; they will make an eternal impact. We'll bear fruit that will not fail—fruit that forms faith in others and flourishes on earth *and* in eternity.

So, let's see our natural gifts as *supernatural*—unique abilities He's put in us to employ *through* us. Let's leave *no* talent uncovered or gift unused—at *any* age. Too many people die with breakthrough-bringing books unwritten or healing-holding songs unsung. Too many people could have had a professional place in their sport but stopped short. Too many people lie in the ground with world-changing inventions or cancer-destroying cures still lying in *them*. The world is aching for hope, healing, and Heaven to break in—and He comes in through the gifts He's given His people. He releases many of *His* gifts through His *peoples'* gifts. So, let's let Him have them *all*. When we surrender our gifts, we step into our *assignments*. The world needs what He'd release through us—even that ability the enemy's belittled. Let's be brave and not take *one* gift to the grave.

He Releases *His* Gifts

The Holy Spirit houses His *own* power-packed gifts, too—ones that He'll give us opportunities to operate in that go beyond our human abilities. In 1 Corinthians 12:8-10, Paul shows us the Spirit's gifts in action: the gift to offer wise counsel, the gift to reveal hidden knowledge, the gift to inspire unshakable faith, the gift to bring healing, the gift to perform miracles, the gift to speak prophecy, the gift to discern spirits, the gift to speak in unknown languages, and the gift to interpret what is spoken. These abilities are not reserved for an elite few; they are given to ordinary believers for extraordinary purposes. Through these gifts, the Holy Spirit continues to make Himself **known** and bring His presence **near**—bearing witness to believers and unbelievers alike that Jesus is *still* active and at work in the world today.

Many people in the Bible placed firm faith in Jesus when they saw a supernatural miracle happen—whether it was a body healed, a prophetic word spoken, or some other wonder worked by the Holy Spirit through a person. This *still* transpires today. The Spirit's gifts can be released to *any* of us. What would happen in our homes, schools, and workplaces if we began to *ask* for and flow in the Spirit's greatest gifts? Maybe we've never pictured the Spirit moving through *us* like this—or maybe we've tried but then doubt drew us back. Some already freely flow in these gifts—but what if we *all* pressed in, hungry to be used in new, unimagined, completely supernatural ways? He doesn't pour out His power on only a few; it's for *any* heart that *asks*. There's no reason this can't be *us*. All that's needed is a deeper understanding and a heart fully positioned to pursue being used in this way—where Heaven's purposes and power can be seen and experienced in full.

Let's remember that the Bible is a book of *miracles*. Story after story, page after page—the Word brims with and boasts of the witnessed wonders of our God. He longs that our very *lives* do, too. The same mighty works we study in the Word can be on display through our lives today. The exact same miracle-working power that poured out of Jesus—and then Peter, Paul, and others—that healed the sick, opened blind eyes, restored the lame, called hundreds to repentance at once, and sparked revival everywhere it was demonstrated can flow in and through us today. We were not given anything less *today* than what they were granted *then*.

In fact, while Jesus walked the earth, He was filled with the *same* Holy Spirit we are. However, Jesus didn't simply have the Holy Spirit inside Him; He *surrendered* so fully that the Spirit completely consumed Him, bursting forth in power that radiated from Him and flowed through everything He did. We can catch this clearly in the account of the woman who had been badly bleeding for twelve years (Matthew 9:20-22, Mark 5:25-34, Luke 8:43-48). No doctor could mend her, and her money had melted away—but someone mentioned that *Jesus* was moving through her town one day. Despite the crowd, her condition, and the crude stigma surrounding her sickness, she sought out *Jesus*, believing that *one* touch of His hem would heal her. Full of faith and fierce courage, she forged through the crowd and laid a finger on the fringe of His robe—and, *immediately*, the flow of blood froze. As soon as she touched His hem, *"Jesus knew at once that someone had touched Him, for He felt the power that always surged around Him had passed through Him for someone to be healed"* (Mark 5:30 TPT). The Holy Spirit's power and presence pulsed through Him—pouring out of Him even without a word. It was drawn by raw, reaching faith. This *same* Spirit—the one who surged through Jesus and spilled out healing at the touch of faith— is the *very* Spirit who now lives and moves within *us* today.

Likewise, Peter—a man who once sold *out* Jesus in fearful betrayal but later sold out *to* Him in faithful surrender—experienced the same surging power at work within him. We read about people laying the sick where Peter would walk *"knowing the incredible power emanating from him would overshadow and heal them"* (Acts 5:15 TPT). When Peter walked by, *"his shadow might fall on one of them [with healing power]"* (Acts 5:15 AMP). Peter was a human who housed the Holy Spirit just as *we* do. Jesus, too, had the same Holy Spirit within who lives and breathes in *us*. What flowed through Peter's shadow and surged through Jesus' touch is the very Spirit alive in us today—ready to move, to heal, and to work wonders through willing hearts. So, let's be *willing*. Let's be *eager* to experience being used to this extent. The Word describes "signs" that will follow believers and lists "gifts" of the Holy Spirit: hands that heal, mouths that speak heavenly languages, authority that casts out evil spirits, words of knowledge that bring freedom, faith that could literally move mountains, and more (Mark 16:17-18, I Corinthians 12:4-11). These gifts flow at the *Spirit's* timing, released through those who willingly *ask* and open their *will* to His work.

For us to become voluntary vessels for His work to flow through, we must rightly picture *where* the Holy Spirit resides: He lives *inside*. Where our minds are—with all its thoughts and plans—*His* is, too. Where our hearts beat—with all its fluctuating feelings—*His* does, too. He even wears our hands like gloves—longing to allow His power to seep through onto hurting bodies. He also dons our feet and fervently desires to direct them where *He* wants to go. The Holy Spirit inhabits and clothes our entire being and is eager to move through every fiber and fold. Remember that He waits on our *will*. We can lean our thoughts, feelings, and even hands into *His* any time we choose—and we can *let* Him move. We can *ask* Him to pour His power through our hands to heal as we lay them on a person and pray. We can *ask* Him for "words of knowledge" to move from His mind to ours—and then mouth His miraculous words to people mired in misery. We can *ask* for messages so anointed that they cause crowds and individuals to radically repent of sin and rush to Him. If we specifically *ask* for this, we will powerfully *experience* this.

We are too often asking Jesus to accomplish what He wants to use *us* to achieve. We pray for peoples' pain to pass, but we seldom expect the Spirit's strength to stream through our stretched-out hands, sparking supernatural healing on the spot. We pray for the Holy Spirit to pull people to Jesus, but do we pursue the powerful word that would win their hearts? We just simply say it and pray it, and then we expect *Him* to do it however and whenever. Yet, all the while, His healing hands are *in* our human hands. His voice is stored and heard *in* our spirits—waiting and *ready* to surge into our minds and spill boldly from our mouths. The Holy Spirit works *wonders* through *willing* people. If we hunger to see His power more fully poured out, we must invite Him to move through us. We can't ask Him to "move in signs and wonders" without expecting to be His instruments. Jesus and Peter surged with the same Spirit we do—but they *eagerly* asked, expected, and embraced being used supernaturally before witnesses. To see the same, we must lay down fear and long for it just as boldly.

We must also spend time in Jesus' *presence.* A person who spills out His Spirit is a person who constantly drinks in His Spirit. If we want to know Him and walk like Him—even to the point of having our hands and lips anointed with the supernatural gifts of the Spirit—we must, *again,* spend time with Him *daily.* If we are still in the fight to forge this habit, *this* is the battle to win first. To *walk* in His power—on any level—we must *sit* in His presence. The one who sits with Jesus daily walks with Him deeply, gets shaped by Him steadily, and moves in His ways supernaturally. Again, the enemy knows this—and that's why he wages war on the *one* thing that fuels it all: our time alone with Jesus. If we lose this, we lose *everything.* Let's guard it and prioritize it—letting *nothing* take its place.

Let's also go after greater *faith* and *courage*. Too many people like being *too* comfortable. We worship a massive, mountain-moving God but also want a predictable, peaceful life. In our quiet craving for comfort and safety, we unconsciously build fences around our faith—restricting how far we'll follow or how boldly we'll believe Him to move. Some draw the line at their lips; they'll whisper prayers in private but won't speak them over others in public. Others speak freely but only stay in the zone of what's safe—not daring to ask for anything too wild or impossible. We pray neat, controlled prayers that do not create the expectation of a miracle happening right on the spot—because, "What if I pray it, and it doesn't happen?" Well, what if it *did?* For us to be like Peter and John in Acts 3—who grabbed the hand of a money-seeking lame man and declared, *"Silver and gold I do not have; but what I do have I give to you: In the name (authority, power) of Jesus Christ the Nazarene—[begin now to] walk and go on walking!"* (Acts 3:6 AMP)—we must have *greater* faith and courage. We must know—like these two did—that witnessing a miracle in front of our eyes will not happen through *"our own power or godliness"* (Acts 3:12 AMP). It *all* flows from the Holy Spirit. Even the boldness and faith they walked in weren't self-made; they were Spirit-given. Let's ask *Him* for an increase in courage. How many prayers never leave our lips because of fear? How many miracles never enter our midst because of timidity? The Lord commands His people to have courage and not fear; timidity is *never* tied to Him (Joshua 1:9, Deuteronomy 31:6, John 14:27, 2 Timothy 1:7). Let's *ask* the Holy Spirit for a holy *boldness* that's only heaven-born.

We must also possess *pure* hearts. Consider what this verse reveals: *"In a wealthy home some utensils are made of gold and silver, and some are made of wood and clay. The expensive utensils are used for special occasions, and the cheap ones are for everyday use. If you* **keep yourself pure**, *you will be a special utensil for honorable use"* (2 Timothy 2:20-21 NLT). Here's a second translation of the end of that: *"Become the kind of container God can use to present any and every kind of gift to his guests for their blessing"* (2 Timothy 2:21 MSG). To walk in the Spirit's special gifts and see signs and wonders flow, we must purposely live with a *pure* heart. We must *daily* deal with all specks and signs of sin, offense, pride, jealousy, judgement, deceit, and greed. We are human beings, and these human things creep up constantly in our hearts. When they show up—even in tiny traces—we must throw them out. The more passionately we keep our hearts pure, the more we're sure to *"see God"* in all kinds of ways (Matthew 5:8). We too often hinder the Holy Spirit by some human hang-up hiding in our hearts and habits. Let's continually ask as David did: *"Point out anything in me that offends You"* (Psalm 139:24 NLT). The Holy Spirit will repeatedly remove *anything* standing in His way in our hearts—making us clean vessels ready to carry and release His miraculous gifts.

To have a pure heart, we must also purge any desire to *impress* people. Wanting to impress others stifles the Spirit's outpouring and offends God's heart. We can either impress people or influence people. The desire to impress is Satan-sent—even matching the motive that removed him from Heaven—while the fire to influence flows from our Father. Remember His heart races with *love* for people. He *is* love, and it motivates all His movements (1 John 4:8). The desire to *love* and *lift* people must lead us, too. As Paul reminds us, even the greatest deeds mean nothing without love: *"If I speak with human eloquence... but don't love, I'm nothing...If I speak God's word with power...but I don't love, I'm nothing...If I give everything I own to the poor... but I don't love, I've gotten nowhere. So, no matter what I say, what I believe, and what I do, I'm bankrupt without love"* (1 Corinthians 13:1-3 MSG). Walking in the Spirit's gifts for show is *nothing.* Walking in His gifts to serve is *everything.* He will hand His gifts out to the heart that is *pure*—and that passionately loves *people.*

Let's remember our Lord's longing to be **known** and **near** to *all* people. We live and work on a mission field full of eyes waiting to witness *Jesus.* We can faithfully teach Him and preach Him, but we will powerfully reach them when they *see* Him. Just as Jesus' teachings and testimonies were affirmed by miracles, signs, and wonders, ours can be, too. There's *more* for us to want and walk in for the sake of *others.* Many hesitant hearts surround us daily, saying on the inside, "I hear people talk about Jesus, but I'll believe in Him when I *really* see Him!" They'll see Him through *us* as we allow the Holy Spirit to fully have us and flow through us to His fullest extent. Let's not *fear* this. Let's *revere* this and reach for it. After Jesus becomes **known** and **near** to us, He desires to become **known** and **near** through us—to *others.* He does this most powerfully through a life that is surrendered in will, bold in faith, pure in heart—and *expectant* to be used for His glory. Through such a life, the Spirit releases His gifts, Jesus is revealed, and many are drawn *near* to *know* Him for themselves.

He Emboldens & Anoints Us

Spirit-led steps often start with shaky knees. It takes *guts* to go where He leads. It can feel like tiptoeing onto a tightrope—our hearts racing, our feelings flooding, and our comfort zone fading behind us. He may prompt us to pray out loud, to prophesy an encouraging word over a friend, or to participate in a small group. He could nudge us to start a conversation about Jesus, to step up and help a stranger in need, or to spend longer time in private prayer. He may call us to preach a message to a crowd, to plan a community outreach, or to prepare for a mission trip to a foreign country. He could lead us to give generously, to go to the front of the church for prayer, or to grow our gifting before watching eyes. He will birth businesses, books, and brilliant ideas through His people—but following Him requires *faith*.

As always, our adversary will aim to stop our Spirit-led steps. The moment the Holy Spirit nudges us, the enemy swiftly shrouds us in a suffocating curtain of fear, freezing us in place. A tangible thought to pray out loud for the struggling store clerk will boldly bolt across our minds, but fear fires up *fast*—making our hearts physically pound and our minds wildly whirl with "what-ifs." *Many* stand still and stuck by the fear Satan sends the second the Spirit speaks—missing a would-be miraculous moment. However, those who press forward find this out: the curtain of fear is *sheer*. The very instant we move to obey—by offering to pray, by opening our mouths to share what He wants us to say—the fear falls dead and *confidence* comes alive. As soon as we begin to speak, courage peaks—and power leaks. Where *we* step out on earth, *Heaven* steps in. Let's know that Satan senses the supernatural surrounding our Spirit-led steps—so, the greater impact our obedience will infuse, the greater intimidation he'll impose. When the Holy Spirit whispers, let's *go*—even with hearts hammering hard—and take the step in *trust*. He will never invite us into a moment or a movement and then melt into the background. He doesn't shove us out to stand or speak alone—or without His anointing. Every prompting is a *partnership*. Even the nudges that ignite our insecurity are *invitations* to step into something supernatural with Him. When we move in obedience, He moves in power—and we never need to fear failure because He *never* fails.

Let's know that Satan doesn't waste his attacks where we're weak; he claws at our *calling*. He'll whisper worry, stir self-doubt and shame, and dispatch distraction directly into the places where our obedience would bear the *most* fruit. Our anointings alarm our adversary. Yet, what the enemy targets, Jesus intentionally chooses. In fact, Jesus doesn't pick the most perfect, polished, or predictable people to carry His power. He uses the *willing*—even if they're weak, wounded, or labeled "weird" by our world. Let's not be surprised if our most-attacked area is *the* particular part of us Christ has chosen to bring change and break chains. Satan senses what we carry and aims to crush it before it's carried out—but he can't cancel what Jesus has *called*.

Remember, too, that the Bible brims with people who were anointed but all-too-human—many of whom questioned their call when it came. Moses' voice oozed with anointing, yet he spoke with a stutter (Exodus 4:10); his hands also dripped with murderous blood, yet he delivered God's people (Exodus 4:10, Exodus 2:11-12, Exodus 3:10, Exodus 4:10). Jeremiah also cowered when his call came—claiming to be "too young"—yet his voice thundered prophecy amid the storms of a rebellious people (Jeremiah 1:6). Then, insecure Gideon hid—deeply doubting God's call—yet he became the mighty warrior he was destined to be after all (Judges 6:12). King David, too, was chosen and called despite his foul failures, but he led with a passionate heart, uniting a nation and pointing to the coming Messiah (2 Samuel 11-12). Then, there's John the Baptist, who lived an eccentric life—dwelling in the woods, donning wild hair and rugged clothes, and dining on locusts and honey—yet he was chosen to preach fiery, fearless messages that forged the way for Jesus (Luke 1:80, Mark 1:4-6, Matthew 3:3). Also, once delivered of demons, Mary Magdalene became the first witness of Jesus' resurrection—the first feet that ran to preach the gospel (Luke 8:2, John 20:16-18). Let's also not forget that Saul—who first killed Christians—later became Paul—who powerfully penned much of the New Testament (Acts 8:1-3, Acts 9:1-19). There's impulsive and flawed Peter, too—who walked on water one second then sank the next—*and* who broke His oath to Jesus and later rose as a rock of the early church (Matthew 26:75, Matthew 14:29-30, Matthew 16:18). In fact, *all* of the twelve disciples Jesus called closely to Him on earth point out that Jesus doesn't appoint and anoint the clean-cut; He uses the cut-ups and the mess-ups, too. So, when the enemy whispers that our flaws and failures disqualify us, we can point to the pages of Scripture—where liars led nations, doubters walked on water, and murderers became miracle-workers—and boldly shout out, "God delights in using the unlikely, and He can use *me*, too!"

When stepping out to be used by the Lord, let's not focus on our perfection—*or* our performance. Let's fixate on Jesus' power. The most power-packed, life-changing sermons weren't preached perfectly; they were prepared in His presence *humbly* and then shared *sincerely*. When telling our testimony or talking about Jesus across a table—let's not worry when we fumble our words; His word is *still* heard. When teaching and guiding conversation in a small group, it doesn't matter if we forget what we meant to say or even go blank when we pray. Jesus *still* moves anyway. We can make a mistake in the song we sing, and it can *still* break bondage and set someone free. We can boldly share a word we believe was breathed by the Spirit—*sure* it's sacred—but still slip in some slight mistakes. If our hearts are pure and our motives right, He'll *still* move with might.

Let's let this truth enlighten and lighten us: *"The Spirit alone gives eternal life. Human effort accomplishes nothing. And the very words I have spoken to you are spirit and life"* (John 6:63 NLT). We are flaw-filled and powerless; *He*, however, is power-filled and flawless. The Spirit *alone* opens eyes and transforms lives. We are simply the imperfect instruments He uses. We can't wait until *we* are "great"—or put-off His purposes until *we* can "perfectly" pull it off. No spiritual fruit comes from *our* perfection—*ever*. A person could preach the most polished, flawless message without one heart budging but then stumble and stutter through a simple sermon and see altars flooded with fired-up people. A "home-run" in delivery doesn't mean a "home-run" was hit spiritually. This principle can apply to *any* step the Spirit prompts us to take. Let's approach our obedience with excellence, but let's also remember that the Lord says this: *"My grace is always more than enough for you, and my power finds its full expression through your weakness,"* and then Paul responds, *"So I will celebrate my weaknesses, for when I'm weak, I sense more deeply the mighty power of Christ living in me. So, I'm not defeated by my weaknesses, but delighted!...For **my weakness becomes a portal to God's*** *power*" (2 Corinthians 12:9-10 TPT). The Spirit's strength shines brightest when we bring Him our shaky voices and trembling steps. He doesn't need our perfection—just our obedience. So, even when fear tries to silence us, stepping out in weakness becomes the very place where His power shows up and flows out—through *us*.

The enemy will aim to stop *all* our stepping out and speaking up—but if we hush him and head into it anyway, he'll attack in a different way. He'll immediately pick apart our *performance*: we talked "too fast," we explained "too little," we came across "too strong," we stuttered "too much," and so on. Let's point both ourselves *and* our enemy to Jesus' *power*—instead of our performance. We may have faltered, but Jesus didn't fail. Every time we step out or speak up, Heaven comes down and crushes Hell. We may not see it with our eyes, but let's sense it in our spirits and let *gratitude* arise. After we've had the Jesus-centered conversation, prayed aloud over the classmate or coworker, spoken a word over the stranger, or preached the message we wrote alone in His presence—no matter how *we* think it went—let's thank Jesus in faith for using it. Let's put the whole moment in His hands and trust that *He* moved and made miracles happen—even if we didn't *see* it. Let's step into every shaky moment standing strong on *His* strength—and step out of it in awe, always giving thanks for His sure and steady stirring. Because when we rely on His power—and *not* our perfection—even our *imperfect* steps become the very footsteps of His unstoppable Kingdom moving forward.

We'll never be picture-perfect, but we're still heaven-sent and Spirit-filled. Because of this, we can walk in courage—a *boldness*—that is Spirit-given. Let's ask Him to totally terminate our timidity. Our Jesus *"has not given us a spirit of fear, but of power and of love and of a sound mind"* (2 Timothy 1:7 NKJV). Fear never flows from our Father. Instead, He equips us with power to stand firm, love to act selflessly, and a sound mind to think and live with clarity—and with courage. The Holy Spirit both *empowers* and *emboldens* His people to do and say things they never could or would without Him. In Acts, we see *"ordinary men with no special training in the Scriptures"* standing up and speaking out with a confidence that even widens the eyes of their enemies (Acts 4:13 NLT). We see them worship and pray—all-out asking Jesus to stretch out His hand to heal—and even buildings bobble as the Holy Spirit breathes out a heaven-born boldness upon them (Acts 4:31). They walked, worked, and worshiped with a *holy* courage lit by the fire of the Holy Spirit, and it led them to stun crowds, confound authorities, and move in signs and wonders. Even when facing fearsome threats and imprisonment, they didn't fall back or flee; they just asked to be filled even *more* completely—and the Spirit ignited them with fresh fire again and again. Their boldness wasn't self-made or personality-driven; it came straight from the Spirit. All they did was *ask* for it and receive it—and *we* can, too. Let's request this kind of Spirit-breathed boldness. When it rises within us, it enables us to speak when we would have stayed silent, to step out and stand strong when we would've shrunk back, and to succeed in what only Heaven could empower.

Walking in this Spirit-given boldness today—just as they did in Acts—means living with a fearlessness fueled by a real relationship with Jesus. The more we sit with Him—praying, listening, studying His Word, and receiving—He frees us from *all* our fears (Psalm 34:4). *Every* encounter with Him in private emboldens us in public (Matthew 6:6). Our sitting with Him will empower us to stand for Him. For teenagers, carrying this courage looks like standing up for what's right—even when the crowd chooses to stay quiet. It's pushing through peer pressure—walking in careful purity and courageous integrity publicly—even if laughed at or left out. It's unapologetically praying for schools and classmates—igniting revival one fire-filled prayer at a time. For parents, this boldness bolsters them to bring up their families with *faith*—pushing back on culture in what they view, where they venture, and how they value and use their time. They courageously create bold boundaries—limiting screens, choosing friends wisely, and pointing their children to truth and a *real* walk with Jesus consistently. This boldness also shows up in boardrooms and breakrooms through Spirit-filled adults in workplaces. They speak with grace, stand with grit, and shine with great resolve that doesn't relax under pressure. Their courage carries honesty into everyday conversations—refusing to hide their beliefs and values—and their kindness conveys Christ in all their interactions. Also, those serving in their churches are sent out of their comfort zones by this same Spirit-given boldness. They teach, welcome, pray, and lead with a courage *they* couldn't create—and as they do, holy growth rises within them and radiates around them. We are *called* to this kind of courage—this divine boldness that transforms fear into faith and hesitation into holy action. When we walk in it, we become living lights, unwaning witnesses carrying the fire of the Holy Spirit into every corner of our world.

Let's remember the point of all of this—the fight to fulfill our call and the boldness to walk in it all. It's all for *fruit.* The greatest fruit we'll ever harvest is human lives. Our giftings and anointings—all our callings—exist *so that* we'd fetch falling-apart and far-off people and bravely *bring* them to Jesus. He's fully filled us with His Spirit *so that* we'd become His hands, His feet, and His mouth—bringing to light His mind, His heart, and His power to everyone around us. Let's long for *all* people to experience Jesus as **known and near.** His heart pants and pounds for *all* to have the relationship with Him they were born to have. Let's have *His* heart. Let's let His *love* move us. Let's burn with *boldness* in sharing Jesus. Let's let nothing silence us, sideline us, or stop us from answering His every call and bearing the greatest fruit of all: *souls* rescued from the Fall, made whole and standing tall.

PART 7

The Promises

CHAPTER TWELVE

Truths to Hold On To

"So now wrap your heart tightly around the hope that lives within us, knowing that God always keeps His promises!...Don't lose your bold, courageous faith, for you are destined for a great reward!"—Hebrews 10:23, 35 (TPT)

He Will Be With Us

Our Father is a promise-maker *and* a promise-keeper. The Bible bursts with powerful promises He presents to His cherished children. His sacred pledges aren't just transactional or impersonal; they are rooted in His love, presence, and commitment to us as His family. They pour from His passion for personal relationship with us. Let's know that He is not like a flaw-filled, fickle man who can forget, break, or delay his promises; He is totally trustworthy, distinctly dependable. He *always* follows through and comes through—punctually *and* perfectly. In fact, here's the promise He repeats most from Genesis to Revelation: *"I will be with you"* (Genesis 28:15, Exodus 3:12, Joshua 1:9, Isaiah 43:2, Matthew 28:20, Hebrews 13:5, Revelation 21:3). Whatever paths we tread, He *promises* His presence will be **known** and *near.*

Let's let this revelation of David resonate with us: no matter where we are, our Father is there, too—and He's *fully* aware of our every care and our every movement (Psalm 139:1-4). David deeply discerned that the Lord delighted in the *details* of his life—even knowing when he's sitting or standing or resting at home or traveling and fully aware of his thoughts and words before they're even thought or said. He even declared this: *"Where could I go from Your Spirit? Where could I run and hide from Your face?...Wherever I go, Your hand will guide me; Your strength will empower me. It's impossible to disappear from You or to ask the darkness to hide me, for Your presence is everywhere, bringing light into my night"* (Psalm 139:7, 10-11 TPT). David understood—as *we* should—that our God *chooses* to be wherever we are. He could remove His presence from any place or person, but when we become His, His Spirit fully moves *into* us and *with* us. He deep-dives into our entire existence and *"delights in every detail of [our] lives"* (Psalm 37:23 NLT). He hears our every sigh, feels our every desire, knows every tiny turn of each thread of our being. Not one crack or corner of our essence or existence is hidden from Him. He knows us fully—and He stays with us faithfully.

In moments of light *and* moments of darkness, let's believe this to our core: our Jesus couldn't possibly be with us *more*. He exists in and experiences *every* moment with us. He even assured us, *"Never forget that **I am with you every day**, even to the completion of this age"* (Matthew 28:20 TPT). Hear Him here, too: *"You always have God's presence. For hasn't He promised you, '**I will never leave you, never!** And I will not loosen My grip on your life!'"* (Hebrews 13:5 TPT). He also tells us this: *"Do not yield to fear, for **I am always near.** Never turn your gaze from Me, for I am your faithful God. I will infuse you with My strength and help you in every situation. I will hold you firmly with My victorious right hand"* (Isaiah 41:10 TPT). This promise persists even when life is perplexing: *"Even though the Lord may allow you to go through a season of hardship and difficulty, **he Himself will be there with you.** He will not hide himself from you... When you turn to the right or turn to the left, you will hear His voice behind you to guide you, saying, 'This is the right path; follow it'"* (Isaiah 30:20-21 TPT). He will *never* loosen His grip on our lives. Even when we falter or fumble, He still holds us fast. When we walk amidst worries and woes, He will only increase His hold and intensify our ability to hear. He won't waver, weaken, or withdraw. He is firmly, unfailingly *faithful*.

So, let's live life *enjoying* His nearness. We truly can walk with Him on earth as we would have in Eden. Jesus has restored *that* kind of closeness—and He's eager for us to enjoy it. We no longer bear burdens or brave battles and breakdowns alone. We don't wake up, walk, or work without Him. We never rise or lie down to rest again remote from Him. He is *there*—literally *right* there. Our Father and our Friend is *with* us. Let's live—let's *delight*—in His steadfast presence (Psalm 140:13). Let's *"celebrate God all day, every day. I mean, revel in Him!"* (Philippians 4:4 MSG). Let's thank Him for breath as we open our eyes and rise each morning—and praise Him as we pour our coffee. Let's invite Him into our meetings, classes, practices, errands, car rides, and chaos. Let's linger to *listen*—between the noise and notifications—and pause to *pray* in the middle of pressure. We can whisper worship as we wipe counters, wait in traffic, and weep in weary moments. Let's lean ourselves towards *Jesus* at every turn, and we'll perceive His presence isn't just a place; it's a Person—dwelling in every detail of our day, *delighting* in doing life with us. He's our *Father* and *Friend*—walking with us just as He wished when this world began.

He Will Take Care of Us

He is a Father who's also promised to take perfect *care* of His children. Just as earthly parents ensure their children are fed, clothed, cleaned, seen, and carefully put to bed, our Father even more so knows our needs and nurtures us. We never need to *worry*. His eye is always on us—never distant, never distracted. He knows our needs—even before we do—and He's already planned to provide. We no longer fend for ourselves or have to fetch or force provision. We work well and *wisely* steward our money—but He promises that even in lack, we will have plenty (Psalm 37:18-19, Psalm 34:10, Philippians 4:19). As His children, we are freed even in our *needs*. He calls Himself our Provider—and His will is that we wouldn't worry.

He says so in Scripture: *"Not even one sparrow falls from its nest without the knowledge of your Father. Aren't you worth much more to God than many sparrows? So, **don't worry**. For your Father cares deeply about even the smallest detail of your life"* (Matthew 10:29-31 TPT). He's aware of our every need and care; even *"the very hairs of [our heads] are all numbered [for the Father is sovereign and has complete knowledge]"* (Matthew 10:30 AMP). Jesus also passionately proclaimed this: *"I tell you **not to worry** about everyday life—whether you have enough food and drink, or enough clothes to wear…Look at the birds. They don't plant or harvest or store food in barns, for your heavenly Father feeds them. And aren't you far more valuable to him than they are?"* (Matthew 6:25-26 NLT). He continued by calling out our cares about clothing—claiming that if He arrayed even flowers more fancily than King Solomon, He'll adorn *us* well, too (Matthew 6:28-30). He wrapped up His stop-worrying speech by contrasting the anxious chase of unbelievers with the quiet confidence of God's children—who don't scramble for food, drink, or clothes, because their Father already knows what they need (Matthew 6:31-32).

Jesus' summative statement for that sermon was this: *"But first and most importantly seek (aim at, strive after) His kingdom and His righteousness [His way of doing and being right—the attitude and character of God], and all these things will be given to you also"* (Matthew 6:33 AMP). Our highest priority must become pursuing *Him,* not money, meals, or modern outfits and shoes. As we prioritize *His* purposes and presence—aiming to live with His heart, His character, and His ways—He will take care of our physical and practical needs throughout our days. As we focus on what matters to Him, He *promises* to take care of what matters to us. When we make His eternal priorities *our* responsibility, our everyday needs become *His* responsibility. He wants our thoughts teeming with Him, not scarcity and survival. He faithfully provides all we truly need—not just to survive but to thrive according to His good purposes. Even when fighting tight finances, we can find rest—and *provision.* As we choose contentment over constant worry, continue to spend daily time with Jesus, keep serving others—and are still careful to make wise decisions with work and money—we can *count* on Him. He can provide through *people* and providential miracles—literally even delivering what we need to our doorsteps. Let's become people who treasure knowing Him and becoming like Him above *all* else—and trust that He will supply everything essential for life and godliness.

Let's also remember that He invites us to *ask* when we have a need of *any* kind—spiritual *or* situational. In Matthew 7:7-8 (AMP), Jesus boldly told this truth: *"Ask and keep on asking and it will be given to you; seek and keep on seeking and you will find; knock and keep on knocking and the door will be opened to you. For everyone who keeps on asking receives, and he who keeps on seeking finds, and to him who keeps on knocking, it will be opened."* He followed this truth with a fact about the Father: *"What man is there among you who, if his son asks for bread, will [instead] give him a stone?...If you then, evil (sinful by nature) as you are, know how to give good and advantageous gifts to your children, how much more will your Father who is in Heaven [perfect as*

He is] give what is good and advantageous to those who keep on asking Him?" (Matthew 9-11 AMP). Just as we expect our children to ask us for what they want and need, our *Father* does, too. In fact, He *welcomes* our requests—and even waits for them, *wanting* to fulfill each one.

James 4:2 (NIV) plainly proclaims, *"You do not have because you do not ask God."* Jesus even declared, *"Yes, ask me for anything in my name, and I will do it!"* (John 14:14 NLT). However, He doesn't grant greedy requests; He graciously honors godly ones. View this verse: *"We can also have great boldness before Him, for if we ask anything agreeable to His will, He will hear us. And if we know that He hears us in whatever we ask, we also know that we have obtained the requests we ask of Him"* (1 John 5:14-15 TPT). The list of "anything agreeable" to Him—things that aptly align with *His* will—include requests like these: salvation for others, spiritual growth and wisdom, strength to resist sin, forgiveness and a clean heart, help in forgiving and loving others, peace in anxiety, healing of any kind, courage in sharing His Word, and more—including *provision* in our daily needs. Bold prayers aligned with His heart are *never* left unanswered.

Not only will He meet these expectations; He'll *exceed* them. Let's let Ephesians 3:20 (TPT) bolster our boldness: *"Never doubt God's mighty power to work in you and accomplish all this. He will achieve infinitely more than your greatest request, your most unbelievable dream, and exceed your wildest imagination!"* We *get* to live like this: with hearts aligned with His will, we can *ask* for even "impossible" needs to be met. We won't receive meager answers; we'll step into a divine partnership where God's limitless power transforms even our smallest prayers into miracles beyond measure. Our Father will answer above and beyond—*more* than meeting every need and abolishing *all* our agitating worry.

He Will Answer Us

So, let's *pray*—without losing heart or calling it quits. Our Father faithfully fills our daily needs—freeing us from fear and weighty worry—but He also miraculously moves the mountains we pray for *persistently*. We will often stand staring at a stuck situation or a stubborn human heart that only our Savior can solve. Without Jesus, people eventually throw up their hands, shrug off hope, and surrender to despair, murmuring, "There's nothing *anyone* can do!" However, Spirit-filled, prayer-powered souls rise to respond with faith and fiery courage. Whether a soul needs saving, a body needs healing, a door needs opening, or finances need supplying—*anything* can happen when a child of God prays.

Jesus told a tale that teaches us still today that we should *persistently* pray. This powerful parable showed the disciples *"that they should always pray and never give up"* (Luke 18:1 NLT). It goes like this: a determined widow keeps knocking on a judge's door—day after day— pleading for justice with steady, stubborn resolve. Though the judge cares nothing for people or God, her relentless persistence presses him until he finally renders to her what she's repeatedly requested. Jesus then pointed out that if even a perverse judge can be pulled and persuaded by persistence, our just and generous God will *readily* and *reliably* respond when His people pray and refuse to give up (Luke 18:2- 7). He sealed the story with this sobering question: how many people on earth will have this kind of *persistent* faith—the kind that fights until things are set right (Luke 18:8)? Jesus urges us to *keep* praying without giving up—not to wear God down but to build *us* up, refining our faith, fine-tuning our trust, and drawing us closer as we wait. Let's become people who pray every day—even when there's delay. Our faithful, listening Father radically responds to His children who continually cry out with unwavering hope. Let's trust in His listening ears, His caring heart, and His perfect timing. Let's be people who believe for the impossible—who pray until the day comes that *He* makes a way.

Some answers arrive quickly while others take time. As we pray—even in the face of delay—let's *know* that He's working. If we could see into the spirit realm and witness what wonderful works are weaved as we relentlessly believe, we'd *never* stop praying (1 Thessalonians 5:17). We'd pray over *everything* every day (Ephesians 6:18). Let's imagine this: as we intercede from our couches, cars, or closets, power gushes and rushes from wherever we are to the place or person over which we're praying. The Holy Spirit follows the flow of our fervent prayers, pouring out power that He then spins over hearts, homes, minds, and situations—shaping them into *His* will. Never forget or doubt this: *"The earnest prayer of a righteous person has great power and produces wonderful results"* (James 5:16 NLT). Our prayers can be propelled like the stone slung from David's sling shot—heading straight to the forehead of a formidable spiritual foe and dropping him dead (1

Samuel 17:49). They can be lifted like Moses' staff raised high above a hopeless situation—parting deep waters and forming a path for a person to forge ahead (Exodus 14:16). They can alter an entire atmosphere like Paul and Silas' ardent worship—shaking foundations and flinging open prison doors for people the enemy meant to keep misled (Acts 16:25-26). Many things are impossible for man— *"but with God, everything is possible"* (Matthew 19:26 NLT). There's nothing that can't be budged, breached, broken off, or blessed when the Father's children *pray* without letting hope give way.

Let's *ask*—and *keep* asking—for parents, children, and friends to receive salvation; for sick bodies and hearts to be healed; for evil trends to end; and for our deepest desires to come to pass—even if it takes days, months, or years. Our prayers shape the scenes of the future. It's as if we're riding a train, gazing and watching out wide windows, wondering what we'll see around the bend. Yet, here's the truth: as Jesus' people, we aren't just passengers; we're *partners*—His co-laborers—in what will appear next. When we stop merely wondering what we'll witness next and start praying with purpose, we can watch in confidence as the landscape ahead begins to reflect the very things we've *been* lifting up in prayer. Let's not just pray *reactively*—only crying out to Heaven when Hell breaks loose. Let's *proactively* pray—faithfully framing the futures of friends, families, and even foes through daily, determined intercession.

No prayer ever prayed ever dies or disappears either. Every Spirit-directed prayer that leaves a human mouth both reaches Heaven and remains before the Father's throne. The writer of Revelation witnessed this: *"The four living beings and the twenty-four elders fell down before the Lamb. Each one had a harp, and they held gold bowls filled with incense, which are* **the prayers of God's people***"* (Revelation 5:8 NLT). He saw this, too: *"Then another angel with a gold incense burner came and stood at the altar. And a great amount of incense was given to him to mix with the prayers of God's people as an offering on the gold altar before the throne"* (Revelation 8:3 NLT). Next, *"The smoke of the incense, mixed with* **the prayers of God's holy people**, *ascended up to God from the altar where the angel had poured them out"* (Revelation 8:4 NLT). Our prayers are not cast aside; they are *collected.* They are so treasured in Heaven that they fill golden bowls with incense held by elders before the Throne. Our faithful prayers rise like holy fragrance—flooding His throne with a sweet, sacred scent that delights the heart of God. They are eternal—*never* wasted. Even prayers prayed long ago still linger in Heaven. They don't disappear; they accumulate and are poured out powerfully before the throne in divine timing. In fact, here's what was witnessed next: *"Then the angel filled the incense burner with fire from the altar and* **threw it down upon the earth***. Thunder crashed, lightning flashed, and there was a terrible earthquake"* (Revelation 8:5 NLT). After the prayers ascended, power avalanched down upon earth—a potent picture of our prayers preceding His powerful movement in our world. *Every* whispered plea, tearful intercession, and bold declaration is heard, held, and honored in the courts of Heaven. Not one is missed; they *all* become miracles.

So, let's become people who *pray*. Let's not pray blanket, generic prayers over people or problems. Let's receive precise phrases from the Holy Spirit—the *exact* words that will rebuild and resurrect what's been long-dead. Remember Ezekiel in the valley of dry bones— how as he prayed word-for-word as the Lord led him, the *Lord* poured out power and performed it. They repeated this process together until—at the end of the story—the bones stood on their feet as *"an exceedingly great army"* (Ezekiel 37:10 AMP). This is a picture of *His* power partnering with *His* prayers poured out of *our* mouths. He can and wants to do the "impossible"—the things we, like Ezekiel, know that only *He* can do—but He does it as *we* pray as *He* leads us. Let's lean in and listen—and then pray as we're led. Let's always ask the Holy Spirit exactly what to say, and as we pray it, He *will* do it.

Since He answers so surely and accurately, let's live turning every *fear* and *frustration* into a prayer. When something heavy hits our hearts, let's be people who immediately hand it to Him—every care, anxiety, worry, or concern (I Peter 5:7). Let's reform every fearful thought into a faith-filled prayer (Philippians 4:6-7). Let's let our frustrations just fuel the fire of our intercession, too. What we want to scream, we can pray. What we want to complain about, we can carry quickly to Jesus. He's the One who can fix the heart and root of every issue. We must also remember, *again*, that we do not fight flesh and blood; we struggle and spar with a spiritual enemy and all of his cohorts on assignment against *us* (Ephesians 6:12). The enemy's aim is to get us exasperated, tired, and *done*. He wants to frustrate us right out the front door of our homes, schools, workplaces, and callings. So, think of his vexation with the one he can't sway—no matter what games he plays. This is who we can *all* be when we habitually pour every frustration into prayer. Literally, let each agitated thought turn seamlessly into an aggressive prayer. Prayer then turns our frustration into fire—a deep desire to see change transpire and the kind of faith that won't expire until it does.

Our prayers release the power that can put every out-of-order person or problem back in order. Prayer calms us down with the peace of Heaven. Prayer fills us with the pulse of Jesus' authority and anointing. Prayer wrecks walls that stand against God's will. Prayer sends Satan sprinting and his schemes spiraling. Perhaps we can't publicly flip furniture in frustration as Jesus did, but we *can* force devils out of places and people through iron-willed intercession (John 2:13-16). Prayer accomplishes what no crying or complaining can. Heaven hears and honors our prayers—*each* one making it to His throne and moving His heart. Let's not treat prayer as a last-ditch lifeline; let's make it our *first* move—our frontline. Prayer isn't a fallback plan; it's *the* force that shatters strongholds, heals hearts, and dashes open doors only God can break through. When we pray, His power pours and paves a way. If His children—who are **known** and **near** to Him—will only *ask*, He will act. He *promises*.

He Will Bless Us

Our Father also promises to bestow His *blessing* on His children. Numbers 6:24-26 (AMP), known as the Priestly Blessing, beautifully captures God's heart toward His people: *"The Lord bless you, and keep you [protect you, sustain you, and guard you]; The Lord make His face shine upon you [with favor], And be gracious to you [surrounding you with lovingkindness]; The Lord lift up His countenance (face) upon you [with divine approval], And give you peace [a tranquil heart and life]."* This beautiful blessing was originally spoken over the Israelites, God's chosen people in the Old Testament. Today, through our relationship with Jesus, this same blessing extends to all who belong to God's family. Upon each of us who carefully, closely lives in *real* relationship with Him, He pours out His protection, favor, lovingkindness, approval, and peace.

The original Hebrew word for "bless" is "*barak*"—a word weighted with wonderful promises. It doesn't signify just a single smile or a wish of good fortune, but an active, ongoing bestowal of divine favor that flows all through our lives. God promises to impart His presence, power, and peace—enabling His people to thrive spiritually, emotionally, relationally, and even physically in His perfect wisdom. His blessing wraps around us like a radiant robe—shielding, steadying, and setting us apart. It shines over our lives like sunlight breaking through storm clouds—driving out fear and forging growth even in grave circumstances. It surrounds us like a covering of favor— opening doors no one can shut, refreshing us in dry places, and ordering our steps with grace and peace. His blessing is not a random moment of goodness; it is the *constant* covering of His care and the evidence of His delight—brightening our lives with His Light.

God's blessing isn't proven by perfect parking spots, prize-winning moments, a padded bank account, or popularity. His favor doesn't mean a life free of trouble; it means His presence travels with us and transforms us *through* it. When we must park far away, we're still close to His side. When we're passed over, we're still carried by His promises. Even when we're not everyone's favorite, we're still chosen and cherished by His heart. His hand even turns hardship into harvest and delays into divine appointments. Outwardly, He provides what— and whom—we need right when we need it. Inwardly, He anchors us with peace, joy, and unshakable hope no matter what's shaking the world around us. His blessing isn't about what's around us; it's about Who's *with* and *within* us.

We don't bear the Father's blessing by just professing His Name. His favor doesn't fall fully over our lives as we just fellowship at church. It doesn't even budge or bend down just because of good behavior. His blessing and favor flows into the life lived in *true*, faithful relationship and obedience to Him—truly trusting Him, wholly walking in His ways, and continually clinging to closeness with Christ. The one who *sits* with Him—leaning in and gleaning every truth and morsel from His written Word and speaking lips every day—and then stands, strides, and serves like Him is the one whose life is drenched in divine delight and direction. We must live in faithful *relationship*—trusting, obeying, and seeking Him daily—opening our hearts to His presence and power so that His blessing can flow freely in and through us. Let's not be those who hand Him only fragments of our lives. Instead, let's surrender it *all*—heart, soul, mind, and every movement and moment— so that we can completely step into the fullness of His favor.

The Father wants to bless each part of our lives with *His* best. In Jeremiah 29:11 (TPT), He addressed His plans for His children's future: *"My intention is not to harm you but to surround you with peace and prosperity and to give you a beautiful future, glistening with hope."* He also expressed this: *"I thought to myself, 'I would love to treat you as my own children!' I wanted nothing more than to give you this beautiful land—the finest possession in the world. I looked forward to your calling me 'Father,' and I wanted you never to turn from me"* (Jeremiah 3:19 NLT). Both verses consummately capture God's heart as a loving Father—desiring intimacy, obedience, and the joy of *blessing* His children with the finest of what He has. He displayed these desires in His deliverance and dreams for the Israelites in the Old Testament. With a mighty hand, the Father freed His people from slavery in Egypt, demonstrating His power and faithfulness (Exodus 6:6, Exodus 12). His goal wasn't just to break them out of bondage but to bring them into *blessing.* He would lead them to the Promised Land, a land *"flowing with milk and honey"*— where they would find full freedom, flourish under His care, and fulfill the dream of a love-filled relationship with their Father (Exodus 3:8 NLT). The same Father who led them still leads us likewise *today*— calling each of us into our own "Promised Land" of purpose, peace, and powerful relationship with Him. For some, it may look like full freedom from fear, radical restoration in a broken family, or wholly walking in a calling they never thought possible, but, in every case, it's a life marked by His presence and provision—and every one of His *promises.*

However, many of the original Israelites failed to follow Him fully into their Promised Land. When they reached the very edge of it, they beheld towering giants, tall city walls, and threatening armies that tore up their faith and tortured them with fear (Numbers 13:28–33). Instead of standing strong on God's promise and power, they stared at their own weakness and the seemingly impossible obstacles, which led them to rebel and refuse to enter (Numbers 13-14). Fear clouded their faith, and grumbling drowned their gratitude. They thought the road to

God's promise would be smooth and simple, but it required steadfast faith and the courage to keep confidently trusting when challenges came. They lacked faith and refused to fight. In response, the Father declared that this generation—except for faithful, fearless Caleb and Joshua—would *not* enter that lavish land (Numbers 14:22-24). They wandered wearily in the wilderness for forty years until they all wasted away and died off. It was their children who courageously crossed over and claimed the land under Joshua's steady leadership (Joshua 1-3). This generation grew up trusting God's promises *fully*—the very ones their parents doubted—and they obeyed His commands *faithfully*. Unlike the older generation, they had courageous hearts ready to follow *and* fight battles in order to fully possess what He'd promised (Joshua 1:6-9, Deuteronomy 1:38). Their faith, obedience, and readiness to trust the Father's leading made *all* the difference.

Today, the Father still leads us towards our *own* Promised Lands—not of geography but of grace, growth, and great purpose. The same choice remains: will we follow Him to His best in our lives or falter in our faith and find ourselves circling in fear, too? His promise may be a godly marriage where two hearts walk in covenant love and grace, reflecting Christ's relationship with His Church (Ephesians 5:25-33). It could be the unmatchable joy of stepping confidently and *completely* into the calling God has placed on our lives, serving fearlessly with passion and purpose (Colossians 3:23). It could be breaking free from the prison of addiction and sin, living in the *full* freedom Jesus bought with His Blood (John 8:36, Galatians 5:1). It may even be simply pursuing peak *physical* health—a body in renewed shape, a diet restructured, and physical pains and problems radically receding (3 John 1:2). Still, just as formidable giants and fortified cities precluded the Israelites' promise, problems could prevent us from possessing ours, too. Doubts that darkly whisper, fears that paralyze progress, toxic relationships that threaten us and twist the truth, old habits that hold us hostage—*these* can be the giants that intimidate us, the walls that seem impossible to scale. Yet, our *promised* places still exist and wait. His *best* in every area waits behind the walls that block our way. Let's decide and declare like David: *"In Your strength, I can crush an army; with My God, I can scale any wall"* (Psalm 18:29 NLT). In the Spirit's strength, we can overcome *any* obstacle and obtain *every* promised place planned and prepared by our Father.

So, let's not *settle*. Too many people begin their journey towards God's best but stop short. Fear, pride, and the pull of the world push them off track. The Israelites literally glimpsed the Promised Land, yet they turned back trembling at giants instead of gazing at the power of their great God and going ahead (Numbers 13-14). Saul, a chosen king, compromised his crown not to opposition but to his lack of obedience; he preferred partial control over complete surrender (1 Samuel 15). The rich young ruler sadly snubbed his best life because his wealth weighed more in his heart than the riches of fully following Jesus (Mark 10:17-22). Also, Demas—a cherished companion of Paul—faded into the background of Scripture because his love for the Lord lost to his love for the world (2 Timothy 4:10). Each of these—and *so* many more—possessed perfect access to promised, powerful places, but comfort, fear, or self-interest persuaded them to park at *partial* possession. Today, we still face these same giants: the lure of ease, the temptation to compromise, and the fear of risk. Our Father promises careers, opportunities, victories, and relationships that are heaven-sent—personally appointed and anointed from *His* hand to *our* lives. They will require faith that presses forward when the road becomes complicated and costly. They will require us to fight our flesh and our fears—as well as our forsaken, false-lipped enemy. They will require fire—both grace *and* grit. Let's become people who see His best, believe it, pursue it, and *never* quit.

Let's know this, too: when hardship hits and hurdles happen, it doesn't mean His blessing has halted. It only means we're about to become *more* blessed. Let's tightly hold on to this truth: our Jesus will always bring His best about in—and *because of*—our worst situations. Let's plant this promise permanently in our hearts: *"And we know [with great confidence] that God [who is deeply concerned about us]* **causes all things to work together [as a plan] for good** *for those who love God, those who are called according to His plan and purpose"* (Romans 8:28 AMP). What people or our enemy intend for our harm, *"God intended it for good"* (Genesis 50:20 TPT). He shows up on the scene of our suffering to supply *"a crown of beauty for ashes, a joyous blessing instead of mourning, festive praise instead of despair"* (Isaiah 61:3 NLT). He even deals out double for our trouble: *"Instead of your shame you will receive a* **double portion**...*in your land"* (Isaiah 61:7 NIV), and, *"I promise this very day that I will repay* **two blessings for each of your troubles"** (Zechariah 9:12

NLT). Job experienced this doubling in his restoration: after he prayed for his friends, the Lord gave him *twice* what he had lost (Job 42:10). Our Jesus also encouraged us with this: *"In the world you have tribulation and distress and suffering, but be courageous [be confident, be undaunted, be filled with joy]; I have overcome the world. [My conquest is accomplished, My victory abiding.]"* (John 16:33 AMP). From cover to cover, the Bible bursts with this beautiful promise: Jesus bends every burden and battle—every *bad* thing—into a *multiplied* blessing.

For those living in close communion and careful obedience with Jesus, every attack only becomes an avenue for increase. Every lack just turns into lavish provision. The enemy's schemes backfire; what he meant to break us only builds us. His attempts to wound us only prune us for greater fruit. His efforts to steal only make *more* room for Jesus to fill. With Jesus, our most awful moments become the birthplaces of His most amazing blessings. Loss makes space. Pain produces purpose. Trials turn into triumphs. The deeper the valley, the higher the harvest. *This* is His blessing on a life that's His—and we can grow so rooted in His goodness and so confident in His care that when adversity arrives, we don't panic. We *praise* instead. We don't fear because we know we're about to flourish. Like all of our Father's promises, *this* one will never fail: His blessing will *always* flow to and fall on those who are **known** and **near**—those who *faithfully* follow Him.

He Will Return

Jesus *promised* to return to the earth again. Before He ascended into Heaven, he assured His disciples, *"When everything is ready, I will come and get you, so that you will always be with me where I am"* (John 14:3 NLT). When He arrives—*right* on time—He won't slip through the clouds quietly; He will split the skies in unmistakable glory. No country, no coast, no corner of the earth will miss His radiant return. He will arrive visibly, powerfully, and gloriously. Matthew 24:30 (TPT) tells us that we *"will see the Son of Man appearing in the clouds of Heaven, revealed with mighty power, great splendor, and glory."* He also won't re-enter earth empty-handed: *"Look, I am coming soon, bringing my reward with me to repay all people according to their deeds"* (Revelation 22:12 NLT). He'll appear with both reward and reproof in His hands. He'll also arrive when our world is torn apart by tribulation, fractured by fake prophets and false "Christs," and unhinged by upheaval and unusual signs in the skies (Matthew 24:1-

27). We must stay steady and standing (Matthew 24:13). We must live watchfully, well-prepared, and wide *awake*.

Not even Jesus knows the day of His Return (Matthew 24:36). The Son stands *ready*, waiting only for the Father's nod—then He'll come swift as lightning, glowing with glory (Matthew 24:27). When He still walked the earth, Jesus warned: *"You also must **be ready all the time**, for the Son of Man will come when least expected"* (Matthew 24:44 NLT)—and Paul later prophesied, *"The day of the Lord will come like a thief in the night"* (1 Thessalonians 5:2 NIV). He'll appear suddenly, unexpectedly, and we must not be found unprepared. The unknown timing of His return isn't meant to be a trick; it's meant to be a test of who's *truly* His. If He declared a clear date, people would wait until the last minute to spiritually stand up straight. His return will be only for those who live *ready*—those who stay step-by-step with the Savior daily—not those who suddenly do it for show or last-minute gain. He doesn't want people to abruptly *act* holy or outwardly religious out of panic or pressure. He desires faithful followers—those who are wholeheartedly watching, working, and waiting for Him. What it really comes down to—again and always—is *relationship*. He's not after rehearsed religion or last-minute, not-really-meant repentance; it's *real*, raw relationship that He reveres. He's coming for the ones already coming to Him daily, the ones who love His presence and live in passionate pursuit of Him. He's returning for those who walk with Him *now*, who wait with lamps lit, who watch with *longing*—not those who withhold and whisper, "Someday…," but those who staunchly shout, "Even so, *come!*" He'll arrive for those who are *already* authentically His.

Yes, Jesus will arrive suddenly—and *strikingly*. His appearance will *"burst forth with the brightness of lightning shining from the eastern sky to the west"* (Matthew 24:27 TPT). Not one eye will be able to deny what it's witnessing in the sky. Every ear will hear a trumpet signaling that the Son has appeared. As He comes conspicuously through the clouds, all feet will firmly freeze and all eyes gaze with amazed awe at the breathtaking scene breaking across the infinite blue above. Imagine the whole wide world suddenly illuminated by a radiant, undeniable light— everyone seeing at once that the King has *come back* in might. The world will stand still and stunned, watching in wonder as He appears in glistening glory, galloping on a majestic white horse and wearing a collection of crowns—each a symbol of His supreme authority (Revelation 19:11-12). Like fire, His eyes will flash and blaze—peering and piercing through every shadow and secret. Like thunder, His voice will roll and resound—commanding attention from every crevice of creation (Revelation 19:12-13). He will not return as the baby born in a barn who became Bethlehem's humble carpenter; He will ride down as the Resurrected King and Righteous Judge—vibrant and volcanic with victory and reclaiming His royal, rightful throne on the earth. All eyes will witness Him, and all hearts will know that the Messiah has kept His promise and radically *returned* (Revelation 1:7).

Jesus will descend from Heaven *"with a cry of command, with the voice of an archangel, and with the sound of the trumpet of God. And the dead in Christ will rise first. Then we who are alive, who are left, will be caught up together with them in the clouds to meet the Lord in the air, and so we will always be with the Lord"* (1 Thessalonians 4:16-17 ESV). Yes, *"in a moment, in the twinkling of an eye,"* those who are genuinely Jesus'—both those still breathing and those lying still in their graves—will be taken up together and transformed in the air (I Corinthians 15:51-52 ESV). While this reunion transpires in the sky, a reckoning will take place on the earth. After the glorious gathering of His genuine people, the King will sit on His throne, and *"all the nations will be gathered before Him [for judgment]; and He will separate them from one another, as a shepherd separates his sheep from the goats; and He will put the sheep on His right [the place of honor], and the goats on His left [the place of rejection]"* (Matthew 25:32-33 AMP). He will distinguish between those who have faithfully followed Him and those who have readily rejected Him. The sheep will hear the words their hearts have hoped for: *"Come, you who are blessed by My Father; inherit the Kingdom prepared for you from the creation of the world"* (Matthew 25:34 NLT). In that moment, they will step into a sorrowless Kingdom, into everlasting joy, into the very presence of the very King they walked with by faith on the earth. Soon, they will be welcomed to the Marriage Supper of the Lamb, where robed saints rejoice, Heaven's hallelujahs thunder, and the Bridegroom's victory and love for His Bride are celebrated *forever* (Revelation 19:6-9).

However, the goats—those who lived for themselves, ignoring both Jesus *and* the poor and least of the earth—will face the justice of the King they never truly *knew* (Matthew 25:41-46). They won't wander the earth; they'll enter eternal separation (Matthew 25:41). In this moment of judgement, no middle ground and no second chances will exist—just the justice of the Holy Judge who sees all and rewards all according to absolute truth. He meant what He said about life on the earth: one path leads to eternal life and the other to everlasting loss (Matthew 25:46). Grace is openly offered, and those who ignore the Cross will eventually bear the cost.

While interpretations of the details and order of end-time events vary, the central truth is unwavering: God's heart beats for *relationship*, and His deepest desire is that His people live in genuine, daily intimacy with Him. Real relationship with Jesus alone redeems and readies hearts to stand before Him and then step into eternity with Him. Though Scripture speaks of coming judgment, trials, rebellion, and the final defeat of evil, these events are woven into a grand tapestry that ultimately points to restoration, righteousness, and *relationship* reigning supreme (Revelation 6-22). Jesus *will* triumph, creation will be cleansed and crowned with perfection and peace once again, and the faithful will dwell in His Kingdom forever (Revelation 19-22). The whole world will again whisper with wonder, and every shadow of sorrow and sin will be silenced. Rivers of life will run relentlessly through this restored realm, trees of healing will bloom beside crystal-clear streams, and the Savior will be steadily *seen*—walking and talking face-to-face with His people once more (Revelation 22:3-4). As eternity unfolds, it will look familiar. It will be a place—a *paradise*—of continual celebration, joy, peace, and unbroken fellowship with the Father. Yes, eternity will echo Eden, but it will never end. Each heart's deepest desires—both the Lord's and His people's—will finally be fulfilled forever. He will be perfectly **known and near,** and relationship—the way it was always meant to be—will be fully restored. Every soul will forever delight in the flourishing friendship they were *born* to have with the Lord.

Let's live *ready* to receive this radical gift when He returns. Yes, the world has waited on His promised return for two thousand years— but He's *still* coming. He's not been slow-paced. He's been patient. He's been compassionate. View this verse: *"A single day counts like a thousand years to Lord Yahweh, and a thousand years counts as one day…Contrary to man's perspective, the Lord is not late with His promise to return, as some measure lateness. But rather, His 'delay' simply reveals His loving patience towards you because* **He does not want any to perish** *but all to come to repentance"* (2 Peter 3:8-9 TPT). He's prolonging the time because He's longing for relationship with more people. As we wait and anticipate His arrival—which will come *"as unexpected as a home invasion"* and include the heavens and earth passing away and all the world being judged— let's live *ready* and *right* (2 Peter 3:10 TPT). Since these are the sure, soon-coming events, let's *"see how vital it is to live a holy life,"* and let's *"be consumed with godliness"* (2 Peter 3:11 TPT). Let's live this way: *"Since you are looking forward to these things, be diligent and make every effort to be found by Him [at His return] spotless and blameless…[having lived a life of obedience to Him],"* and let's *"consider the patience of our Lord [His delay in judging and avenging wrongs] as salvation [that is, allowing time for more to be saved]"* (2 Peter 3:14-15 AMP). While we wait for His glorious return, our calling is to walk wisely, to live as *wholly* His—mindful of holiness in every moment and matter. At the same time, we are to intentionally invite and warmly welcome *others* to experience Jesus as **known** and **near**—into the same kind of personal, life-transforming, heart-deep relationship with Jesus *they* were born to have, too.

Even Jesus shared a story about *actively* waiting for Him like this. He spoke of ten virgins—or bridesmaids—who were waiting for the bridegroom to arrive so that they could enter the soon-coming wedding feast (Matthew 25:1-13). Each held a lamp, but only five were wise and brought extra oil to feed their flame and keep it alive. The foolish five brought *none*. While waiting longer than expected for the bridegroom's arrival, they all drooped in drowsiness and drifted off to sleep. Then, at midnight, a sudden shout shook them awake: *"Look! The bridegroom [is coming]! Go out to meet him!"* (Matthew 25:6 AMP). Each wise virgin bolted to her feet, trimmed and lit her lamp, and rushed out *ready* to meet Him. The foolish five saw that their flames were no longer alive and begged for some oil from those who were well-prepared for this unmissable moment. They did not have enough to spread around and share, so they sent them to the store to buy more. However, as they dashed away, the bridegroom arrived without further delay; He invited the prepared to come His way and welcomed them into the wedding feast happening *that* day. After they stepped in, the door was solidly shut and securely locked behind them. Later, the ones who had been oilless returned breathless, *begging* for the door to be opened for them. Yet, the Lord rightfully replied, *"I assure you and most solemnly say to you, I do not know you [**we have no relationship**]"* (Matthew 25:12 AMP). Jesus sums up His story with this solemn statement: *"Therefore, be on the alert [**be prepared and ready**], for you do not know the day nor the hour [when the Son of Man will come]"* (Matthew 25:13 AMP). Notice again that it is a real *relationship* alone that makes us *ready* to stand before Him.

Let's not pass by *any* of Jesus' points in this powerful parable. First, let's understand that not all who appear to be believers are *truly* right and ready. All ten virgins seemed similar on the outside—but only five were truly alive and ready on the inside. Our churches and Christian circles brim with believers who seemingly serve Jesus but don't *seek* Jesus. They have a public reputation for being alive but have no real relationship with Jesus in private. Let's revisit Jesus' most weighty warning—that not everyone who calls Him "Lord" will go to Heaven but only the ones who actually *do* His will; He continued by explaining that many will stand before Him and describe what they did for Him in *public*—preaching, prophesying, and praying for miracles—but then He'll direct their attention to what they didn't do in *private*: get to *know* Him (Matthew 7:21-23). The way we constantly keep our supply of "oil" is to keep sitting alone with Jesus daily. Our entire lives must be arranged around *this* activity as our highest priority—even the very times we retire to bed at night and rise in the morning each day. Remember that Jesus met the eyes of a devoted yet distracted Martha, then nodded to the peaceful Mary seated at His feet—quiet, attentive, *hungry* for intimacy—and said she had found the *"one thing worth being concerned about"* (Luke 10:42 NLT). Day after day, time alone with Jesus *always* stands as our highest and holiest priority.

Jesus also points out that intimacy with Him cannot be *borrowed*. The wise virgins could not give their oil away. Their personal oil could not be put into another's unlit lamp. A walk with Jesus is a *personal* path; no one else's journey can substitute, support, or shadow our own. On that final day, we cannot stand silently before Him, stretching out a finger and pointing to our parents, pastors, or particular godly friendships who had intimately known Him. We cannot just lean on *their* faith and not forge our *own*. Though we cherish and admire their close connection with Christ, their relationship is not *ours* to claim. No matter how deeply our loved ones know Him, they cannot transfer their trust or testimony to us when we stand before the Throne. We must know Him—truly and tenderly—*ourselves*.

Through this persuasive parable, Jesus declares, too, that there's a *deadline* for our personal preparation. Once the door was slammed and shut to the virgins, it was irrevocable. The moment was *final*. A sudden *second* is coming when our opportunity to repent and ready ourselves through a *real* relationship will end. This tense tale of the ten virgins is a warning and a wake-up call. Jesus *will* come back—and when He arrives, it will be too late to arrange and assemble ourselves aright. There will be no reaching for a friend's forged faith, no running out to retrieve what we didn't have ready. We prepare ourselves through a real *relationship* only—one that is dedicated to Jesus *daily*, one that sits and seeks Him, one that listens and learns from Him, and one that then rises to radically obey Him in the power of His Holy Spirit. Those found walking like this will be welcomed into the joy of His Kingdom.

So, let's live daily like He's coming back *today*. What will matter the most when we stand before Him should matter to us most *every* second. Let's let His return *burn* in our hearts. Let's *constantly* think about the coming King. Let's daily draw near to Him and drink in the oil of His Spirit. He alone can keep us aflame like this: *"Be enthusiastic to serve the Lord, keeping your passion toward him boiling hot! Radiate with the glow of the Holy Spirit and let him fill you with excitement as you serve him. Let this hope burst forth within you, releasing a continual joy. Don't give up in a time of trouble, but commune with God at all times"* (Romans 12:11-12 TPT). The powerful oil that pours over our relationally rooted lives will make us glow and blaze with the joy of Jesus while we wait for His return. To live ready is to *really* live—grounded in a relationship where He's truly **known** and always **near**. Living like this leaves us *nothing* to fear.

Heaven Awaits

Jesus' greatest promise is a *place*—the unending paradise prepared for His people. He has promised us a home in *Heaven*. There, golden streets glimmer beneath skies of endless sapphire, and the light of the Lamb dances across every surface, warm and radiant as a gentle sunrise. Majestic music swells in the air—instruments, voices, and laughter melding together into melodies that deeply delight ears and hearts. Rivers shimmer like liquid crystal and carry the fragrance of blooming gardens—while every breeze whispers peace, joy, and love. Each face shines with glorious gladness, and every heart beats in perfect rhythm with the lavish love of Jesus. Wonder unfolds endlessly—each moment more miraculous than the last. When we arrive here, we'll finally feel at *home*. At last, we'll feel fully and truly ourselves, entirely **known** and **near**—closer to Jesus than we've ever been—and we will have all eternity to explore the endless beauty of this *promised,* heavenly home.

In this promised place, perfection will delight every one of our senses. Our eyes will widen in wonder at golden streets that gleam and glow— *"pure gold, like transparent crystal"* (Revelation 21:21 AMP)—and at radiant rivers that run in rippling rhythm, *"the river of the water of life, clear as crystal, flowing from the throne of God and of the Lamb"* (Revelation 22:1 AMP). Our ears will surge with sounds that soar like a symphony: the deep, glad thunder of countless voices *"crying out with a loud voice, 'Salvation belongs to our God who sits on the throne, and to the Lamb!'"* (Revelation 7:10 ESV)—woven with angelic anthems and the gentle hush of holy stillness. The air itself will feel alive—warm with welcome, weightless with wonder—no shadows or sorrow, only light, for *"the glory (splendor, radiance) of God has illuminated it, and the Lamb is its lamp and light"* (Revelation 21:23 AMP). Perfect peace, too, will pulse through every place and person, for *"He will wipe away every tear…and there will no longer be sorrow or anguish, or crying, or pain"* (Revelation 21:4 AMP). Within us, jubilant joy will rise without end. We will feel fullness without limit or end—fearless and free *forever.* Here, all hearts are whole, joy is unbroken, and Heaven's holiness and harmony will be our *home.*

In Heaven, He also promises to give us glorious new bodies— no longer weak or worn but *whole,* strong, and shining with the splendor of Jesus. Scripture says, *"Our earthly bodies are planted in the ground when we die, but they will be raised to live forever. Our bodies are buried in brokenness, but they will be raised in glory. They are buried in weakness, but they will be raised in strength. They are buried as natural human bodies, but they will be raised as spiritual bodies"* (1 Corinthians 15:42-44 NLT). Our heavenly bodies will experience no more sickness, no more frailty, no more aging—only strength that never fades and joy that never ends. Still, even in our transformed bodies, we will readily recognize and rejoice with those we have loved. Just as the disciples knew Jesus after His resurrection (Luke 24:30-31), we, too, will know one another in Heaven. Paul even assured us of our perfected perception in Heaven: *"Now I know in part [just in fragments], but then I will know fully, just as I have been fully known [by God]"* (1 Corinthians 13:12 AMP). We will no longer just *partially* perceive and understand our God and our loved ones; in Heaven, we'll know them *fully*—more familiar and intimate with *both* in Heaven than we ever were on earth. Heaven will be filled with joyful reunions—families embracing, friends laughing, and forever worshiping side by side. Every face will be familiar, every heart whole, and every soul shining in the presence of Jesus forever—*together*.

Heaven also holds other holy gifts for us. For instance, heavenly homes await us—prepared by the heart and hands of our Savior, who said, *"In My Father's house are many rooms…I go to prepare a place for you"* (John 14:2 NIV). These dwellings will be real and enduring spaces—places of belonging where light abounds, joy is shared, and every heart finally feels at home. Still, our homes are only part of the promise; Scripture suggests that believers will also participate in heavenly service, entrusted with roles of purpose in Christ's Kingdom. Some will help guide and teach, assisting saints to grow in understanding of our infinite, glorious God (1 Corinthians 12:4–7; Matthew 19:28) while others may serve in ways that reflect Christ's righteous rule, leading in justice, worship, or stewardship over what God has made. Every role will be purposeful and intentional, a place where God-given gifts are fully employed and joyfully expressed. Heaven will mirror what the Church was always meant to be: every believer living side by side in perfect peace, love, and unity, all using their unique gifts to serve freely in His Kingdom. Wherever we dwell or serve, our hearts will be fully at ease and endlessly glad. No task will weary us; no moment of fellowship or service will diminish delight. Every second of labor or laughter will deepen joy, awaken wonder, and draw forth ceaseless worship of the One who has given us this eternal life—the most glorious, awe-filled gift *ever* promised.

He'll also hand out heavenly *honors* and holy *rewards* for the way we invested our time and talents and endured adversity on earth (Matthew 16:27, Revelation 22:12, Matthew 6:19-21, 1 Corinthians 3:10-

17). In Heaven, faithful service will be richly rewarded, for *"the Lord will reward everyone for whatever good he does"* (Ephesians 6:8 NIV). Those who remain steadfast under suffering will receive *"the crown of life"* (James 1:12 ESV), a sign of love that lasts forever—and those who long for Christ's return will inherit *"the crown of righteousness"* (2 Timothy 4:8 NIV). Those who shepherd and serve with pure motives will shine with *"the unfading crown of glory"* (1 Peter 5:4 ESV). Every hidden act of kindness—like giving quietly to the poor, praying faithfully for others in private, or fasting in secret—will be seen and celebrated by the Father (Matthew 6:4–6). Every moment of endurance, every word of encouragement, and every gift of generosity given out of *genuine* love becomes treasure stored in Heaven, *"where moth and rust cannot destroy, and thieves do not break in and steal"* (Matthew 6:20 NLT). Beyond crowns and commendation, Christ promises participation in His reign, too: *"If we endure, we will also reign with Him"* (2 Timothy 2:12 ESV)—sharing in His authority and the eternal rule and rewards reserved for the faithful. To store up treasure in Heaven, then, is to live with eternity in mind: to love lavishly, to serve selflessly, to give generously, and to walk faithfully—knowing that every small seed sown on earth will bloom into everlasting reward in the radiant presence of Jesus. Every heavenly honor and reward reflects God's perfect justice and overflowing grace, reminding us that Heaven is a place where faithfulness is treasured, selfless service is celebrated, and every heart is fully known, fully loved, and fully honored by Christ Himself.

Still, the most precious part of the promise of Heaven is to be in the very *presence* of Jesus Himself—to be fully, perpetually *near* Him. The sweetest splendor of Heaven will not be the streets of gold or the songs of angels but the Savior Himself—seen, spoken with, and sweetly embraced at last. We will no longer walk by faith and *not* by sight (2 Corinthians 5:7); instead, *"we shall see Him just as He is [in all His glory]"* (1 John 3:2 AMP). We'll see Him dressed in a royal robe wrapped with a gloriously golden sash, His hair *"glistening white like snow,"* His eyes *"flashing like a flame of fire [piercing into our beings],"* and His face shining with *"Shekinah glory"* like *"the sun shining in all its power"* (Revelation 1:13-16 AMP). He'll look upon us with *love* that is titanic yet tender, holy yet healing. To see the striking but sweet smile of our Savior, to hear His victorious voice, to hold His scarred yet sovereign hands—*this* will still our hearts and satisfy every longing over and over, forever and ever. As

Love itself wraps His arms around us, His nearness will undo every ache of absence, and His embrace will anchor us in endless peace. Yes, we will *"[be privileged to] see His face"* (Revelation 22:4 AMP), and with every glance, worship will well up in us like a rushing river, joy will leap like lightning, and love will pour forth in unceasing praise to the Lamb, our Lord, our everlasting Love and Light. Beyond the crowns and treasures Heaven holds, the highest honor and our deepest delight will be this alone: to see **Jesus** face to face, to be fully *known*, and to dwell forever *near* the One our hearts have *most* longed for and adored.

CHAPTER THIRTEEN

Stay Close

"Don't throw it all away now. You were sure of yourselves then. It's still a sure thing! But you need to stick it out, staying with God's plan so you'll be there for the promised completion. It won't be long now; He's on His way! He'll show up most any minute…We're not quitters who lose out. Oh, no! We'll stay with it and survive, trusting all the way!"—Hebrews 10:35-39 (MSG)

Endure to the End

Let's not miss *any* of this. Let's not miss **Jesus** on earth *or* in Heaven in all His holiness. Let's not miss *Him*—our glorious, gracious Jesus who waits to welcome us home to Him both here on earth and later in eternity. The fight of faith is fierce, the battle often biting and bewildering, yet Scripture calls us to *"fight the good fight of faith"* (1 Timothy 6:12 NIV). *This* is the fight worth every fiber of our being: to daily spend quiet, hungry moments with Jesus; to linger and listen when He whispers; to walk fully led and empowered by the Spirit; to obey *His* voice no matter the cost; and to remain relentlessly, increasingly close to Him. We were *born* for this. We were *made* to have hearts set wholly on Him, lives aligned with His will, eyes fixed on eternal places and prizes. Yes, the enemy prowls, the flesh falters, and the world wounds—but each struggle, each step, each steadfast surrender draws us nearer to the crown of joy, the treasure of His presence, the indescribable delight of being fully **known** and **near** to Jesus. The prize is infinite, the reward incomparable, and the fight—though fierce—is incredibly and eternally *worth it.*

Let's not shrink. Let's not surrender. Let's not step back when storms sharply strike, when we sinfully stumble, or when our hearts senselessly stray. Every trial, every test, and every misstep is a stepping stone towards *more* of our Savior who shouts, *"I will never leave you, never! And I will not loosen My grip on our life!"* (Hebrews 13:5 TPT). Scripture also assures us that *"He who has begun a good work in you will [continue to] perfect and complete it until the day of Jesus Christ [the time of His return]"* (Philippians 1:6 AMP). He promises to use even our failures and unforeseen adversity to graciously grow us from glory to glory (2 Corinthians 3:18). If we will *stay close,* life with Jesus gets deeper, richer, sweeter with every step and in every season. We will know Him more consummately, understand Him more clearly, delight in Him more completely—and we'll live more and more *courageously.*

Let's lean into a life lived on *this* truth: *"So why would I fear the future? Only goodness and tender love pursue me all the days of my life. Then, afterward, when my life is through, I'll return to Your glorious presence to be forever with you!"* (Psalm 23:6 TPT). Our God will never give up on us; He will persist in pursuing us with a personal, powerful love that never pauses or perishes. Let's have hearts that mirror His: we, too, will never quit, never shrink, and never cease to love Him. *Nothing* will pull us away—not our failures, not our doubts, not our hurts, and not our enemy. We will stand *firm.* We will stay *faithful.* We will live planted in His presence and rooted in His love, flourishing in His purposes. Then, at the end, the holiest, highest prize awaits: we'll see **Jesus**, behold His glory with our own eyes, and be finally, fully home with Him.

We'll be with the One who first molded Adam and Eve in His image in Eden, the One who bled and shed saving grace on the Cross, the One who has drawn us and called us to *intimacy* with Him through every quiet breath and heartbeat of our entire lives. Since the crux of creation, He's called *each* of us to know Him, to trust Him, and to walk closely with Him each and every day, from sunrise to sunset—all the way into eternity. When we get there, we'll forever dwell in the deep, dazzling joy of being truly **Known and Near**—cherished, embraced, and fully alive in the *relationship* with Jesus we were born to have.

Katie Rockett is a teacher, pastor, and lifelong lover of words whose greatest joy is helping people discover that Jesus is not distant or abstract; He is deeply personal, unmistakably present, and wonderfully *real* and near. She teaches at a Christian school where her days are spent shaping young minds and shepherding young hearts, believing that encounters with Jesus early in life can change *everything* that follows.

After growing up in East Texas, Katie attended Centenary College in Shreveport, Louisiana, earning degrees in Music and English, and also studied abroad at Oxford University. These years refined her love for people, truth, and the written word. As an adult, she has faithfully served in ministry within the local church—receiving pastoral ordination in 2012—and in Christian education. For people of all ages, her heartbeat remains the same: to open the Word of God and invite people into a transforming *relationship* with Jesus.

Writing has been a quiet companion to Katie since childhood, and years ago, she sensed a clear call to write books centered on life with Jesus. The idea for *this* book was first stirred more than twenty years ago, growing slowly and prayerfully over time. Her hope is that these pages clearly illuminate God's invitation to *relationship*—revealing both the *cost* and the immeasurable *gift*—and that they speak with grace and truth into every challenge and season a believer may face.

Katie is happily married to the kindest husband and is the grateful mother of three beautiful children. She delights in preaching, teaching, creating, writing, taking long walks, and enjoying the sacred stillness of her country home—surrounded by trees, quiet, and the beauty of Jesus. The message of her life and work is simple: Jesus can be **known** and **near**, and all people—young and old—can find and flourish in the relationship with Jesus they were *born* to have.

Katie is deeply grateful for the opportunity to steward these words in print and looks ahead with prayerful hope to sharing future books through **Draw Near Books**—as the Lord leads.